BROWN'S BRITAIN

BROWN'S BRITAIN

ROBERT PESTON

✳ SHORT BOOKS

First published in 2005 by
Short Books
15 Highbury Terrace
London N5 1UP

10 9 8 7 6 5 4 3 2 1

A CIP catalogue record for this book
is available from the British Library.

ISBN 1-904095-67-4

Printed in Great Britain by
GGP Media GmbH, Poessneck, Germany

JACKET DESIGN: NICK CASTLE
INDEX: ANNIE WILLIAMSON-NOBLE

For Siân, Simon and Max

CONTENTS

INTRODUCTION

I nterviewing Gordon Brown on the record, for publication, is usually a maddening process, always heavy-going, rarely fun. Each time I go in filled with unwarranted optimism, thinking, "This time he'll let rip about what he really thinks about the Prime Minister" or "This will be the one interview in ten years that includes a terrible gaffe."

And each time I'm subjected to a sermon on his latest obsession, delivered without hesitation, though usually including a fair amount of repetition. I've been lectured by him on the imperative of forcing the unemployed to find work, the importance of compelling companies to compete more aggressively, the supposedly pernicious economic implications of early drafts of the European constitution, and the limit of the writ of markets in the provision of public services, among many other weighty and worthy themes. His small talk is ponderous, his jokes taken from a personal archive that's replenished too rarely, his apparent obsession with football no more remarkable than the next man's.

According to Derek Scott, a former Downing Street aide, the Prime Minister moans that speaking to Brown is frequently like having a conversation with the speaking clock (*Off Whitehall*, 2004) – which is fair in the sense that in response to almost any tricky question that is put to him, he has in his mental locker a safe answer that he prepared earlier. Over the years for example, whenever I pressed Brown about the issue of the moment, such as whether the UK would join the euro, out would come the same stock phrases about the economic tests needing to be met (and it turns out he was just as unforthcoming with the Prime Minister). There were no slips, but also little evidence of his substantial intellect (as it happens, in the last year of so – since the birth of his son – he has lightened up and engages in a more active way with his interlocutors).

However, everything he says is meant, so a non-answer he gave me on September 24, 2004 was just about worth turning up to hear. It was a Friday at 6.45pm. I was sitting on a slightly worn, blue, Victorian-style armchair - the kind you expect to see in the lobby of an unpretentious four star hotel - in his private meeting room in the Treasury, with its views over St James's Park, its dazzlingly white walls and a giant expressionist canvas which is electric blue (mostly) with green and pink rectangular blue splodges (whose provenance I've never bothered to check but is too loud and overbearing for the smallish space). Three pictures of his son, John – who was about to celebrate his first birthday – were carefully arranged on an otherwise empty occasional table. Brown junior has the more delicate eyes and nose of his mother, Sarah, combined with the powerful mandible of his father's side. It was the day after the funeral of Gordon Brown's mother and he was looking exhausted and upset. She had been frail for some months and Brown had stayed in Scotland for the summer – forgoing his habitual summer holiday in New England – in order to spend precious weeks with her in her birthplace of Insch, near Aberdeen.

Labour's annual conference was due to start two days later and Brown had decided to give just one press interview, in advance of a week that would have a significant bearing on his future in politics, on the prospects that he would one day fulfil his long-held ambition to be Prime Minister. Relations between Brown and the serving premier, Tony Blair, were as bad as they had ever been. Only days earlier, Blair had undermined Brown by bringing back into the Cabinet a conspicuous critic of his policies and modus operandi, Alan Milburn, and then insulted the Chancellor by putting Milburn in charge of Labour's general election campaign, a role that Brown had filled in 1997 and 2001. Also it was widely believed among MPs and journalists that Blair had recently reneged on an agreement he had made with Brown in 1994 – and re-pledged at least twice since – to stand down before the general election. Brown feared that Blair would endeavour, at the annual gathering of Labour's activists which was to take place in Brighton, to marginalise him further, by painting him as a political dinosaur opposed to essential modernisation of public services. So here I was – with Patrick Hennessy, my colleague from the *Sunday Telegraph* – expecting him to trot out a tedious message on the imperative of the Party remaining united in the run-up to a general election that would probably be held the following year (he didn't disappoint: "I think unity around our values gives us the best chance of moving forward so that our first and second terms are followed by successes in the future," he said).

Of rather greater interest to us were recent newspaper reports that in the spring he had talked Tony Blair out of "pre-announcing" an intention to resign as premier and leader of the Labour Party (or declaring after Easter in 2004 that he would quit that same autumn). It was a slightly mad story, which I struggled to believe – since it was so difficult to understand why, after all those years of yearning to be Prime Minister, Brown would actually work against his own hopes by urging Blair *not* to tell the world that he was off. However, as I learned about the context in which it all took place, I became convinced that it was true (the incident is described on pages 335-43). Anyway, by the time of our interview with Brown, I already knew a fair amount about the conversations between Blair and Brown on the fraught issue of when Blair would stand down, having talked at length to their colleagues. So I was being disingenuous in probing the Chancellor about it – although it was worth a bit to have Brown say something even mildly indiscreet and disloyal on the record.

What he should have said to me, if he had wanted to kill the story dead, was that it was all a load of trivia and nonsense. What he actually said was:

I've never in the past gone into talking about these things and rumours and speculation and talking about private conversations I may or may not have had with people. The one thing I am clear about is that my responsibility is two fold: it is to stand up for what I believe is right for Britain and to uphold and work for the unity of the Labour Party...

You know of your experience of talking to me before, I've never been drawn into public debate over issues like this. My business is to get on with being Chancellor of the Exchequer and doing the best for Britain. I believe that the challenges facing Britain can not only be met, but met in such a way that Britain can be one of the global success stories.

For a politician as anal and cautious as Brown, this was the equivalent of a very loud "YES! I DID PERSUADE TONY NOT TO ANNOUNCE HIS DEPARTURE AND NOW I AM IN AGONY ABOUT IT." And later in the interview, when we asked him if his 20-year relationship with Blair was as strong as ever and whether they still trusted each other, he could not bring himself to answer in the affirmative. "I think the record speaks for itself: people must judge that on the basis of what's been achieved" was his non-sequitur of an answer. So we tried again: did he and Blair still seek each other's counsel? "I've got my job to do and he's got his job to do," he replied. "It's as simple as that."

In that answer, Brown captured the truth of his unique relationship with Blair. Apart from the unmissable implication that they had fallen out of love with each other, he was also stating that he does not feel beholden to Blair. And why should he? For more than 7 years he has operated with greater independence from his Prime Minister than any Chancellor of the Exchequer has ever done. There have been many powerful Chancellors in the history of British cabinet government, but none has enjoyed the autonomy and influence of Brown. Also, for all his negative qualities – his excessive introspection, his mistrust of people outside his immediate circle, his inflexibility – he is a rarity in an age of political pygmies: a serious politician with big ambitions to improve society.

This is where I should admit to a certain naïveté: almost since I first spoke to him in 1993 (when he was Shadow Chancellor and I was trying to persuade him to give me colourful quotes to insert into an investigative piece I was writing for the *Financial Times*), I've felt that there was an historical inevitability to Gordon Brown becoming the British Prime Minister. To a greater extent than any other politician I have encountered, his entire life has been an apprenticeship for that momentous job.

There are plenty of serious commentators who think my instinct is wrong, that his moment has passed and that he will turn out to be the best Prime Minister Labour never had. Just at this moment, the weight of evidence may be on their side, in the sense that Blair has at last made it crystal clear that he is not going to smooth the way for Brown to take over. Far from quitting before the end of his second term of office, as he promised Brown he would do, Blair is now intent on fighting and winning a third term – and then serving almost all of that third term. So if Blair has his way, the leadership will not fall vacant for another three years or so. Who knows whether at that far-off time, as measured by the politician's faster-ticking clock, Brown will still stand head and shoulders above all other pretenders to the crown?

But Blair may not be in control of his own destiny as much as he would like. Brown has now set himself up as the official opposition to Blair within the very heart of the Cabinet. The coming year will see not just the beginning of a battle for the future leadership of the Party but also a struggle for the Party's soul, as Brown and Blair offer strikingly different visions of how Labour policies and doctrines should evolve. So it is an apposite moment to assess Brown's contribution to Labour's revival during its wilderness years in the 1980s and early to mid 1990s, to ask what he has achieved as the longest serving Chancellor this century, and to examine what his activities in government can tell us about the kind of Britain he would try to fashion as Prime Minister.

And here's the nightmare that occasionally troubles the Prime Minister's equanimity. Even if Brown doesn't make it to 10 Downing Street, there is a chance that this Labour government will be remembered as Brown's rather than Blair's – although Brown himself is fearful that chancellors and their foreign counterparts, the Finance Ministers, are always remembered as historical footnotes, never as the individuals who define an age (he believes, for example, that it's unfair for Clinton to receive the credit for all the economic successes achieved by the US administration in the mid to late 1990s, when Robert Rubin and Larry Summers, as Treasury Secretaries, were enormously influential). Thus even if Lawson, as Chancellor in the mid-1980s and before, made a major intellectual contribution to what became known as Thatcherism, it was a contribution to his Prime Minister's brand, not his own. That's why Brown will not rest until he has made it to Number 10, or has been persuaded that his chance of doing so has receded to zero.

Most of what follows is about Brown, the public man, the politician. Very little will touch on his private life for two reasons. My fuddy-duddy view is that the private sphere, even for politicians, is only rarely of relevance to a judgement about whether someone is fit to hold high office. That is not to say that a politician's conduct outside of the job is never pertinent to the electorate's judgement of him or her. Crooks and scoundrels should be hunted down and expelled. But Brown is neither, unless I've been asleep for a decade.

And there is a rather less high-minded reason why I have largely eschewed his life outside politics. Whenever I've given it a moment's thought, his personal life always seemed unexceptional and dull. There was, for a while in the 1990s, gossip around Westminster that he is gay, which is what MPs and advisers – with too little to occupy them – always say about someone in their forties who is not married. The rumour was fed by his political opponents, keen to play on an unattractive homophobia in the Labour Party. As it happens, it was nonsense. But even if it was true, I cannot see why that should affect a judgement of him as a potential Prime Minister. To his credit, he has always been remarkably unruffled by the bitchy rumours, which shows an unwonted absence of homophobia for an MP (the talk was probably slightly more annoying for his wife, Sarah Macaulay: when she was still his girlfriend, she pressed on me slightly more information than I could ever have wanted about his heterosexual prowess, in the slightly naïve belief that I am the sort of club-bable hack who would prop himself up on the bar of the Commons press gallery and retransmit the glorious details to my colleagues and rivals).

On the other hand, the slur against him that he is "psychologically flawed" – made in January 1998 by "someone who has an extremely good claim to know the mind of the Prime Minister" – might seem to relate to Brown "the man" as opposed to Brown "the public figure". But evaluating that charge is plainly in the ambit of this book, because it's all about his qualities as a pretender to be premier and was levelled at him by a political rival (albeit an anonymous one). The description was given to Andrew Rawnsley and appeared in his *Observer* column on January 18, 1998 (and also featured in his book, *Servants of the People*, 2000). It was widely believed to have been said by Alistair Campbell, then the Prime Minister's closest adviser as his Press Secretary, although those close to Brown think the phrase was Blair's own.

At the time it was a barb forged in the frustration of an acutely dysfunctional relationship between 10 Downing Street and the Treasury. The government consisted and consists of two great fiefdoms, one around Blair and one around Brown. And although they were notionally in alliance in a battle against the Tory opposition, there have been many occasions when a power struggle between them seemed to take precedence. This tension – often creative, sometimes destructive – has been a defining characteristic of this government. It stems, in part, from the circumstances in which Blair usurped (in Brown's view) the Labour leadership in 1994. So this book's one intrusion into the semi-private sphere is an examination of the relationship between Brown and Blair, which is much closer than is normal in politics. It may be an overused metaphor to say that they have had a long and turbulent marriage, but it's no less true for that. The hurt that used to be manifested by Brown was that of the spouse who has been cheated on. The guilt regularly manifested by Blair is that of the spouse who's done the cheating. They are in this thing together, and if one of them is psychologically flawed, they both are.

This is not to suggest that Brown is the easiest or most relaxed man to deal with. But his faults are recognisable and are far outweighed by his strengths – which are an ability to see the big picture, a wariness of the easy option and a determination to plan for the long term. Strikingly, the poise he had before surrendering the Labour leadership to Blair has returned since the birth of his son, John, on October 17, 2003 (also, the terrible sadness for him of the death in earliest infancy of his first child, Jennifer, in January 2002, helped him to put personal ambition into perspective). The notion that his greatest foible, a difficulty in trusting people who are not family or very longstanding friends, should disqualify him from being Prime Minister is absurd – although his hard shell and ungregarious nature have made it harder for him to reach the top, because he has needlessly alienated colleagues and people who might have been useful to him.

***

My second reason for concentrating on the world of politics is that this is Brown's world. He lives and breathes it, rarely leaves it: he's always "on". One illustration of that tendency was given to me by one of the tiny circle who attended his wedding to Sarah Macaulay on August 3, 2000. On the night before the big day, there was a dinner for friends and immediate family. But – after the news of the impending nuptials leaked – Brown felt obliged to leave the meal, in order to brief his allies in the Labour Party and in the media. Public life takes precedence, almost always.

He is dedicated to the Labour Party in the way that his father was to the Church of Scotland. In fact, what infuriates Blair and his closest allies is the way that Brown has defined himself, with no trace of doubt or irony, as the living embodiment of the spirit of the Labour movement, the bulwark against the instincts of a Prime Minister who – in Brown's view – is too prone to forget that he was elected to lift up the poorest. But it's this blurring of personal ambition and ambition for his Party that makes Brown hard to measure. What comes first for him, self-interest or party-interest? He would say that the Party should and does take priority, that when his own interests have conflicted with those of Labour he has made the important personal sacrifice. This is his own rationalisation, for example, of why he didn't in the end challenge Blair for the leadership in 1994. On the other hand, Tony Blair sitting in 10 Downing Street would equate loyalty to party with unquestioning loyalty and deference to him – and Brown has never manifested those qualities. Even so, Brown has had plenty of opportunities to inflict serious and possibly fatal wounds on Blair and he's always resisted that temptation. Has his motivation been disinterested? Not completely. He's calculated that the mortal blow to Blair would also wreak terrible damage on Labour – and he does not want to inherit a party that has made itself unelectable. He wants to be Prime Minister, not leader of an opposition party.

The true measure of Brown is in what he has done in government and opposition, his policies, his speeches, his management of the Treasury, his engagement with the rest of the Cabinet. In my assessment, I've had unprecedented access to unpublished policy documents prepared by him and his team in the run up to New Labour's 1997 landslide election victory. And I've spoken to many people who know him well and work, or have worked, closely with him. Many of these would only talk on condition of anonymity, which is a journalistic convention I dislike but was the only way to extract apposite information in the paranoid state of British politics.

To be clear, this is not a comprehensive "life of Brown", nor is it an official biography. Brown has been aware that I was doing it, however, and – given the astonishing loyalty to him of his friends, political allies and family – it would have been much more difficult to write if he had discouraged members of his close circle from speaking to me (which he has done with previous books about him). I have, of course, also interviewed ministers and senior officials who would not count themselves as his friends or supporters, some of whom would ally themselves with the opposing camp of Tony Blair, and others (more than you might think) would see themselves as neither Brownites or Blairites. The judgements in the book are all mine.

For what's it's worth, I emerged from the evaluation process more impressed with Gordon Brown than I had been. In a political world where image and spin counts for so much, he has big ideas which he pushes through relentlessly. The giving of control over interest rates to the Bank of England, the merger of the tax and benefits system through the creation of a system of tax credits that provides £16bn in subsidies to 20m people, his veto on joining the single currency: these are substantial initiatives (for better or worse). He's redolent of Thatcher in his ability to think strategically, in his horror of U-turns, in his enormous drive and capacity for work. Like her, he has a powerful sense of his own Britishness – though, inevitably, his definition of the qualities associated with this nation is starkly different from hers.

One of his weaknesses is also very Thatcherish: a them-and-us mentality, a suspicion of anyone who's not an avowed ally, an excessive propensity to see plots against himself. Related to this, he's fiercely loyal to those who have passed the test of friendship (especially those who fought alongside him in the cockpit of Scottish politics during the 1980s or the more recent generation of combatants in the campaign against 10 Downing Street) – and he will endeavour to seek promotion in government for them long after they have proved themselves to be mediocre or even an embarrassment to him. On the other hand, he is an identifier of genuine talent, such as Douglas Alexander, a rising young minister, Geoff Mulgan, who worked for him as a special adviser and was a stalwart of Downing Street and the Cabinet Office from 1997 to 2004; Yvette Cooper, a junior minister in the office of the Deputy Prime Minister; and her husband, Ed Balls, the former Chief Economic Adviser to the Treasury and the parliamentary candidate for Normanton in Yorkshire. His political relationship with Balls – who acquired the sobriquet "the Deputy Chancellor" till he resigned in June 2004 – is particularly close.

Balls was a remarkable special adviser, in a government which gave greater power and prominence to special advisers than any previous one. He was the perfect foil to Brown, steeped in the technical detail of economic policymaking in a way that Brown isn't, and able and willing to take much of the management and administrative burden off a

Chancellor who prefers not to get bogged down in the nitty gritty of day-to-day decision-making. What's more, Balls, too, sees the big picture – and in the coups, such as empowering the Bank of England to set interest rates, there's as much Balls as Brown in the development and execution (though, inevitably, the actual decision had to be the Chancellor's).

Sir Andrew Turnbull, head of the home civil service, put it like this in November 1999 (in an interview in the *Guardian*): "Ed is like an extension of Brown. You bolt on an extra server and increase the capacity." So this book is also to an extent about Balls, partly because he's been Brown's constant companion for more than a decade and partly because he's still the other half of the double act, even as he seeks election to parliament. If Brown enters 10 Downing Street, it's a racing certainty that Ed Balls will be close at hand, giving form to Brown's vision – though the relationship between the two is changing, as Balls endeavours to create an identity for himself in the public sphere.

And what is Brown's vision? It's more pragmatic than poetic: it's to lift up the dispossessed and reduce inequality, without scaring too many voters at the apex of the income scale that they will be penalised and without damaging the competitiveness of the UK in a way that harms rich and poor alike. And the main means – which is also an end in itself – has been to reduce unemployment (when you ask Brown to list his achievements, seeing the UK return to full employment – as near as damn-it – is usually at or near the top). Reducing inequality in Britain – that's at the heart of it, although he has other concerns, such as a long-held sincere passion for alleviating the desperate poverty of Africa and less developed countries.

Is Brown's credo all that different from Tony Blair's? Well, it would be absurd to argue that there is a great ideological gulf between them. But Brown is more anchored and less of an opportunist than Blair. And over the past couple of years, during a period when his ambitions for personal advancement were being checked, Brown has gone back to first principles, in an attempt to root his own policy initiatives – and his reactions to the policies formulated by others – in an explicit set of rules about the appropriate relationships for our time between individual, community, local government and national government. He's been developing theories of what it is to be British, and how to amend the constitution to rebuild the trust of an apathetic electorate in both politics and politicians. His journey of intellectual rediscovery also includes looking at why some public services would be damaged by allowing them to be bought and sold in a market place, and how to restore the public service ethic to pride of place in schools and hospitals.

Perhaps most important of all, his quest for a political lodestar has been an implicit and devastating critique of the core of Blair's political modus operandi. It is a repudiation of "triangulation," a strategy imported from the US by Blair and his friend and counsellor, Peter Mandelson, which broadly says that a successful policy is one that could almost have come from the locker of your political opponent – so in Blair's case, it's a policy that the Tories find hard to attack, but which alienates Labour's more left-wing members. One classic example of the approach in action was the imposition of variable tuition fees for university students, which prompted a political storm in 2003 and early 2004. Brown acknowledges that the triangulation strategy is successful to the extent that the policies generated by it tend to win support from the media, especially the more right-wing newspapers. But his concern is that it is not a rational way to run a country or to create policies that command broad and deep support, such that they stand a chance of outlasting a change of government or a change of ideological fashion.

If his quest for the big truths is of more recent origin, he's diverged from Blair in one other respect over a much longer period. Brown has consistently been more of an activist than Blair in the battle to close the gap between haves and have-nots: he has less confidence than the Prime Minister that everyone prospers when the economy grows. Thus to the very last, the Prime Minister was uncomfortable with his Chancellor's decision in 2002 to impose a 1 per cent National Insurance levy on individuals and businesses, to pay for a huge increase in spending on the National Health Service. And Blair tried to limit the scope of the £5bn windfall tax on the privatised water, energy and telecoms companies, which was needed to pay for the New Deal measures to reduce youth and long term unemployment.

But in contradiction to a widespread view, I have never detected the slightest sign that Brown would relish imposing higher taxes on the wealthy just for the sake of it: he is a meritocrat; he believes rewards should accrue to those who exercise their talents; and he is neurotically fearful of the damage that can be done to the poorest through a policy of redistribution that would drive wealth creators to countries with lower taxes. Even so, Brown is more recognisably in the Labour tradition than Blair. For Brown inequalities can be justified, but only if they are demonstrably in the interests of the least fortunate. In that context, any version of socialism that harms the dynamism of the economy has little appeal to him. Back in 1997, in a speech to commemorate Anthony Crosland (a Labour cabinet minister of the 1960s and 1970s, who – like Blair – went to a minor public school and Oxford, but – like Brown – tried to formulate a workable politics of redistribution), Brown summed up his own mission as well as anyone has:

> There have been left-of-centre politicians who have espoused socialism but failed to meet the test of credibility. There have been those who have presented themselves as credible by abandoning socialism. The real challenge of left-of-centre politics is to be socialist and at the same time credible.

> If Brown amounts to anything it is that he is the credible socialist.

***

From 1995 to 2000, when I was political editor of the *FT*, I saw a great deal of Brown. The change that came over him in that period, compared with his personality before he decided not to challenge Tony Blair for the leadership of the Labour Party in June 1994, was startling. He became manifestly less relaxed. Every thought and deed was controlled. He retreated into himself and became much duller. The deal with Blair for not standing in the contest (usually called the Granita deal, which is a shorthand I will use) was a good one: he was given unprecedented autonomy as Shadow Chancellor and Chancellor. But it did not compensate for the bitter hurt of betrayal by his oldest and closest political friend, Blair.

Over the past year or so, Brown has broken free of the tyranny of resentment and regret. He's been liberated by Blair's second betrayal, his ripping up of the Granita agreement. Blair's decision to govern more independently of Brown has persuaded the Chancellor that there is almost no possibility of there being a smooth, seamless transition from Blair's premiership to his. If there's no point in waiting for Blair to anoint him as the successor, Brown can be truer to his own beliefs in words and deeds.

He still dearly wants to be Prime Minister and is building a platform and preparing a manifesto. Brown recognises that time is increasingly precious for him, because there will come a moment – and it may not be that far off – when voters become sick to death of him, simply because he has been splashed all over the television screens and newspaper front pages for more than a decade. These days, all politicians have shorter useful working lives than their predecessors: voters become bored with seeing them all the time – or at least that's Brown's thesis.

And if it doesn't happen, if he never leads Labour and the country, well I don't think he will flagellate himself to death in the way that he once would have done. In fact, according to his friends, there is a possibility that he will wake up one morning, decide "enough is enough", and do something completely different. But whether he becomes Prime Minister or withdraws from the field of domestic politics, he can look back on the last few years with satisfaction. In 1994, he lost the leadership and won power. This book is about what he did with that power.

CHAPTER ONE
An inherited mission

"In some quarters even the idea that a Labour spokesman can have family connections with business is still regarded as incredible." Thus, on November 11, 1996 at the Confederation of British Industry's annual conference in Harrogate, Gordon Brown attempted to wear a smart capitalists' outfit. It was the denouement of a surreal episode that had shown Brown at his worst: trying to prove he's something that he's palpably not (an entrepreneur manqué); dragging his family into an unconvincing personal reinvention; humanising himself with all the subtlety of Mr Spock in *Star Trek* endeavouring to manifest emotions. It was less than a year before the 1997 general election. And Brown was making one last push to show the business community that it really had nothing to fear from a New Labour government. How better to reassure them than to testify that he had inherited wealth-creating DNA from his mother? So on November 7, his hulking minder of a press spokesman, Charlie Whelan, confided a great discovery to me: Brown's mother had been a director of a small builder's and timber merchant. Hey presto, Brown, the dutiful son of the Boss, was born.

The authorised statement from Brown on all this aimed – without success – not to exaggerate the claim: "I certainly am an MP and not a businessman, but I think it would be true to say that business is in my blood," he said. And what a remarkable person his mother had been: she was "probably, at the stage she became a company director, one of a small number of women who were company directors". And here was the reaching-out to the plutocratic audience: "I was brought up in an atmosphere where I knew exactly what was happening as far as business was concerned. I was aware of all the difficult decisions that businesses had to make and you couldn't escape the fact that there were challenges that they had to face."

Now the first rule of politics – or possibly of life – should be "don't mention your mother without checking with her first." Within minutes of Brown's remarks appearing on the Press Association's wires, Andrew Pierce, a quick-witted writer on the the *Times*, telephoned the future Chancellor's octogenarian parents. Elizabeth Brown, speaking from her retirement home in Aberdeenshire, told Pierce: "I don't know why Gordon is saying all this. It's all a bit embarrassing. I was not a working director at all. It was a small family firm. I was not very important. I merely performed some light administrative duties when I was there, which was far from all the time. I went away when I got married. I was only a director on paper. That is the truth. I would hardly have called myself a business woman." Did she recall the business atmosphere of the family hearth that had such a profound influence on her middle son? "No. My husband was first and foremost a Church of Scotland minister. He preached for more than 40 years. There was no time for business." And that, of course, is the truth of it. As Andrew Brown, the Chancellor's brother, said in a tribute to his mother at her funeral in September 2004, she was the tireless minister's wife, at his parishes in Govan, Kircaldy and then Hamilton.

The daughter of John and Jessie Souter, she was brought up in Insch in Aberdeenshire largely by her mother, after her father died when she was 10. And she was the first member of her family to leave the area, when – during the Second World War – she moved to London to work in decoding intelligence. By 1945, Elizabeth Souter was also a sergeant in the Auxiliary Territorial Service. However she was a shy woman, who hated public attention. In fact it was in part to protect her from possible invasions of her jealously guarded privacy that Gordon Brown, in 1978, turned down the opportunity of securing a safe Labour seat in Hamilton, where his father was the minister at St John's Church (though the principal reason was that he was already the candidate for a less-safe seat in Edinburgh and felt it was wrong to desert it so soon after being chosen).

But if the Reverend and Mrs Brown were not entrepreneurial capitalists in tooth and claw, nor were they socialists or died-in-the wool Labour supporters. Elizabeth Brown came from largely Tory stock. And the approach to politics taken by her husband, John Ebenezer Brown – whom she married in July 1947 – was to vote for the man, rather than the Party. His sons believe John Brown voted Labour immediately after the War, but probably for the Liberals on other occasions. And when he was working in Hamilton, they think he voted for a Conservative councillor who was a member of his congregation. His children sum him up as a "small l" liberal.

It would be true to say that the most important influence on Gordon Brown's political outlook was his father, who was a Calvinist devoted to the welfare of his parish. What he passed on to Brown was a devotion to public service and a powerful vocation to serve others, but through secular institutions rather than ecclesiastical ones. Gordon Brown is a Christian, although not a proselytising one. He doesn't accentuate his religious leanings in his public image, unlike Blair, and his speeches contain little ecclesiastical imagery. But a childhood in the company of a sermoniser wasn't entirely wasted: on September 26, 2004, he looked utterly at home standing in the pulpit of a great barn of a church in Brighton, declaiming to a congregation of anti-poverty protesters about the need to write off the debts owed by impoverished nations. Scots often describe Gordon Brown as a typical "Son of the Manse" (if you type that phrase into Google, Brown pops up as the sixth reference out of 21,600). For him, the Labour Party, rather than the church, became the institution through which he gained a sense of his own identity. His devotion to it is almost religious.

One of his most prized recent finds is an extract from a local newspaper dated July 1997 and headlined: "Proud father praises speech". Brown did not know that his self-deprecating parents had ever made any public statement in support of his chosen life in politics. There is a slight implication that, like many buttoned-up fathers of that post-War generation, John Brown found it hard to articulate praise for his children in private. So the voice from the past in the small square cutting is a treasure for the Chancellor. It's redolent of the simple virtues that a minister would want to see in his children (which cannot always have been easy for them to live up to) and says:

> I think he spoke very well. I thought his suggestions were very good. I thought it was a very sensible budget. He said what he wanted to do was act fairly and I think he was trying to do that.
> I felt he came across very well. He spoke very wisely and quite humbly. I don't think there was any sort of show about him or anything like that. I don't think he had any jokes at all, as far as I can remember. It was a good speech, well put together.

However, what the father failed completely to pass on to his son was his teetotal ways – although Brown junior has never been one to while away the hours in the bars of the House of Commons (rather to the frustration of a succession of parliamentary private secretaries, his eyes and ears in the Commons, who wish he would do himself more favours by lubricating a few backbenchers). And as for sparking his interest in politics, Brown gives much of the credit for that to his older brother, John.

Brown also attributes his political awakening to the great mood of change of the early 1960s (few young men of any intellectual pretensions claimed a bond with the etiolated Tory party of Douglas-Home) and the proximity of his childhood home in Fife to traditional textile, mining and manufacturing industries in palpable decline. Within the family as a whole, there is also a powerful memory of the poverty encountered by John Brown at his first parish of Govan in the 1940s and early 1950s. There were doubtless other early influences too, but those will do. And it's striking that a concern for the plight of the unemployed, a view of

Labour as primarily the party of full employment, is the leitmotif of Gordon Brown's life in politics.

What's equally conspicuous is how little he has moved from where he started, his childhood home of Kirkcaldy, which is an old industrial town in Fife on the eastern seaboard of Scotland. Brown's constituency of Dunfermline East is close to where he had a comfortable upbringing, as is his Scottish home on the Firth of Forth. His forebears on his father's side had been tenant farmers in the vicinity for at least a couple of hundred years. Gordon Brown is not a great one for tearing up his roots, in his politics or in his life.

The Rev. John Brown was ferociously intelligent but rejected the opportunity to be an academic, according to Gordon Brown's childhood friend, Lord (Murray) Elder, who has been around for most of the big moments in his life (Elder was Chief of Staff for the late John Smith when Smith was the Labour Party leader and Brown was the Shadow Chancellor). The scion was even brighter, according to Elder – who insists, however, that he, Elder, was the cleverer of the two bright boys in one subject, maths. But, in the circumstances in which he found himself, Brown regarded his precociousness as something of mixed blessing. At the age of 10, a year younger than normal, he was put into a special stream for "gifted" students at Kirkcaldy High School. It was an educational experiment that the teenage Gordon Brown was to lampoon. "I was a guinea pig, the victim of a totally unsighted (sic) and ludicrous experiment in education, the result of which was to harm materially and mentally the guinea pigs" Brown says in a paper he wrote in 1967 (which was obtained by his biographer, Paul Routledge: *Gordon Brown*, 1998). "At 10 years with nothing but anticipation, I began my course of senior education. At 16, I had more problems than I had years." Here was the angst of the tortured adolescent. There follows a lament for his many classmates who fell by the wayside under the strain of being forced to achieve too young. But there was no escape from Gordon Brown's terrible fate as a prodigy.

At this same age of 16, in October 1967, he followed his older brother John to Edinburgh University, the youngest fresher since 1945. In a manifestation of the closeness and competitiveness of the siblings, all three brothers went to that university and all three were to edit the student newspaper. Curiouser still, Gordon and his much younger brother Andrew Brown were both on the governing body of Edinburgh University in 1975, Gordon chairing it as rector and Andrew as president of the Student Association (they've remained close and Andrew worked for his brother as a parliamentary researcher in the 1980s, when Gordon shared an office with Tony Blair: but the younger Brown was more likely to have a beer with the gregarious Blair than with his earnest older brother).

Gordon Brown had the predicted brilliant academic career at Edinburgh – he took a first in history – but there was near-disaster within days of arriving. He was having difficulties seeing and was diagnosed as suffering from retinal detachment, which was probably caused by being kicked in the head several months earlier in a school rugby game. Brown missed the entire first term, as doctors at Edinburgh Royal Infirmary battled to restore his sight. It was too late for the left eye, which Brown can no longer use, but further operations four years later saved the right one (shortly after becoming political editor of the *FT* in the mid 1990s, I learned never to sit on Brown's left side during one of his press conferences if I wanted to attract his attention).

The other manifestation of Brown's precocity was in politics. He dates his first serious interest in politics to the autumn of 1963, when at the age of 12 he offered his campaigning services to Andrew Forrester, Labour's candidate in the Kinross and West Perthshire by-election. It was being held so that Sir Alex Douglas-Home, recently chosen by the "magic circle" of Tory grandees as Conservative leader and Prime Minister, could have a seat in the Commons (he had given up his earldom and right to sit in the Lords). For a child with a preternaturally acute sense of social justice such as Brown, Home represented everything that was wrong with the distribution of power in 1950s Britain. Labour under Harold Wilson symbolised everything that was modern and exciting.

The contest, which turned out to be the last hurrah of a Tory Party that had been in office too long, was a national event. The Scots poet, Hugh MacDiarmid, stood for the Communists; the Scottish National Party fielded a journalist, Arthur Donaldson; and Willie Rushton, the satirist from the magazine *Private Eye* and BBC TV's "That Was The Week That Was", was an independent candidate. Home romped home: Labour came in third.

At Edinburgh University, Brown was a skilful pamphleteer against a governing body that he perceived as reactionary. One notable success was forcing the university to dispose of significant investments in apartheid South Africa. And, inevitably, he became chairman of the university Labour club. His most celebrated coup, however, was to harness student discontent to secure the election of one of their own to the post of Rector. Traditionally, the title had been largely honorific and the elections had been a bit of fun and pageantry. In 1971, Brown put up a serious student candidate – his close friend Jonathan Wills – who was duly elected (in a contest, by an odd coincidence, against Willie Rushton). And the following year, the long-haired malcontent Brown – incongruously flanked by nubile and mini-skirted Brown's "Sugars", who wore T-Shirts screaming "Gordon for me" – ran for the post and trounced his opponent (Sir Fred Catherwood, a high-minded business-man of the kind whom these days would be assiduously courted by New Labour). It was also around this time that Brown made an important friend-for-life in Wilf Stevenson, who had become the researcher of the student association having read chemistry at Oxford. They counselled each other through break-ups with girlfriends and went on holiday together to Italy and the US. These days, Stevenson runs what is a *de facto* personal think tank for Brown, the Smith Institute, named after the late Labour leader, John Smith.

So by the early 1970s, Brown was well on his way to being a big fig-ure in Scottish politics. However he insists there was nothing inevitable about his becoming an MP; he could perfectly easily and naturally have remained a university lecturer. This is a slightly unconvincing conceit, particularly since he believes that politics is always a vocation, never a job. If you don't want to change the world, then stay away, would be his view. Anyway, at the age of just 23, he almost became a candidate in the second general election of 1974, when Harold Wilson's Labour won a slim majority over the Tories. And then, having failed to seize the opportunity in Hamilton, he stood as the candidate for Edinburgh South in 1979 and lost. Possibly for the better in terms of acquiring skills and experience, he had another four years of almost-real life, if working in television (which is what he threw himself into after more than a decade of academic life, including a stint as a lecturer at Glasgow College of Technology) can be described as such. Had he been an MP in 1979, he would have had a valuable four-year headstart against Blair in the race to lead the Labour Party, but Brown consoles himself that these would have been four years of misery: the Labour Party from 1979 to 1983 was on a suicide mission, as it vainly tried to come to terms with the new political order inaugurated by the advent as Prime Minister of Margaret Thatcher.

As for the life of the mind, he was – and is – a voracious reader. These days, the intellectual influences he acknowledges are the "safe" British democratic socialist writers, including Anthony Crosland, RH Tawney, GDH Cole and Douglas Jay. A paper he wrote in 1994 for the Labour think tank, the Fabians, as a kind of rite of passage between Old Brown and New Brown (called "Fair is Efficient") includes this from Tawney: "A society is free in so far, and only in so far, as within limits set by nature, knowledge and resources, its institutions and policies are such as to enable all its members to grow to their full stature, to do their duty as they see it and – since liberty should not be too austere – to have their fling when they feel like it" (*Equality*, 1931). He's also prone to use a rule of thumb borrowed from John Rawls, the US political philosopher of the moderate left, when testing whether to stamp on particular inequalities (the Brown version of Rawls's famous fairness dictum goes like this: "As long as you are satisfied about people's individual liberties being protected and safeguarded, inequalities are justified if they are in the interests of the least fortunate").

This mature, sensibly social democratic Brown is recognisable in the fizzing, fiery Brown of 30 years ago. But he was, back then, also having a "fling" with the more flamboyant thinkers of the European left. In 1975, while working on his PhD thesis about the links between the Labour Party and trade unions in Scotland, he edited a series of essays by Scottish left wing intellectuals on the future of their country, which was to resonate north of the border for quite a few years. It was called *The Red Paper on Scotland* and Brown's own contribution – which pays homage to the Italian communist intellectual, Antonio Gramsci, rather than the Labour public schoolboy, Anthony Crosland, whom he would later laud – is a paean to nationalisation and economic intervention. He's also surprisingly tolerant and understanding of the desire of some Scots for independence (later he would become an anti-separationist and arch devolutionist). My favourite Brown quote from the *Red Paper* was him fearing that it was "increasingly impossible to manage the economy both for private profit and the needs of society as a whole". Today, even if you held a pistol to his head, he would say the opposite, that failing to manage the economy for private profit would be to damage all members of "society", poor and wealthy alike.

That said, Brown always preserves something from his past when periodically he feels obliged to remake himself. So the *Red Paper* talks sentimentally about "the gap between what people are and what they may have it in themselves to become". And 22 years later, in a tribute to Crosland's concept of "democratic equality" given in February 1997, Brown says: "I believe that everyone should have the chance to bridge the gap between what they are and what they have it in themselves to become."

So what did Brown have it in himself to become? In the early 1980s, he was a producer of political, consumer, literary and sport programmes for Scottish Television. Then in 1983 at the age of 32 – when the Thatcherite Conservative Party was at its most rampant – he became the Labour MP for Dunfermline East. He wanted to be a great parliamentarian, like his hero, James Maxton, the Glasgow MP of the 1920s and 1930s who was chairman of the Independent Labour Party. Brown was steeped in Maxton lore, having studied him for almost 20 years and eventually – in 1986 – publishing a readable biography of the great parliamentarian and maverick socialist. He admired Maxton's humanitarianism, his use of a platform in the Commons to rail against the unemployment that blighted whole communities. And he shared his view that the drive for greater equality was not an end in itself but was "for the sake of liberty". Brown writes:

Cold, bureaucratic centralised state socialism held no attraction for him. For Maxton, the only test of socialist progress was in the improvement of the individual and thus the community. Greater educational opportunities would not only free people to realise their exceptional talents but allow common people to make the most of their common humanity, and ordinary people to realise their extraordinary potential.

The future Chancellor could equally well have been writing about his own credo. But there was one crucial difference between Brown and Maxton. Brown was intent on holding the reins of power in order to make a difference. Maxton's tragedy, and that of the Independent Labour Party (of ILP), was in being too far from the madding crowd, in being disconnected from the mass of working people. By contrast, the mainstream Labour Party thrived, on Brown's analysis, because of its umbilical link to the "mass support of the trade union movement".

In the 1930s, in its not-so-splendid isolation, the ILP became the refuge of "ultra-left theorists". It retreated into sterile ideological debates with which the vast mass of voters could not possibly connect. Inevitably, Maxton had a slightly self-indulgent existence on the backbenches, till his death in 1946. The ILP could therefore be accused of "committing political suicide for the sake of ideological purity" (*Maxton*, 1986). Brown was intent on making sure that his own fate would be very different. He would never sacrifice power for an arcane point of principle – though the process of melding ideology with the pragmatism that delivers electoral success has always been painful for him.

***

It's one of those curious political paradoxes that in Labour's darkest hour – Thatcher's landslide victory of June 1983 – the seeds of the party's eventual revival were planted, with the arrival at Westminster of Brown and Tony Blair. Both were elected on the back of the most socialist, idealistic and unrealistic manifesto ever put to the British people by Labour. It called for wholesale industrial intervention, withdrawal from what was then called the European Community and unilateral nuclear disarmament (the "practical" Brown crafted his personal message to voters so that they could be in no doubt that he would battle to preserve jobs for his constituents in the "defence industries" of the naval dockyard in Fife, whatever the official policy on nuclear disarmament – and, as it happens, most of this message is an early version of the theme of his political life, that only Labour can "end the scourge or mass unemployment"). Labour's significant leftward shift was in precisely the opposite direction to where public opinion in general was heading – and, if it hadn't been for its bedrock of trade union support, Labour might have been consigned to the dustbin of history by the upstart Social Democratic Party founded by its right-wing, pro-European refuseniks. At this dire time for the Party, it's extraordinary that Blair and Brown should have found each other so quickly and agreed to share a room in the Commons.

Blair was in a way the more unusual new boy – not because he was a public schoolboy and graduate of St Johns College, Oxford (Labour's cabinet was littered with class traitors in the 1940s and 1960s) but because he came to politics relatively late and was not steeped in Labour lore (in many ways, he would have been a natural for the SDP). Back then, there was no doubt that Brown was the senior partner of the duo. It couldn't be any other way, since he had longer and deeper experience of the Labour Party, he'd read all the relevant history books, and his media experience was more extensive. Blair's genius, which would not become apparent for

33

almost a decade, was as a performer on television and a seducer (not, of course, in a literal sense) of journalists. He would become the political equivalent of the classless breakfast television presenter: reasonable, reassuring, safe.

When Brown began his parliamentary journey in 1983, he wasn't particularly left-wing by the standards of Labour at the time – though he was well to the left of the Labour émigrés in the SDP, David Owen, Roy Jenkins, Shirley Williams and Bill Rodgers. But the Brown of two decades ago bears only a faint familial resemblance to the austere Chancellor of 1997. He set out his stall in a book that he edited with Robin Cook – the Scottish Labour MP with whom he has had a fractious relationship for 25 years – called *Scotland: The Real Divide*. At that moment, he was a proponent of explicit, whopping rises in taxation whose point was to redistribute income from the relatively well-heeled to the poorest and neediest – which was no more than a reflection of where the mainstream of Labour Party opinion was at the time. The notion that economic growth on its own would be strong enough to generate sufficient incremental resources for the poor was rejected by him, as it has been consistently in his career. But his prescription of the time – a sharp rise in income tax rates (at the time the top rate of tax was 60 per cent, 20 percentage points above the current level), increased social security payments and a national minimum wage – would make him blush now. Of these policies, only the minimum wage was implemented by Brown 15 years later in largely unadulterated form.

His speeches in these early years were littered with statements that jar with his activities as Chancellor. Thus since 1997 he has linked the size of tax credits and a pensions credit received by any household to the size of the income of that household. This is means testing, whether he likes it or not (and he doesn't, because of the historical baggage, especially the concept of the "undeserving poor" that is associated with the phrase, "means testing"). Yet in the 1980s, he constantly attacked ministers for introducing more means-testing into the benefits system. Back then, he was also critical of initiatives to make it harder for the unem-

34

ployed to claim social security payments without looking for work – which was to be the very spirit of his 1997 New Deal for the unemployed. And he was outraged when income tax rates were cut in 1988 while public services were allegedly being starved of funding – but he has never reversed those tax cuts and in March 1999 he took another penny off the basic income tax rate (while, as Chancellor from 1997 to 1999, he put a massive squeeze on public expenditure).

But if he's not been completely consistent over 20 odd years in parliament, he's been a less opportunistic politician than most of his contemporaries. And since 1990 or so, his steadiness in pursuit of his goals has been peerless. His political life is more about continuity than about U-turns, especially when it comes to the point for him of being in politics. Throughout his career, he has always been convinced that the surest and best way to help the poor is to help them find jobs. If his policies for doing that underwent a change, that should not be a surprise, given that the political and economic landscape is unrecognisable from how it was two decades ago. In the early 1980s, an aspiration to implement proper, old-fashioned socialism in one country or in Europe as a whole was almost practical. Capital and talented individuals could not easily relocate to a more benign economic climate if a British government put taxes up above the international norm. But these days, globalisation – or the creation of a worldwide market place for products, services, people and finance – severely restricts the ability of any administration of any persuasion to engage in traditional social engineering without hobbling the economy (recent British governments of all shades have gauged their success not in the gap between rich and poor, but by the number of Japanese and Korean manufacturers they have wooed to our shores). The levers available to any Chancellor or Prime Minister have been reduced.

If Brown's rhetoric of the mid 1980s was still in the mainstream, "old" Labour mould, it was lively and effective. He also had a knack of obtaining leaks from the civil service of statistics or documents that undermined government policy (the facility with which he did this may explain why he has a horror of committing anything even faintly sensitive to paper and why as Chancellor he has only ever written to colleagues at moments of extreme annoyance about the policies being promoted by Blair and 10 Downing Street). This effectiveness in the Commons mêlée quickly brought Brown to the attention of the Party's then leader, Neil Kinnock, who – in 1985 – made him a junior member of the trade and industry team under John Smith. Brown had already turned down a frontbench job in the shadow Scottish Office team, because he did not want to be typecast as a "Scottish" politician, having determined (correctly) that his Scottishness would be a handicap to the fulfilment of his ambitions. This preference for being seen as British first and Scottish second has endured.

It was around this time that a crucial event in the remaking of Labour took place: Peter Mandelson was appointed its Director of Communications. Mandelson's contribution – which Brown enthusiastically embraced and encouraged at the time – was to force the leadership to take far more account of the mediation of television and newspapers in the presentation of policies to voters. It was all very well having policies that played well to the instincts and prejudices of longstanding Labour Party members. But what was the use of them if they were going to be torn apart by the *Daily Mail* and the *Sun*? As the 1980s moved towards the 1990s, Brown, Blair and Mandelson became co-conspirators in a plot to modernise Labour. And they mutually reinforced each other's standing in the Party and in the wider world. Or, to put it more simply, Brown regarded Mandelson as a close ally and intimate friend.

Meanwhile, the big political trend was the onward march of Thatcherism, even as Thatcher's own immolation loomed nearer. In the June 1987 election, Kinnock saved Labour from extinction and saw off the challenge of the SDP (which had to come to terms with never being more than an influential third force in British politics and soon merged with the Liberals – though arguably it achieved a victory of sorts in converting Tony Blair to much of what it held dearest). Kinnock had shown courage and perspicuity in driving the extreme left Militant Tendency from the Party. But the Tories still won a huge majority, of 101.

From this moment, a more familiar Gordon Brown starts to emerge. His stentorian tones had been resonating in Scotland for some years. But he became an increasingly influential British politician after 1987, when he came eleventh in the annual poll of Labour MPs for places in the Shadow Cabinet (he won 88 votes, seven less than his longstanding rival, Robin Cook). Kinnock was forced to put him on Labour's front bench and made him Shadow Chief Secretary to the Treasury, responsible for reining in the spending ambitions of his frontbench colleagues. Brown – whose immediate boss was once again John Smith, the new Shadow Chancellor – had been given a sensitive responsibility. Much of the Tories' successful propaganda in the 1987 election was about Labour's profligate public spending plans and the alleged inevitability that a Kinnock government would have to impose swingeing tax rises. Brown's job was to ensure that at the subsequent election there would be fewer such hostages to fortune, by reining back Shadow ministers who dreamed up any expensive new initiative. It was the kind of role that ought to have annoyed his colleagues – and indeed would do so, in spades, when he returned to this thankless task with a vengeance as Shadow Chancellor in 1992. In those days, for both Labour and its opponents, the Party was a high-spender or it was nothing much at all. The idea that it wouldn't want to spend vastly more than the Tories just didn't compute. Somehow, though, Brown's popularity didn't wane. In fact, in the succeeding three years, he became the rising star *par excellence*.

Part of his success was due to him still singing the traditional Labour refrains. Thus in the debate on Nigel Lawson's famous tax-cutting budget of March 1988 – when the basic and top rates of income tax were reduced to 25 per cent and 40 per cent respectively – Brown ridiculed what he described as a redistribution *from* the poor *to* the rich. For most Labour MPs, this was almost poetry. But his big break was a sad and prophetic one.

In October 1988, John Smith had a heart attack, which incapacitated him until the following January. As his temporary stand-in, Brown was a *tour de force*. In the important debate on the Chancellor's autumn

37

statement, he savaged Lawson – whose reputation was formidable – for profligacy and abandoning the old and needy. His parliamentary colleagues were electrified. Just two days later, he came top of the annual Shadow Cabinet elections, which was a notable achievement for an MP only in his second term.

These were the years of his maximum popularity, never to be relived. He was the coming man in the Party, the darling of the media, the great hope of anyone who feared that Labour incompetence was allowing the creation of a Tory one-party state. In November 1989, Brown was given the more glamorous job of Shadow Trade and Industry Secretary, having topped the Shadow Cabinet poll for the second successive year. He excelled in the role, which makes it all the more amusing that since becoming Chancellor in 1997 he has more or less neutered the DTI, absorbing the more interesting policymaking bits of its portfolio. These days, he even muses about abolishing the entire department. Anyway, by 1990, political commentators and his fellow MPs were talking of him as a future Labour leader – which is when patrons and mentors, such as Neil Kinnock and John Smith, started to eye him more warily as a potential rival.

Meanwhile Blair was also beginning to make his mark. In the 1989 Shadow Cabinet contest Brown's junior colleague and friend came fourth and – as Shadow Employment Secretary – he ended the Party's support for the closed shop. More significantly, when the Party tested the televisual appeal of its frontbenchers on groups of floating voters (in the focus groups that became notorious in the mid 1990s), Blair was their favourite by a significant margin. At an indeterminate point after 1992, Brown's pronounced and proud Scottishness, in comparison with Blair's rootless and bland Englishness, became perceived at the top of the Labour Party as a handicap for someone with ambitions to go right to the apex of *British* politics.

In spite of Brown's apparently sterling work earlier as Shadow Chief Secretary, Labour's campaign in the general election of April 1992 was yet again undermined by Tory charges that it was planning punitive tax rises. Although John Smith's shadow budget contained relatively few uncosted spending commitments, it called for a new 50 per cent top rate of tax on those earning more than £40,000 a year and the removal of the earnings ceiling on which National Insurance contributions were paid (which effectively meant a higher tax charge for those whose pay was more than £21,000 a year).

Millions on low pay would have benefited, from higher child benefit, increased pensions and a substantial increase in the basic income tax allowance. But effective scare stories ran in the press (especially in the *Daily Mail*), which helped the Tory leader, John Major, to get the vote out. As it happens, Brown and Blair tried to persuade Kinnock and Smith to dump the shadow budget at the end of 1991 and refocus Labour's election campaign on how it would spur economic growth and create employment. To no avail, although Brown himself was permitted to hold his own press conferences in the run-up to the general election – well away from Labour's main ones – where he would highlight the Tories' allegedly poor unemployment record. His reward was a gradual deterioration of his relationship with Smith – who stood to benefit if Labour lost the election and if Kinnock quit as leader, and was therefore vulnerable to the embarrassing charge that he retained the shadow budget precisely because it was unpopular.

The Tories won again, with a small parliamentary majority. But in one respect Major's achievement was astonishing: the Conservatives received 14.1m votes, more than for any party in at least 50 years (and 2.5m more votes than Labour received). Kinnock could not stay on (especially after the hubristic triumphalism of a notorious rally in Sheffield during the campaign).

When he stood down, there was immediate speculation that Brown would challenge for the leadership. "Basically in the run up to 1992 there was a big debate about whether Gordon should run against John Smith" says a senior Labour official. "Blair was urging him to do so. Gordon refused. But I think there was always a fear in some parts of John Smith's world that that's what would happen or might happen." Brown's close allies insist that he never seriously thought about it, that his settled view from the off was that it was "Smith's turn". Their conspiracy theory is that the notion that Brown wanted to challenge Smith was put about by his political enemies, who wanted to further complicate their relationship. They tell murky tales of dark dealings by the Scottish political mafia and a brotherhood of members of the Boilermarkers union (the GMB) – but it's long ago and memories of who said what to whom are confused in the mists of old and bitter hatreds. What is clear is that Brown never made any practical preparations to enter the contest, in the sense that he never instructed his most loyal lieutenant in the Commons, Nick Brown, to take soundings in the parliamentary Party.

On the other hand, Tony Blair agonised over whether to go for the deputy leadership. According to Blair's biographer, John Rentoul (*Tony Blair*, 1995), he was torn between the desire to carry the flag of the "modernisers" at the top of the Party and a fear of upstaging Brown. Blair's friends say that this was the moment that he made a personal sacrifice so as not to upset the balance of his relationship with Brown – and it was clear that it would be the last such sacrifice. Brown's colleagues say that version is balderdash, that Brown talked Blair out of running to protect his old friend from the humiliation of losing. "We talked Tony out of running for the deputy leadership, not because we were jealous of him, but to protect him," says one. "He couldn't win. We had Tony's best interests at heart." Blair probably couldn't have secured the post without the endorsement of John Smith, who wanted to have Margaret Beckett as his number two. When Smith persuaded Beckett to stand, Blair decided not to enter the lists. Smith and Beckett were duly elected. These days Brown's friends regret that Blair took their advice. "I wish we had let Tony run," says a senior MP. "It would have been better for us if he had lost and been humiliated."

The new leader gave Blair and Brown two of the great opposition posts, those of Shadow Home Secretary and Shadow Chancellor respectively. In theory, at a relatively youthful 41, this was a great achievement by Brown. However it inaugurated two black and scarring years for him.

Brown was persuaded that Labour had simply not been rigorous enough in persuading the electorate that the economy was safe in its hands and that it wasn't a vindictive imposer of taxes on the successful and the aspirational. So he tore up Smith's shadow budget. Gone were the explicit plans to raise tax rates. He then proceeded to use his new authority to block any attempts by his front bench colleagues to come up with policies that had spending implications.

Previously, Labour had concocted initiatives that would be implemented only "as resources allow". But Brown believed this formula provided ammunition for the Tories to foment fears of Labour's profligacy – the Conservatives could and would put a price on Labour's conditional policies and would then present them as Labour's "secret" plot to spend, spend, spend. Given Labour's spendthrift history, many voters would be minded to believe the charge that it would throw financial caution to the wind, once it had the reins of power. The only way to allay their fears was to impose a ban on any polices that would cost money – which Brown duly did.

Someone who knows him well explains the pressures he faced: "We refused to make spending commitments. We then rejected a return to crude Keynesianism, a massive injection into the economy, which was being recommended (notably by Peter Hain, then a backbencher who made a lot of noise). And we made our employment creation dependent on responsibilities through the New Deal, which was very controversial (especially for Brown, who had savaged the Tories in the 1980s for putting pressure on unemployment claimants to take jobs with threats to cut their benefits, but was now on the verge of emulating them)". Inevitably, he felt isolated, says this minister: "It was a pretty unhappy time, because basically you took on people from the left and then you were undermined by the right. I mean that's what happens. You've just got to live with that."

But for all the alienation of his friends and colleagues, Brown wouldn't budge. He was making an almost religious atonement for the sins of Labour's past. He put on a hairshirt and insisted the rest of the

Party did too. And he further alienated many of his natural supporters in parliament and the country by adopting a very macho stance on Britain's membership of the European Exchange Rate Mechanism (see pages 182-86). In essence, he was defending an over-valued pound that was crippling the British economy. For many Labour Party members, he was betraying the workers who were being thrown out of manufacturing jobs as their companies found it impossible to compete with sterling so strong.

His motives were for the best. Brown was trying, in just a couple of years, to build a reputation for Labour as a hardnosed manager of the economy. Although staying in the ERM may well have been an intrinsically bad policy, he didn't want anyone to allege that Labour was "as usual" going for the soft option. Calling for devaluation would have been seen as just that – especially since for 70 years, almost every Labour administration had faced extreme pressure to devalue sterling and had always buckled. A friend of his explains the dilemma:

> If Gordon could have been told unequivocally that we were definitely going to leave the ERM, he might have taken a different strategy. But he didn't know that. In fact many people advising him at the time were telling him differently... If Labour had gone out in advance and advocated devaluation, it would have been seen as unpatriotic. And if it turned out that devaluation was unnecessary, we would have totally cemented ourselves as the Party of devaluation.

That said, even his colleagues concede that his execution of this policy left something to be desired: "The criticism you can make of Gordon at that period is that once you have made that decision, you should probably sit tight. And probably he paid a certain price in credibility by putting out lots of press releases when there wasn't much to be said."

Anyway, this scattergun approach to public relations came to an abrupt halt in early 1994, with the arrival of Charlie Whelan as his spokesman and Ed Balls as his economic adviser. Their role was to give more discipline and shape to Brown's political mission, although he had already put in place the building blocks that would eventually persuade voters that the economy was safe in his hands. Many Labour MPs and party supporters, however, couldn't see the truth that he was working to serve their interests. They felt hurt and confused by what they saw (mistakenly) as his rejection of a basic commitment to expand the state for the good of the least well-off. Few understood his view that "big government" would only be possible again when Labour had won back trust through proving its economic competence. Brown's stock in the Party started to fall, while he stayed true to his mission to redeem the economic credibility of his Party – little knowing the sacrifice he was making.

CHAPTER TWO

Losing the leadership, winning power

The thesis – that Labour would never again be able to achieve its social objectives unless and until it had become a credible manager of the economy – was implicit in an influential pamphlet Ed Balls wrote at the end of 1992, called "Euro-Monetarism: why Britain was ensnared and how it should escape". The seeds of Brown's policy towards monetary union and – more importantly – his transfer of the control of interest rates to the Bank of England were both sown by this paper, published by Labour's most venerable think tank, the Fabian Society, which Balls discussed with Brown while he was drafting it (see pages 118-21).

When he wrote it, Balls was a 25-year old leader writer on the *Financial Times* who was flirting with the idea of going into politics. And, slightly oddly, it was the *FT*'s then editor, Richard Lambert, who seemed to be encouraging Balls along the political route when he told him that the Shadow Chancellor was sniffing around him (Lambert is now a member of the Bank of England's monetary policy committee, having been appointed by Brown and Balls in 2003).

What happened was that Lambert had been chatting to Swraj Paul, the wealthy Asian industrialist and longstanding Labour supporter (who became a working peer in 1996). Paul had informed Lambert that Balls was going to be approached by Brown – which duly happened (Balls was probably recommended to Brown by Gavyn Davies, the influential City economist who was to have a brief and lively spell as chairman of the BBC from 2001 to 2004, and by Geoff Mulgan, an adviser to Brown who became one of Blair's most influential recruits to Downing Street after the 1997 election).

Balls met Brown for the first time in October 1992 and then spent a year as his informal adviser, regularly going down to Westminster in the early morning for 90-minute chats, before bowling along to the *FT* for the leader conference at midday. The *FT* was an inordinately civilised place to work back then, a refuge for gentleman journalists (no longer, alas). At this stage he hadn't completely decided to quit journalism and might well have stayed at the *FT* if he had been given his dream job of Africa editor. But in the event, he decided that the opportunity to help shape the agenda of the first Labour government in almost 20 years was too good to miss. So he resigned from the *FT* in October 1993 and formally left the paper three months later. For the following three and a half years, Swraj Paul effectively paid his salary, as a donor to the Industrial Research Trust, which covered the expenses of Brown's office in opposition (according to a friend of the industrialist).

Like Brown, Balls has been politically active most of his conscious life. He told me in an interview in 2004 that as a child growing up in Nottingham he wanted to be an MP (though he toyed with being a doctor until he learned that he couldn't cope with the sight of blood). His father, an academic zoologist, was chairman of the local Labour ward and Balls joined the Party at the age of 16. However, his school, Nottingham High School, was considerably more elitist than Brown's. It is a fee-paying, boys' day school with a royal charter from Henry VIII and alumni who include Ken Clarke, the former Conservative Chancellor, and Lord Richardson, a one-time governor of the Bank of England.

In the year above Balls was Ed Davey, who became a Liberal Democrat MP and a spokesman on local government issues. Davey, the school's head boy, gave a leg-up to a future political opponent. "He had a whole set of detailed 'A' Level history notes which his brother had given him, and he passed them on to me," Balls recalls, before making the inevitable tribal jibe*: "They were the last sensitive or useful papers he has ever given to me – and he's certainly got none back."

Balls followed his father to Keble College, Oxford – which is a heavy-drinking rugby college, without a particularly distinguished intellectual pedigree. As a student, Balls manifested apparent political ambivalence by joining the Labour club and the Oxford University Conservative Association – which didn't in fact reflect any uncertainty about where his allegiances lay, but showed a ruthless determination to hear the speeches of as many senior politicians of whatever shade as possible (and learn from them). He immersed himself in university politics, rather than party politics, and is remembered by contemporaries as being both sickeningly self-confident and too self-consciously grown-up for most tastes (in a dispute over room rents, he upset fellow students by being emollient to the college authorities: Balls would say he was just being realistic). His real political awakening, however, stemmed from a post-graduate stint at Harvard on a Kennedy Scholarship, where he was tutored by the future US Treasury Secretary, Larry Summers. "When I went to Harvard I thought it was a possibility I would go to the Treasury as a civil servant [he had passed the civil service entrance exam after leaving Keble]," Balls says. "But by the time I came back to the UK, there was no possibility I was going to do that. I'd seen British/American politics."

His salient characteristics are that he's immensely hardworking, devoted to Labour's cause, fiercely loyal to Brown and possessed of armour-plated, lethally sharp elbows. He's obsessed with football and supports Norwich City, the team of the town of his birth. As an occasional player for the *FT*, the Hampstead Heathens (a trendy amateur side) and the parliamentary lobby (for which he was a ringer), he would hang around in front of goal. "He has an acute footballing brain, but his body can't always keep up," says one of his team-mates. There's a drum-kit in

* The quotes from Ed Balls that follow are hitherto unpublished extracts from an interview he gave me for the *Sunday Telegraph* in July 2004, after he resigned from the Treasury.

the top floor study of the tall modern house he occupies with his wife – the minister Yvette Cooper – on the outskirts of Castleford, in Yorkshire, where he does the cooking at a huge annual, American-style barbecue, which she throws for local Labour dignatories and party members in their large garden. At the time of writing they have three children under five.

They love big, bustling events: his January 1998 wedding in Eastbourne was an immense affair, thronged by hundreds of relations, politicians, academics and journalists, which included fairground attractions and assorted ethnic food stalls. "If we give a party we like to do it properly," Balls says. Superficially it was the complete opposite of the small, hush-hush wedding of Brown to Sarah Macaulay in August 2000 at his Fife home. But the Browns' supposedly more intimate affair became a national media event, mobbed by snappers and hacks, who were not discouraged from hanging around outside for a sighting of the newlyweds.

Anyway, while Balls was settling into his new existence as Brown's adviser, factotum and all-round sounding board in early 1994, Blair's reputation was going from strength to strength, especially among the London-based journalists who shape opinion. Looking back on this period, Brown and his advisers believe they made an elementary mistake in giving Blair a relatively free run in schmoozing so-called opinion formers. "Gordon always believed that he would sort out the policy and that Tony would sort out the London-side of the politics, which in retrospect was rather naïve," is how one of Brown's friends puts it.

Among the wider electorate, Blair's fist-in-velvet-glove approach to home affairs was also playing well. It remains particularly irksome for Brown's friends and family that it was Brown who invented Blair's famous catchphrase, "Tough on crime, tough on the causes of crime." One says: "Gordon actually created Tony's platform, both by arguing with John Smith after the 1992 election that he should be given the shadow home portfolio and then by penning the 'tough on crime' slogan. The debt has neither been acknowledged or repaid."

At the end of 1993 and beginning of 1994, there was a climate of mistrust at the top of the Labour Party. There had just been a bruising fight at Labour's 1993 annual conference to introduce greater democracy into the election of candidates and of the Party leader, commonly described as the battle over OMOV (or One Member One Vote). In the end, John Smith had pushed through a slightly tawdry compromise reform, against considerable opposition from the trade unions. This was a significant victory for him, but for Blair and Brown – arch-modernisers and proponents of putting greater distance between the Party and its trade-union founders – it did not go far enough.

Labour was now well ahead in the opinion polls, but Blair and Brown did not believe electoral victory could be assured in the absence of an unremitting struggle to wrest control of the Party from its trade union founders and dump obsolete ideological baggage. Smith, by contrast, wanted to call a halt to the internal strife. Now it's difficult, for those outside the crucible of Labour politics, to grasp the extent of the personal antagonism that a dispute of this sort can engender. Brown came to believe – with good reason – that Smith's supporters and apparatchiks were out to damage him (around this time, one of Smith's allies was allegedly propagating the silly idea that Brown is gay – which, in the Neanderthal Labour Party of the early 1990s, was unhelpful to him). Some of Smith's people regarded Brown's rejection of the pre-election shadow budget as a direct criticism of their hero, since it had been his shadow budget. And they were increasingly neurotic about whether Brown might challenge Smith for the leadership one day. So, for all sorts of reasons, Brown's stock was unusually low in the Labour Party. But it didn't bother him as much as it should have, as one of his friends explains:

At the time, we did not think John Smith was going to die. Well probably if we had reviewed the medical position we might have. And Gordon
obviously knew about all this far more than we did, and probably should
have thought about it more. But we thought there were still two years till
the election. The Tories were in a useless position. Gordon had gone

through a difficult period and was going to come out of it.

The assumption was always that Gordon would be the next leader, not Tony, in everybody's mind, including – as we thought – everybody on the Blair side. If we had said back then, 'If John Smith went down now, how would things look?' – I don't know what the answer would have been. We had never really asked that question. He [Smith] wasn't going to die. And in any case, Gordon was going to be the leader, so therefore it was irrelevant.

But there was more to it than that, as one of Brown's confidants – who took contemporaneous notes about the relationship between Brown and Blair – explains. He says that – in all the talk about a deal on the succession forged in 1994 between the two pretenders for the Labour throne – an earlier explicit deal has been ignored:

The original pact was undoubtedly that Gordon would stand when the leadership became vacant and Tony wouldn't. The deal was that Tony would have his chance later. This provided protection to Gordon. It explains why he felt able to make himself so unpopular with Labour MPs by driving through reforms to economic policy which many of his colleagues hated. The deal was his protection, his insurance, for making himself so unpopular.

Another friend of Brown, an MP who has been close to him for years, confirms the existence of this agreement, but says that it had a date-limit of the subsequent general election, at which point it would expire. However, it was still in force in 1994, or at least that's what Brown believed.

On the other hand, he seems to have turned a Nelsonian eye towards the behaviour of his long-time room-mate, since Blair for a couple of years at least had been manifesting an intention to emerge from the long shadow cast by his friend. Blair had, as we've seen, flagged up his political ambitions in 1992, when agonising about whether to run for the deputy leadership. Even so, one of Brown's friends insists: "We had no idea that Tony Blair's side had made a decision that that's what they were going to do [ie challenge for the leadership]. They had a plan of how they were going to do it. We were far behind the curve."

***

When Smith died of a massive and unexpected heart attack at 9.15am on Thursday May 12, 1994, Brown was knocked for six. To some extent, he regarded himself as Smith's protégé – although all relationships within the incestuous Scottish Labour Party are complicated by petty rivalries and insecurities. The blow was all the greater, because his discourse with Smith had become strained in the preceding months by Smith's reluctance to go all the way in overhauling the Party's antediluvian constitution and his conspicuous lack of support for Brown's reform of economic policy ("They were still friends," says a colleague of Brown, "but political discourse was not easy"). Brown's personal life was also unstable at the time: he had wound up one longstanding relationship (with a lawyer called Marion Caldwell) and had resumed another one, with the broadcaster, Sheena McDonald. "He was not in great shape," says one of his intimates.

Brown spent much of the fateful day expressing his debt and gratitude to Smith by writing obituaries. For just a few hours, he believed there was plenty of time to prepare for an eventual leadership contest, because of his conviction that Blair would honour the agreement that he would be the sole candidate of the modernising wing of the Party. But after Brown gathered together his closest supporters to discuss tactics for the campaign, he had a rude awakening. There was a bandwagon rolling for Blair in the media and parliament: Blair would almost certainly run – or at least that's what journalists were predicting and what Brown was told by his savvier allies in the Commons, such as Nick Brown.

The Shadow Chancellor felt betrayed, devastated. And what's fascinating is that he did not direct his visible anger towards Blair. His fury was instead channelled towards Peter Mandelson, who didn't manifest the unquestioning loyalty to his cause – which Brown felt entitled to expect – and who would go on to secretly manage Blair's campaign (using the twee sobriquet, "Bobby", after JFK's brother). A friend of Brown says they knew of Mandelson's role long before it became public:

> He was exposed in the leadership campaign as this Bobby figure. But from our point of view – from where we sat – from the moment John Smith died he was working for Blair, I don't think there was any doubt about that. It was just our assumption... As far as we were concerned, Peter Mandelson was doing Tony's media: that's just the way it was.

Mandelson himself insists that he was as surprised as Brown when Blair was described in the press as the front-runner to succeed Smith, almost a shoo-in. He claims that he had not noticed the extent to which Blair's stock had been rising as Brown's fell. And that it was only after consulting the late Donald Dewar, the former First Minister of Scotland who was an influential frontbencher, that he had concluded that Brown was unlikely to win. Also, Mandelson dates his irrevocable fallout with Brown as having taken place almost four months later, in September 1994 – after Blair had won the leadership – at an "away day" to discuss the Party's future. In the unlikely setting of Chewton Glen, a lavish hotel in Hampshire, Brown allegedly made an inappropriate proposition to Mandelson to the effect that if they acted as a cabal of two, they could control the Party. Mandelson replied that he could not undermine Blair in that way – and it was at that moment, he feels, that Brown began to view him as the enemy.

Whether it took place in May or September, the estrangement of Blair and Brown was a defining event in the creation of new Labour. The sheer hatred and mistrust of Mandelson that was engendered in Brown was poisonous to him and the Party for years. If Mandelson was no longer with him, he had to be against him – which was an analysis that became self-fulfilling. From now on, every negative press article about Brown would be attributed by his circle to the malign influence of Mandelson. And every time Blair endeavoured to push a policy disliked by Brown, the future Chancellor and his allies would see Mandelson pulling the strings, urging Blair on. Brown had regarded Mandelson as an ally and a friend. It's understandable that there should be an emotional side to their relationship, in that they had been brothers-in-arms in the painful struggle against the tyranny of Labour's unreconstructed socialists. But it wasn't rational for Brown to blame Mandelson more than Blair.

It was a classic case of displacement. Brown couldn't have faced up to his fury with Blair, because that would have been the end of his career, if Blair were to win the leadership. The stakes were less high in an open conflict with the newly elected MP for Hartlepool. "Brown was genuinely hurt by Mandelson's behaviour," says one of his old friends. "I must admit I thought it was a bit exaggerated, but it was very real. And it has rankled for years." The marriage metaphor is quite difficult to eschew. Brown and Blair were the married couple, Mandelson the mistress who transferred allegiances. The marriage survived, largely because the mistress could be blamed for all its problems.

But the defection of Mandelson does not explain why Brown decided to give Blair a free run, why he didn't run against him. Brown had felt for years that leading Labour was his destiny and then opted not to stake his claim. What on earth dissuaded him? Apart from anything else, Brown was steeped in Labour history and was acutely aware that there is a long tradition of reformers and modernisers destroying each other's prospects by competing against each other. One famous example was in the 1976 leadership contest after Wilson resigned, when three authentic giants from Labour's right wing – Roy Jenkins, Denis Healey and Tony Crosland – all put themselves forward. The result was that the vote of progressive-minded MPs was split between the three of them and Jenkins – the strongest of the three – could manage no better than third place in the poll. Jenkins withdrew from the contest, leaving the field clear for the "unity" candidate, Jim Callaghan, to win.

There was no real dishonour in the context of Labour history for

Brown and Blair to fight each other. It wouldn't have been pretty, and many of their supporters would have been upset. But it would have been in the spirit of a party forged out of personal animosities and clashing egos. What's more, unlike the self-indulgent self-destruction of Labour's intellectual right-wing in the contest of 1976, it was unlikely that a contest between Blair and Brown would have allowed a third candidate to emerge victorious: on this unique occasion, dividing the vote of the progressives probably wouldn't have been a disaster for both because there was no potential runner of their stature and popular appeal who could bring together the bickering factions.

So why didn't he enter the lists? The ungenerous explanation – which is the one propagated by Blair's supporters – is that Brown recognised that he couldn't win, that Blair had become too strong in the preceding months. But the facts are not conclusive on that. It's true that Blair had the edge over Brown at the time (indeed, I remember saying to myself, within seconds of hearing that Smith had died, that Blair would probably succeed him – as well as feeling more upset about Smith's death than I might have expected, since in my rare professional encounters with Smith I had found him very irascible). But the result of elections is frequently different from the odds at the outset of campaigning (as Labour learned to its cost in the 1992 general election).

Brown's stock may have been down, but it was not at rock bottom. For a start, there was a caucus of Labour MPs – not all of them Scottish – who were devoted to his cause. And, although much has been made of the fact that in the 1993 elections to Labour's National Executive Committee, Brown came in last place of those chosen from constituents' votes, behind Blair, the difference between them was tiny: Brown received 414,000 votes, compared with Blair's 421,000. However, in the equally important elections to the Shadow Cabinet of October 20, 1993, Brown – in fourth place with 160 votes – performed significantly better than Blair, who came sixth with 142 votes (what's striking about that poll is that the two zealots for abandoning Labour's traditional ideological baggage, Brown and Blair, were beaten by a trio of more left-wing contenders, who would soon be unflatteringly labelled as "old Labour": Robin Cook, way out in front in first place, with Frank Dobson and John Prescott joint second with 163 votes each). In other words, the most current real polls of two of the constituents of the electoral college that chooses the Labour leader had one group, the rank-and-file, opting for Blair, and another group, the MPs, going for Brown.

On that basis, the outcome would have been decided by the trade unions. And it is by no means certain that they would have chosen Blair, given that Brown was much more recognisably one of them (for all that both Brown and Blair were keen to reduce the unions' grip on the Party). So the major differences between the two of them in the middle of May 1994 was that Blair had the explicit and implicit backing of most newspapers – which made the climate less benign for Brown – and that he seemed to recognise immediately that this was his moment. Meanwhile, Brown was in a state of some personal confusion, forced to come to terms with the untimely death of one friend and the apparent treachery of two more important ones.

Towards the end of the month, a BBC survey of the three sections of the electoral college showed that Blair had a lead. But Brown and his advisers, headed at this moment by Nick Brown (who would become Chief Whip in 1997), were persuaded they could win. They might have been wrong, but I don't think Brown withdrew because of a fear that he faced a humiliating defeat. Interestingly, such was the verdict of the political commentator Andrew Marr, whose assessment of the balance of power within Labour has normally been astute. Writing in the *Independent*, he said: "Had he stood, he might have run Tony Blair quite close. Plenty of serious people in the Party thought he could have won. Now he will never know."

Brown's explanation for his withdrawal is that he could have won only by forming alliances with traditionalist elements in the Party to whom he did not wish to be beholden (either in fact or in anyone's perception), by summoning up what his friend Nick Brown calls "forces of darkness". He believes his appeal to so-called old Labour was stronger than Blair's.

And Nick Brown – whose skills in the mischievious art of drumming up votes are finely honed – advised him at the time that deals were there to be done with trade unions and the left. But, if he had won on that basis, his debut at the helm would probably have been marred by conflict. If he had pushed ahead with modernising the Party, which he would have done, he would have been accused of treachery by many of those who voted for him. It was not a stable foundation for forming a government of long duration. A colleague of Brown elucidates:

> He knew quite quickly the extent of the operation being done [that Blair was gearing up to go for the leadership]. He knew also that if he had made a decision to go for it, he could have – on this point different people have different views – he could have beaten Blair. But what would have had to have been done to get to that point would have been so destructive to modernisation and to the future of the Labour Party, that he couldn't have been part of it.

There may be an element of *ex post* rationalisation in this account. But I don't doubt Brown's sincerity when citing this motive. And his precept, that he would never want to inherit the leadership of a splintered and warring party, was later to dominate his behaviour in government, forcing him to hold back when sorely tempted to launch an open war against a Prime Minister whose policies he increasingly resiled from. The paramount importance of party unity became almost an article of faith for him. It did not stop him fomenting dissent against Blair when he profoundly disagreed with the direction of a new policy (such as a plan for the *de facto* privatisation of hospitals in 2002). And it did not stop him furthering his own cause as the supposed natural successor to Blair. But as soon as he has ever calculated that his and his supporters' actions would leave him in charge of an unleadable party, riven by internal strife, he has pulled back (most famously, when he urged Nick Brown in early 2004 to cease opposition to the introduction of so-called top-up fees for university students).

This is no rose-tinted view of Brown as a saintly political figure, always altruistically sacrificing his personal interests for the party. He was and is demonstrating behaviour that he would regard as self-interested, on the basis of his years of academic study of Labour's long and unedifying history of civil wars. Brown has only ever wanted to be leader and Prime Minister on his terms. In 1994, those terms were that the Party must unite around the need to "modernise", to abandon the ideological trappings of its origins in the class war of the early 20th century. He did not think that would be possible if he won the leadership as the de facto candidate of the unreconstructed left against the fresh-faced, representative of Middle England, Tony Blair. And in that spirit, for the succeeding decade until the autumn of 2004, he worked to secure an elegant and non-disruptive handover of power from Blair to him, to minimise the risk of damage to the Party's integrity (although he has recently had to abandon the idea that Blair will anoint him as his natural successor and acclaim him as the heir to a modernised Labour Party that they both created; and he has belatedly come to terms with the painful reality that, if he does become Prime Minister, the prize may come only through strife — see Chapter Ten.

Back in 1994, there was supposed to be no campaigning for the leadership in the immediate aftermath of Smith's death. All the potential candidates acceded to a request by Labour's then chairman, David Blunkett, that no-one would declare they were running or start to garner votes until after June 9, which was the date of elections for the European parliament. However, there was plenty of jockeying behind the scenes and a frenzy of speculation in the press. By Monday May 15, just four days after Smith's death, Brown was working on a twin-track strategy. He was at his home in North Queensferry with Andrew Brown, who took a week off from his job in television to help his brother at this crucial time. Brown *minimus* is, in fact, one of the few reliable witnesses of a series of events — the complex choreography of the discussions and meetings between Blair and Brown about which of them would be the candidate — whose import has since been hotly disputed. He was with his sibling around the clock and he wrote down what he saw and heard.

Andrew Brown's view is that the most important negotiation on the leadership question between Blair and Brown took place over three and a half hours late at night on May 15, more than two weeks before the famous *dîner à deux* at Granita in Islington, which has since – and slightly misleadingly – entered into the folklore of the Labour Party as the night of "the deal". Blair had flown up to Edinburgh to pay his respects to John Smith's widow, Elizabeth, and was staying at the home of a wealthy lawyer, Nick Ryden, who was an old friend from their schooldays at Fettes (Blair stayed there again on May 20, on the night after Smith's funeral). At around 9pm, Brown was driven – by one of his oldest friends, Dr Colin Currie, a consultant in geriatric medicine who has written thrillers under the pseudonym, Colin Douglas, and has helped Brown on his speeches for many years – from his home in Fife to Ryden's Victorian tenement house.

The essential elements of the power-sharing agreement between these two men, which was to determine the future of the Labour Party and the future of the UK, were thrashed out here. This has never been disclosed before, because both Blair and Brown would even now be embarrassed to admit that only a few short days after the death of John Smith they were carving up his legacy. But it would have been absurd – almost dishonest in respect of their own relationship – for them not to discuss this so early. For more than a decade, they had been a double act in British politics, ebullient Labour twins fizzing with optimism and ideas, as close to each other as any two MPs can be. There was no possibility of them delaying discussion of the resonant subject that mattered most to each of them.

It was a private tête à tête, with no one else in the room, as were all their subsequent conversations prior to the announcement on June 1 that Brown would not contest the election. What they eventually agreed therefore – as Blair, the lawyer, knew well – would be a million miles from a witnessed legal contract. It was vulnerable to the different interpretation of the two parties, and their views of what transpired – both then and since – have been coloured by their conflicting interests. And it was made all the more complicated in that one of the parties, Brown, was feeling let down by his closest friend, and the other – Blair – wanted to assuage the guilt he felt for the pain being experienced by Brown.

At this first important meeting, Blair played the card that he was better placed than Brown to avert any kind of serious contest for the leadership. He was, he argued, on better terms with the Party heavy-weights, John Prescott and Robin Cook. If he stood, but Brown didn't, they could probably be persuaded not to mount their own respective challenges. As it turned out, Blair was wrong: Prescott stood for both the leadership and the deputy leadership (he became deputy), as did Margaret Beckett (the acting leader after John Smith's demise). There was also a discussion of what Brown's role would be in a Shadow Cabinet or Cabinet *were* he to let Blair have a clear run.

Brown's negotiating position was conditioned by his anger that Blair was in the process of reneging on what he regarded as a promise that he was to have been the sole candidate. So, as one of his confidants recalls, any new agreement between them had to be completely deliverable and unambiguous:

Because Gordon felt betrayed, he made sure there was an explicit deal with Tony. He made clear to Tony that the betrayal was terrible. It was only because he had trusted that Tony wouldn't run that he had for two years been acting against his own interest, in the way he pushed through unpopular reforms to Labour's economic policy. He felt deceived, Tony had cheated him.

So Gordon needed an explicit deal, because Tony had turned him over. And the deal was that he needed the power and freedom to estab-lish his own political identity under Tony's leadership; he couldn't be subsumed as just another member of the Tony Blair team. That was the over-riding priority, to have total autonomy over the social and econom-ic agenda.

Despite the fraught antecedents, the mood of this initial meeting was apparently fairly amicable. Brown took a taxi back to his home at around 12.30pm, arriving there at 1pm – when he immediately confided in his brother. Brown was excited, because he sensed that big opportunities were opening up for him even if he were not to become leader. He told Andrew Brown that Blair had promised that he would have the kind of independent power he wanted, in the event that Blair took the helm. However, Brown had not yet made a commitment that he wouldn't enter the contest.

The following day, Blair and Brown met again, this time at Brown's North Queensferry house. Andrew Brown picked Tony Blair up from Elizabeth Smith's home in Edinburgh, deposited him with his brother, made them coffee and then left them to it. The mood this time between them was more difficult and their negotiation adjourned after just half an hour. Blair was ushered out to the garden in a manifestly tense and nervous state, where Andrew Brown tried to make small talk with him, while Gordon Brown made a series of telephone calls to his allies. It was at this meeting that Blair first mooted that he wouldn't want to be leader for more than ten years, thus implying that he would quit before the end of a second term of a Labour government (on the assumption that Labour was lucky enough to win two terms).

After this inconclusive meeting, Andrew Brown drove Blair to the airport. They knew each other well, from Brown's days as a political researcher at Westminster for his brother in the mid-1980s. Andrew Brown's impression was that Blair was under great pressure from his friends and supporters to secure Gordon Brown's promise not to run, which he had failed to do. But what he mostly manifested in this car journey was remorse for the hurt that his own ambition was causing his friend. "I love Gordon," he told Andrew Brown. "He is the best mind the Labour Party has ever had."

It was "bad luck", said Blair, that Brown was out of favour. He, Blair, had not sought the greatness that was being thrust upon him. It was just one of those things. He had always planned his career on the basis that he would probably be a cabinet minister one day and then he would have liked to have gone off to Brussels as a European Union commissioner. But events beyond his control – especially the widespread perception that Labour needed a leader who would appeal to the small "c" conservatives of Middle England – were pushing him in a different direction. What also struck Andrew Brown was that Blair made clear his concern that if there was a fight between Brown and himself, Brown might well win. There was no hint from Blair that he thought the leadership was in the bag.

The negotiations between Blair and Brown continued along the lines laid down on May 15 and May 16 for another fortnight. There was a parallel series of conversations between two of their closest aides, Sue Nye and Anji Hunter, who ran their respective offices. According to a government member, Blair would say to Hunter, "Look I've got a young family, I'm not going to go on forever," with the express purpose of this being passed on to Nye, for transmission to Brown. "Tony was quite explicit that they were both young enough for Gordon to be able to succeed him and that he would support Gordon as his successor," says a friend of the Prime Minister.

***

Eventually Brown decided not to challenge Blair. He communicated this to his closest allies at a dinner on May 30 at Joe Allen, the American-style restaurant in Covent Garden. Also there were Nick Brown, Charlie Whelan and Murray Elder. Brown and Whelan made a last-ditch attempt to persuade Brown to run, insisting that he could win. Elder – who had known Brown since childhood and could therefore read him as well as anyone – told them to pipe down. However, Nick Brown, had a particular reason for wishing to know precisely what the Shadow Chancellor was going to do. He had been organising Gordon Brown's support and needed permission from him to release a gang of MPs from their individual pledges to vote for him in a leadership contest. Some of these MPs had been drifting away from Brown in any case, because they could read the runes and did not want to be seen to be backing a non-runner. Far better for the ambitious to throw their weight behind the coming man, Blair, whose own lieutenants, Alun Michael and Peter Kilfoyle, were aggressively rounding up MPs prepared to nominate him for the contest. Brown gave Nick Brown the nod to tear up the pledges.

Gordon Brown's failure to campaign as systematically or aggressively as Blair in the preceding days made his decision not to run something of a *fait accompli*. Even so, Blair appears to have been unaware of this, when the two met the following night at Granita, in Upper Street in Islington, North London, on May 31. Granita (which is now closed) served the characterless but fashionable "modern European" food that proliferated in the early 1990s — and its décor was also that clinical, unthreatening, European "modern" look. It was supposed to be a private talk, but Brown — as an act of mischief, to destabilise and discomfort Blair, which it did — walked into the room with Ed Balls. In fact, the principal reason Balls had accompanied him was simply to make sure that Brown reached the right restaurant: Brown was a stranger in modish Islington (where the Blairs had their home), he had never been to Granita before and his colleagues did not have enormous confidence in his orienteering skills. After a drink, Balls was relieved to take his leave of the two. The atmosphere was tense and it was clear this was a conversation that only the duo could have. Although the meeting had been billed by Blair as a discussion about what policies should be adopted by a modernising leadership, Brown was aware that what Blair really wanted to know was whether his friend would stand aside.

Since that famous dinner there have been various versions of what was said and why. Was there a formal deal that Blair would make way for Brown at some later date? Did Brown secure promises about the extent of his power as Shadow Chancellor and future Chancellor? This is what actually happened.

Blair was still not confident that Brown would remove himself from the race for the leadership, and he was not taking for granted that he could beat Brown. In fact, to his credit, Blair never complacently or arrogantly assumes that he'll be the victor in an election, whatever the polling data says, and in this case the data was mixed (thus Blair manifested a profound lack of confidence that Labour would win the 1997 general election, even when all the polls indicated there would be a landslide in his favour, and for years after that crushing victory he behaved as though his grip on office was hanging by a thread). Or to put it another way, in elections he leaves nothing to chance. So if Brown was a potential obstacle in the path of his personal triumph, he would do all he could to secure the removal of that obstacle. Striking a deal with Brown is completely consistent with Blair's record of ruthless pragmatism.

As for Brown, he had firmed up in his mind what he wanted from Blair in terms of the powers he would have as Shadow Chancellor and – if all went well – as Chancellor. He was looking for a formal agreement about how things were going to be done under Blair as leader. What he cared about was whether he would have sufficient autonomous control of social and economic policy and whether he would be consulted when important appointments were made to party and government posts.

Did he also go to Granita determined to ask for a promise from Blair that he would quit as Labour leader at a specific moment? Brown's friends say that's not the case. One says: "Gordon never ever went asking for any agreement about the succession. I think it was implicit that, as and when the time came, he would be well-placed. But Gordon never went seeking a date." The conversation at Joe Allen the previous night had all been about the importance of securing more conventional spoils from Blair in return for the Brown team's co-operation, as one of Brown's allies recalls:

Gordon talked to us about what we should get out of Tony for not running. It was 'we', but to be honest I never thought he could deliver on more than some role for himself. Tony would want to keep Gordon on side. But the rest of us wouldn't matter. I always thought Gordon could only cut a deal for himself, not for the rest of us. And we have ended up paying quite a price for being his supporters. But that's always the way when you back the loser. The complaint of the Brownites is that we paid a high price for him not running."

Brown's supporters insist that he never *asked* for a promise from Blair that he would fight only two elections, that he would stand down during the second term of a Labour government. They insist, rather, that the promise was *given*, freely and unsought. Is this credible? I think so: Brown is not a dishonest man, although he has a history of being naïve about his relationship with Blair.

By way of support for my view, I can reveal that Gordon Brown immediately debriefed Nick Brown on what had been agreed at Granita, when he saw him later that same evening at yet another restaurant, Rodin, opposite the Palace of Westminster in the atrium of 4 Millbank (also "modern European" in style; also defunct). Brown could not have done much eating at Granita, because he had a second meal there with his girl-friend of the time, Sheena McDonald. She sent a bottle of champagne over to Nick Brown, who was sitting at another table. Gordon Brown then told Nick Brown that not only had Blair promised that he would only fight two elections as leader but that he would endorse Brown as leader when the time came.

Was this a deal, a contract? Not in any legal sense. Apart from anything else, it's either silly or profoundly hubristic (and certainly undemocratic and unconstitutional) to think that two men eating bland "European" food at a fashionable North London restaurant could determine who would be premier a decade later. But does that mean that what Blair said was of no consequence? Was Brown foolish to attach any weight at all to Blair's offer to make way for him at some indeterminate point between 2003 and 2004? Gordon Brown takes the old-fashioned view that friends should not say things to each other which they don't mean. Of course, friends in practice do that all the time. But that doesn't mean there is no obligation on the promiser to keep the relevant promise.

What's striking is that Brown's friends are split down the middle over how Brown should have reacted to Blair's mooted treaty of succession.

One says that it was perfectly reasonable of Brown to take it at face value: "There is no doubt that a deal on succession was being offered... But the interesting question is why, given that it wasn't necessary or being sought, it should have been offered... He was clear to Gordon not simply that they would work together on policy but also that he was not intending to fight the third election." Another is a little more cynical about the whole affair:

The deal was always Gordon getting complete control of economic policy. That's all it was. I'm sure Tony said something like, 'I won't go on forever, I'll stand down in the middle of the second term,' or something like that. But it wasn't something you could hold him to. It was the sort of thing you say to your oldest friend and ally to keep him happy. Or at least it is the sort of thing Tony says.

For Brown and his friends, Blair has an annoying habit of making big promises and then – in the style of the lawyer he was trained to be – subsequently pointing to small print that proves the contract null and void. Even more infuriating for Brown is that he's been characterised by Blair's supporters in respect of the Granita deal as a whingeing supplicant trying to enforce a mythical promise – whereas the true position, Brown feels, is that it's Blair who has acted without honour. A friend of Brown's says:

The popular impression – of Gordon demanding a date [for Blair's departure] in 1994, being given it, and then him repeatedly raising it with Tony ever since – is a fiction. It was actually the other way around. It has always been Blair asking for Gordon's co-operation. And Gordon saying, 'Of course I'll work with you, so long as we are clear that where we are going is the right direction, consistent with our goals.'

They [Blair's allies] tried to invent this idea of Gordon as the person desperate for the deal, and Blair resisting and saying it was never true. That was a combination of [Blair's] guilt and an attempt to get out of it.

So if the promise on the succession was freely offered by Blair, what then were Brown's actual conditions for withdrawing from the contest? Well they stemmed from Brown's fundamental lack of trust in Blair's commitment to an agenda based on social justice – and they were designed to give him unprecedented power as a prospective Chancellor. It was at this moment that he became the real power in the land over the domestic agenda in a future Labour government. His ostensible motive was that he saw his destiny as the protector of the Party's traditional values. This had been made clear on May 22, nine days before the Granita meeting, when he set out his ideological stall at the annual conference of the Welsh Labour Party in Swansea. Brown was at his most tub-thumpingly evangelical:

When I see children trapped in the grinding humiliation of family poverty, frail pensioners having to decide whether to be hungry or to be cold, people young, fit and willing to work reduced – in this year of 1994 – to homelessness and begging in the streets. When I see our public services neglected, battered by ideology and corrupted by the abuse of blatant patronage, and while at the same time I see homes standing empty, North Sea billions still squandered year after wasteful year, international companies using and abusing Britain as a tax haven, millionaires paying no tax whatsoever, directors of the privatised utilities overpaying themselves so grossly. When I see the waste, the short-termism and the costly failure of self-regulation in the City of London. When I see this gross disparity between the accumulated excess of wealth and power and the gaping sorrows of the left-out millions. And when I see what the Tories have done to our social cohesion and our sense of community, I know that for the Labour Party the hour has come.

And then he used the "S-word", which Blair would eschew forever after: "For socialists it is the future that must be served... This party – united and revitalised – can unite and revitalise Britain."

The speech was disingenuous, to the extent that it implied a zeal to redistribute wealth from the well-heeled to the needy through higher taxes in the traditional Labour way, which Brown already had profound doubts about. But the rest of it summarises many of the policies that Brown would pursue over the following years: the levying of a windfall tax on privatised utilities, to provide subsidies for new jobs; investment in training and education; integration of the tax and benefits system. In other words, Brown's longstanding obsession with promoting full employment was taking concrete shape in the form of practical policies.

But if Brown had a clear idea of the political journey he wanted Labour to take, he did not have the confidence that Blair as leader would see it through. "Even then, Gordon did not believe that Blair was truly committed to Labour's values," says one of his colleagues. Or to put it more starkly, he thought that his old friend was too right wing. Brown wanted a guarantee that Labour would remain more or less on the true progressive path, as interpreted by him in the light of prevailing economic and political conditions – and, as luck would have it, such a guarantee would reinforce his own power, both in opposition and government. So Blair conceded that a briefing note for the press would be drawn up, giving a commitment to implement Brown's agenda (such briefing notes are a favourite device of Brown: they are created as an aide memoire for senior Labour protagonists, to ensure that journalists are delivered a consistent and coherent message).

Blair asked Mandelson, who was at his home in Hartlepool, to write up this note. The vital passage (which was leaked to the *Guardian* newspaper in June 2003) went like this:

Both (Blair and Brown) recognise the importance of the partnership they have built up and of the Smith legacy of unifying the Party and making use of all its talents.

In his Wales and Luton Speeches, Gordon has spelled out the fairness agenda – social justice, employment opportunities and skills – which he believes should be the centrepiece of Labour's programme and *Tony is in full agreement with this* [my italics] and that the Party's economic and social policies should be further developed on this basis.

When it was sent to him, Brown said it was not good enough. What was wrong with it? Well, in his biography of Peter Mandelson, Donald Macintyre (*Mandelson*, Harper Collins, 1999) says: "The principle argument was over Brown's insistence that he should be guaranteed not only the Chancellorship but also autonomous control over the whole regime of economic policy." But Brown's allies say that's not quite right. What was in dispute was not simply the guarantee of his autonomy and power as Chancellor: it was the guarantee that his social justice agenda would be pursued. Anyway, Brown made an amendment to the text that he regarded as essential. In place of "Tony is in full agreement with this" he scrawled "Tony has guaranteed this will be pursued." The document was then faxed back to Mandelson by Sue Nye, Brown's Political Secretary (and wife of the economist, Gavyn Davies).

Having spoken to Nye, Mandelson asked Blair whether he would agree to the amendment. Blair refused, saying it would be wrong to limit his room for manoeuvre as a future Prime Minister. However, Brown would not let it drop and Nye pressed Mandelson again, who spoke to Blair again. "Tony thought about it for, oh, 15 seconds and said 'no' again," says a friend of the Prime Minister. "What's interesting is the extent to which he was already thinking about what would be appropriate after the election."

Even so, Brown took the view that Blair had not told him directly that he could not live with the amendment, so Brown proceeded on the basis that it had been agreed. "The moment that note with the amendments was sent up to Peter, we operated on the basis that it was the text," says an ally of Brown. And the more germane point is that it describes what happened in practice: Brown, as Chancellor, had unprecedented control over the future Labour government's economic and social agenda, almost the full gamut of domestic policy. Still, Brown left nothing to chance. He ensured that a near verbatim account of his version of the agreement was provided to Peter Riddell, the *Times* columnist who at the time was seen as the public chronicler of Labour's evolution. In his column on June 2, Riddell wrote:

The word yesterday was that messrs Blair and Brown would operate as a partnership, with the latter the driving force on the economic side. Mr Blair, it is said, has *guaranteed* [my italics] Mr Brown that the latter's 'fairness' agenda, broadening employment opportunities and improving training and skills will be the centrepiece of Labour's economic and social programme.

***

From the very moment that Brown made way for Blair on June 1, there were tensions between their two camps. Thus, at the suggestion of Andrew Brown and Charlie Whelan, Blair and Brown themselves agreed to be snapped by press photographers at 3.30pm that day – which was timed to coincide with the release by Brown of his statement that he would not be running. However, Blair's aides then tried to call off the photoshoot. And it was only after pressure was exerted by Brown that the press event happened (by the gates of the member's entrance of the House of Commons) – though it took place at 4.45pm, well after the news had been announced.

The uneasiness of the relationship between Brown's people and Blair's became a conspicuous and unalterable fact. And yet, in the elements that really matter to Brown, the Granita agreement has held up well. As this book will show, he has been master of the domestic agenda. Brown gave control of interest rates to the Bank of England: Blair was notified of the change, rather than seriously contributing to it. Brown merged the tax and benefit system, in the most radical overhaul of the welfare system since the 1940s: Blair watched powerless to prevent this channelling of billions into subsidies for those in work through tax credits, about which he had profound doubts and which he is still reluctant to laud in public. Brown levied billions in a one-off tax on the utilities in order to fund employment creation through the New Deal: until its very announcement, Blair tried to limit the scope of the tax. Brown kept sterling out of the euro and took complete control of the process of deciding whether we will ever join the single currency: Blair had almost no say over a question he regarded as the most important of his career.

This is not to dismiss Blair as an insignificant Prime Minister. If it's too early to form a definitive judgement of his interventions in Bosnia and Iraq or the reinforcement of British ties with the US of presidents Clinton and Bush, there's no doubting these are the actions of a Prime Minister anxious to make his mark on the world. And, like it or not (I don't, as it happens), Blair's war on the libertarian tendency in the Labour Party is not trivial. Meanwhile, he was always persuaded of the need to significantly increase expenditure on health and education – though he largely left to Brown the decision on how and when to relax the constraints on public spending.

But my contention is that the years from 1997 will be viewed as marking a far more significant break from the domestic agenda of Thatcher and Major than is now appreciated. And whether it's an expansion of the public sector, a new stability in the economy, or a channelling of massive subsidies to the working poor, these are largely the achievements of Brown. So, arguably, these have been Brown years, not Blair ones. And, as a minor postscript, Balls will be viewed as among the most influential of all New Labour's army of advisers and spin doctors (apart from anything else, Balls's quiet role in creating an independent Bank of England will be more comprehensible in years to come than Alistair Campbell's aggressive approach to news management).

Of course, there have been moments when Brown felt that Blair was reneging on important elements of the Granita deal. One was the ministerial reshuffle of July 27, 1998 which brought Peter Mandelson into the Cabinet as the Trade and Industry Secretary. At the time, it was fashionable in the media to use a business analogy to describe the balance of power between Blair and Brown: Blair was the Chairman and Brown the

Chief Executive. And it propagated a view that the real locus of power was the Treasury – which must have been galling to the Prime Minister, but was probably even more galling to his main aides, especially Alastair Campbell, Sally Morgan (his longstanding Political Secretary) and Anji Hunter (who for donkeys' years ran Blair's political life and was his *de facto* gatekeeper). So Blair's aides tried to regain the upper hand by changing his ministerial team, to parachute his supporters into more of the strategically important posts, or – more accurately – by presenting a ministerial reshuffle as an anti-Brown reshuffle (which included letting it be known that Morgan, Campbell, Hunter and Jonathan Powell, Blair's Chief of Staff, had organised a coup to squeeze out Brown's alleged cronies).

With the benefit of hindsight, it's clear that the scope of the ministerial changes was less damaging to Brown than he was prepared to concede or 10 Downing Street wanted to admit. For different motives, it suited Brown's people and Blair's to manufacture a row. But Mandelson's arrival in the Cabinet, in an economic post which would give him an interface with the Treasury, was genuinely unwelcome to the Chancellor. And Brown was also maddened by the removal of Nick Brown, one of his closest and oldest allies, from the post of Chief Whip (in which he could be Brown's eyes and ears among Labour MPs). Nick Brown was moved to the less glamorous post of Agriculture Minister, after having incensed Mandelson, Alastair Campbell and Blair for giving an on-the-record interview to Paul Routledge for his 1998 biography of Brown: the book was perceived as having destabilised the government by disclosing for the first time Brown's bitterness at the way Blair had seized the leadership. This was something of a miscarriage of justice, since Nick Brown was almost certainly not responsible for communicating the more resonant details to Routledge.

It was difficult for Nick Brown to quit the government in disgust, since technically he was being offered a promotion. At the time, the Chief Whip had an odd status: the holder of the post was not formally in the Cabinet, though he or she attended Cabinet meetings. The

Agriculture Minister was, however, a full Cabinet member. After seeing Tony Blair for three hours between 10pm and 1am on the Sunday night of the eve of the formal reshuffle, Nick Brown gritted his teeth and took the job – though he could not resist asking Blair if he was being moved because of his annoyance at Routledge's book, to which Blair replied, "You surely don't think I could be so petty?" Nick Brown was, unusually, stuck for a response. What's also striking about this incident is that it shows how Gordon Brown engenders loyalty. It was he who got Nick Brown into the mess by asking him to talk to Routledge, but Nick Brown has never held a grudge against him and remains one of his most steadfast supporters.

Anyway, the reshuffle, in Brown's view, was a rare and genuine breach of the Granita pact. He might not have asked for a promise about succession, but he certainly did demand to be consulted on important ministerial and party appointments. He felt that an overt sacking of people close to him, briefed as such to newspapers, was not consistent with that (this clause in the Granita agreement also explains why in November 2003 he very publicly signalled his annoyance with the Prime Minister for twice blocking his appointment to the National Executive Committee, the body that oversees the Labour Party).

Brown was convinced that Campbell and Mandelson were going out of their way to undermine him. He understood why they were doing this. It was maddening for them that Brown's Treasury simply never took instructions from 10 Downing Street. "Within a world in which the opposition was weak, the media was all over the place and the majority was huge, the Treasury was the only department which just didn't do what it was told – and that caused huge frustration," says a senior government official. But Brown was adamant that he had a licence from the Prime Minister to do his own thing, and there was no possibility of giving it back.

CHAPTER THREE

Capturing the Treasury

Gordon Brown's dominance of the domestic agenda of the government – his exploitation (plus a bit) of his interpretation of the Granita deal – was facilitated first by the astonishingly detailed policy work that was done for him, largely by Ed Balls and Ed Miliband (another brainy adviser), in the run-up to the 1997 general election. But it was his wholesale capture of the Treasury – the greatest of all ministerial departments, whose origin is traceable to the Norman Conquest – that turned Blair's promises of autonomous power for Brown into a defining characteristic of Tony Blair's government.

When Brown arrived, the Treasury was obsessed with the battle against inflation, with whether interest rates should be moved up or down, and with setting the following year's public spending totals. As the holder of the purse strings, for years it had power but little respect. Its reputation in the rest of Whitehall, and in the country at large, was lamentable. Its brand was as the institution that only said "no". Other departments would put forward exciting and imaginative plans to build new railways or order world-beating equipment for the military: the role of the Treasury was to tut tut and point out that such plans were poor value for the taxpayer's pound.

There is still a legacy of negativism in the Treasury. Officials remain wary of huge transport projects, for example, and are constantly nagging the Ministry of Defence to exercise greater financial discipline when ordering multi-billion pound pieces of kit. There's also a tendency to be wary of ideas that weren't first dreamed up by Brown or his Treasury officials. But the department is unrecognisable from the austere, narrow-minded, darkling place I first started to visit regularly about a decade ago. First of all, its writ runs much further. Under Brown, mostly for the better (but not always), it has

• merged the tax and benefit systems and has endeavoured to destigmatise the provision by the state of financial help to the working poor, through the creation of tax credits

• "targeted" billions of pounds in succour to families with children, again largely through tax credits

• tried (and largely failed) to increase saving for retirement by poorer people though the introduction of a raft of new savings plans (stakeholder pensions, individual savings accounts, and – latterly – the "Sandler" range of simple financial products)

• created a so-called minimum pension guarantee which introduced greater means testing (though the Treasury prefers to call it "targeting") into state pension provision

• made it compulsory for young benefit claimants to take a job or receive training, through the New Deal

• ushered in severe new punishments for businesses that rig markets and beefed up the powers of competition watchdogs

• bullied firms into adopting new non-statutory rules governing the composition of their boards, enhancing the role of non-executive directors

• rehabilitated the international development agenda within government and led international initiatives to reduce the burden of debt on starving African countries

• set the parameters for liberalising the planning laws

• laid out a long-term plan for investment in science

• intervened and influenced every government domestic debate of any significance, from the funding of universities and reform of the National Health Service to the introduction of identity cards

Over almost eight years, the Treasury has annexed for itself agendas that ought to belong to other parts of Whitehall. On expensive and symbolically important initiatives, such as the New Deal for the young unemployed and long-term unemployed, it has worked in partnership with the relevant Secretary of State and his or her department – which was David Blunkett and the Department for Education in the case of the New Deal during 1997/8. In fact, the Treasury has usually insisted on being the senior partner.

In some cases, the policy-making arms of ministries – such as that of the now-defunct Department of Social Security – have been made more or less redundant by the elongation of the Treasury's reach. Entire departments – including the Department of Trade and Industry and the Department of Work and Pensions (born out of the DSS) – have periodically acted as *de facto* subsidiaries or executive agencies of the Treasury, with the junior function of giving life and form to Treasury ideas. For example, a much more aggressive approach to promoting competition – at the heart of the DTI's ostensible responsibilities – has been introduced in phases since 1997. And all the important intellectual preparation came from the Treasury and a think tank, the Smith Institute, whose purpose is to provide ideas for Brown. In fact, the individual who provided the momentum for the competition reforms doesn't even have a formal role in government. He's Irwin Stelzer, an economist and adviser to the media tycoon, Rupert Murdoch, who oversaw a series of seminars on competition policy and competitiveness for the Smith Institute at 11 Downing Street in 2000 and 2001. Largely at Stelzer's urging, it is now, for example, a criminal offence punishable by imprisonment for directors of firms to collude with their rivals to fix prices and rig bids for contracts. Also it was the Treasury which pressed for the main competition watchdogs, the Office of Fair Trading and the Competition Commission, to be given greater independence from government and enhanced resources. Throughout the process of making these changes, the role of the DTI was to execute a programme laid out for it by Brown and the Treasury.

Traditionally, Labour governments have agonised about whether the Treasury is too powerful and should be broken up into a finance ministry (in charge of taxation and balancing the books) and an economics one (helping to promote economic growth). The idea that there needs to be a counterweight to the allegedly Tory instincts of the Treasury stems from Labour's first experience in government in the 1920s, when its Chancellor – Philip Snowden – pushed through spending cuts on the urging of his officials at a time when the economy desperately needed to be reflated. This created the powerful myth that a betrayal of Labour's values always begins in the Treasury (actually, it probably begins in the weakness and lack of confidence of its Chancellors). So in 1964, Harold Wilson's government created a Department of Economic Affairs under Labour's deputy leader, George Brown, whose purpose was to promote growth (in 1947, Stafford Cripps had been made Minister for Economic Affairs, working to one side of the Chancellor, Hugh Dalton, but the separation of functions lasted for just six weeks). It was an unhappy innovation, which set up a fatuous power struggle between the DEA and the Treasury over which of them set the priorities for the British economy. Before the 1960s were out, the contest had been won – predictably – by the department that held the purse strings, the Treasury.

Even so, just before the 1997 general election, Peter Mandelson and Roger Liddle, implied in their book *The Blair Revolution* (Faber, 1996) that the power of the Treasury should be offset by a strengthened Cabinet Office which would be "akin to a Department of the Prime Minister and Cabinet, charged with actively carrying forward the cross-departmental policies agreed by the Cabinet." And in 2001, Blair came close to transferring the Treasury's control of public spending – and the position of Chief Secretary – to the Cabinet Office. And, as recently as 2004, Blair – advised by Lord Birt, the former director general of the BBC – considered forming a strengthened economics unit within Downing Street so that he would be better equipped to vet and challenge

Treasury initiatives. But Brown has pressed on regardless, creating a Treasury whose writ runs further than it ever has before, beyond the domestic territory guaranteed by the Granita deal and even into areas of the international agenda (including aid to impoverished nations and all aspects of euro policy).

Brown's eureka was to recognise that less is more, that to give up some responsibilities – notably the control of interest rates, but also important areas of financial regulation, such as oversight of insurance companies – would reinforce the powers that matter. As described in Chapter Four, he has surrendered one of the responsibilities that previous Chancellors and Treasury Permanent Secretaries have prized above all else: the ability to raise or lower interest rates. This most tangible manifestation of the Treasury's muscle was handed to the Bank of England as Brown's very first decision in government. It was liberating, because it allowed both the new Chancellor and officials to step back from day-to-day exigencies and plan for the long term. One official explains:

> Before 1997, the Treasury was obsessed with interest rates. Even if Ken Clarke (the previous Chancellor) only spent a few hours a month focused on the next move in interest rates, the process tied up much of the Treasury machine. It monopolised the attention of people like Alan Budd (the Treasury's Chief Economic Adviser from 1991 to 1997). It is far better to be freed of the short-term decision making, so you can think about the economic framework.

One effect of the interest-rate sacrifice was to give Brown and the Treasury greater independence from Downing Street and far greater authority over other departments. "There was a huge strengthening of the power of the Treasury in economic policy relative to Number 10," an official says. In particular, Brown was insulated from the pressure that his predecessors felt from their respective Prime Ministers to cut interest rates or not raise them for political reasons, rather than economic ones. "Throughout that whole period of the setting of interest rates, the bane of a Chancellor's life was getting these calls from Number 10," recalls an official. "That can't happen any more." And the newly empowered Bank of England was recast as a wonderful bogeyman for the Treasury to cite, when endeavouring to dissuade the rest of government from adopting an initiative it disliked. Ed Balls put it like this in an article in the *Observer* newspaper (August 8, 2004): "Far from weakening the ability of the Treasury to ensure public spending discipline, the risk that the Monetary Policy Committee [of the Bank of England] might respond with a rate rise has proved a useful and effective deterrent to profligate departmental proposals on more than one occasion." One of Balls's colleagues elucidates: "Independence strengthened the Treasury's hand more generally in respect of economic policy, fiscal policy, public spending and the minimum wage. In the old days, the Treasury sanction was not a credible threat. But suddenly we were in a position where we could say: 'If you do that and it is perceived as imprudent, well the Monetary Policy Committee might raise interest rates. It's out of our hands'."

There have been other examples of Brown and the Treasury being empowered by the imposition of rules or reforms that appeared to limit their room for manoeuvre. The classic example is his so-called fiscal rules, which impose a ceiling on the amount the government can borrow over the course of the economic cycle and on the magnitude of public sector debt relative to the size of the economy. Although there are reasonable doubts about whether Treasury definitions of borrowing are as rigorous as they might be, these rules are coherent and sensible – and they too give greater credibility to the Chancellor when negotiating with colleagues on how much their departments should spend. "Perhaps the importance of them is that they reinforced the authority of the Treasury," says an official. "And a weak Treasury is a disaster, because policy making gets hijacked by Number 10. The fiscal rules were good for our authority."

With this redefinition of what the Treasury does has come a change in its priorities. The interests of the current Permanent Secretary, Augustine "Gus" O'Donnell, run wider than his predecessors, in part because his time isn't monopolised by a ceaseless struggle against incipient or actual inflation. The austere, anti-progressive Treasury of Snowden in the 1920s has largely been buried. O'Donnell talks of the constructive interplay between lifting up the neediest in society and economic growth, a viewpoint which he thinks can be in the Treasury's soul. And he is comfortable debating at private seminars about how to combine flexible, US-style labour markets with an effective social safety net, an issue far removed from the concerns of previous Treasury mandarins. If he hadn't provided dedicated service to the previous Tory administration (he was a beleaguered Press Secretary to John Major, when Major was a bruised and battered Prime Minister), there might be a question about whether his outlook is just a bit too "New Labour".

And there has also been a transformation in the look and feel of the place. In 2002, 900 officials moved from the front of the imposing early 20th century building on Whitehall to the back on Horse Guards Road, overlooking St James's Park, as part of a £141m gutting of the interior (the ambitious redevelopment was done in partnership with a private sector group, Exchequer Partnership). Another 300 joined them from a satellite building in Victoria, but total staff numbers have subsequently been cut to around 1050. The internal reconstruction swept away a Kafkaesque rabbit warren of musty, dimly lit rooms running off interminable corridors. The new Treasury – designed by Norman Foster – is all about large open-plan spaces and light from windows at the top of a central atrium. Senior officials don't have to operate "open door" policies for their senior staff, because they sit at desks in the middle of giant rooms reminiscent of City trading floors: there are no doors to close (some of these changes were being mulled in 1995, before Brown arrived, but they never happened, because senior officials became bogged down in implementation disputes).

The Chancellor has preserved his privacy in his office: he's not really an "open plan" kind of politician. But his working area is smaller, more informal and is far less overwhelming than the one he inherited. The space is reminiscent of the suite of smallish offices occupied by the master of a medium-sized Oxford college – filled with the mementos and detritus of a life in politics (such as the trophies commemorating his victories as Scottish Politician of the Year) rather than the quasi-baronial hall of his predecessor. There are politics and economics books everywhere. And the other conspicuous trait is that tough, no-nonsense women dominate the private office where his life is managed (the most important and prickliest of these is Sue Nye, wife of Gàvyn Davies – former Chairman of the BBC – who has been an important factotum for him since 1992).

Brown has eschewed the pomp and ceremony of his predecessors, including the official use of Chevening, one of the government's large country houses. "In the era of Lawson, Lamont and Clarke (Brown's three Tory predecessors) they used to have these meetings at Chevening two months before the budget," recalls an official. "They would have an intensive day of meetings. The Chairman of the Inland Revenue would be there and the Chairman of Customs and Excise. Then spouses and partners would come down for dinner. This was a regular feature going back years and years and years. Now obviously Gordon has never done anything like that."

There's much less formality in general. Only ten years ago, the most senior officials were aloof and remote figures. Even the brightest of the new entrants did not expect to be granted the privilege of actually talking to those in the more senior grades till they had completed years of apprenticeship. Here's the reminiscence of one of these fast-stream officials who joined two decades ago: "After I joined the Treasury, I think it was ten years before I talked to anyone over Grade 3... Frankly it was a 1950s organisation, no longer fit for the purpose. The organisation was over-rigid, there were too many layers. It was full of Oxbridge males. It was not good at communicating with the outside world. It was very secretive. It had to change."

At the top, it's still pretty much a pale-skinned boys club. Just a fifth of the senior positions, called directors, are filled by women, though the proportion was a paltry 9 per cent in 2000. And, as of March 31, 2004, there wasn't a single member of an ethnic minority or a disabled person in one of these top jobs (defined in the civil service as grades G and H). But the proportion of women and ethnic minorities lower down – in the so-called feeder grades – has risen. So it's likely that the Treasury will in time become a less monochrome place.

In other ways, though, there has already been a passing of the baton to a new generation. Bright younger officials, such as Nick Macpherson and Tom Scholar, have been promoted into strategically important positions. And a series of outsiders have been brought in, including John Kingman (from BP), Nick Stern (from the World Bank), James Sassoon (from UBS) and Shriti Vadera (also from UBS). Meanwhile O'Donnell – a passionate Man Utd supporter whom Brown and Balls have been friendly with for years and who became head of the Treasury in 2002 at the age of 50 – is less remote and more easygoing than the traditional mandarin. "When I first arrived, I remember being described as a rough diamond in my first assessment," he told the *Guardian* in 1999. However, the fact that he went to a voluntary-aided Catholic boys' grammar school in Battersea, South London, and then to Warwick University, rather than more elitist institutions, has been the Treasury way for some years: all three of his immediate predecessors, Sir Andrew Turnbull, Lord Burns and Sir Peter Middleton are grammar school boys and, of these, only Turnbull did his undergraduate degree at an Oxbridge college, which was Christ's College, Cambridge.

Building on the foundations laid by Burns and Turnbull, O'Donnell and his senior management team have striven to encourage team work and break down the traditional hierarchical barriers to communication between officials of different ranks – although some officials complain that he has not done enough to demolish the big baronies within the Treasury, to promote co-operation between separate units. Like a business with half-an-eye on fashionable management theory, these days the Treasury's senior echelon, its directors, even hold open days during which anyone can fire questions at them about anything.

Brown is conspicuously comfortable with the re-made Treasury and it appears to be at ease with him. One of the Post-It notes on his brain says "I must remember to praise the department" and he does it at every available opportunity. The respect is mutual. Senior officials admire him for his "rare ability to create a framework in which we can work and plan for the long term" (in the words of one). Another puts it slightly differently: "We love working for a strong Chancellor. And the Treasury will always support a strong Chancellor. Although we are trying to be more open and less arrogant, ultimately we love an intellectual punch up, we relish knocking down someone with the opposing view. The Treasury elite loves winning arguments."

Here is where a nagging doubt must arise about whether the creation of a Brown Treasury has been unambiguously positive. Some former officials fear that Brown and Balls have fashioned the Treasury into a political tool of New Labour. As this chapter will show, these are reasonable concerns. But I don't believe the big issue here is one of improper behaviour by Balls and Brown. With minor lapses in the field of media relations early on in the lifetime of the Blair government, they have been fairly scrupulous in observing the conventions governing the relationship between political appointees such as Balls and career civil servants. Moreover, within the framework set by Brown and Balls, officials bring plenty of ideas to them, rather than vice versa. However – and this is crucial – they are a formidable and determined intellectual force. In the post-war period, probably only Nigel Lawson in the mid-1980s, before the collapse of his anti-inflation policies, commanded quite so much respect within the institution. What this means is that there may be no one in the Treasury capable of challenging them on a point of principle – so the Treasury of today largely shares their values and exists primarily to execute their will.

If you believe that the role of the civil service is to implement the programme of elected politicians, that's absolutely fine. "If you are a democrat, it's quite difficult to object to what Brown and Balls have done," says a former mandarin. But there is a second sense in which the sway of Brown and Balls within the institution may have been too great. There is a risk that they have robbed the Treasury of the confidence to take the initiative. One day soon, there will be a Chancellor less sure of where he or she is going than Brown. Historically, the Treasury's role has been to fill in the gaps when second rate, prevaricating Chancellors – the post-war norm – have been at the helm. Whether Brown and Balls have nurtured the Treasury's ability – in extremis – to create a sense of purpose for politicians who do not enjoy the same strength of purpose is doubtful, to put it mildly.

***

In today's government, the Treasury is a model of cohesiveness and stability, the underpinning of the Chancellor's power. By contrast, the institutions designed to serve the Prime Minister, in the Cabinet Office and 10 Downing Street, are an amorphous court, thronged by courtiers vying for the Prime Minister's favour (as Derek Scott's memoir of his time as Blair's economic adviser, *Off Whitehall*, makes clear). This divergence between the two great central institutions would have been difficult to predict in 1997. Back then, the Treasury was emerging from one of its blackest periods, following the failure of its macroeconomic policies in the late 1980s. And, when Brown unpacked his bags, his plan appeared to be to marginalise the traditional civil servants instead of inspiring and converting them. Rather than capturing the Treasury, his aim seemed to be to make it redundant, by conducting all his important business through a cabal of close political allies, notably Balls, Whelan and Geoffrey Robinson – the gang nicknamed the "Hotel Group" by alienated Treasury officials because it often hung out in Robinson's sprawling, airy apartment overlooking Hyde Park which was high up in the Grosvenor House Hotel.

If Treasury officials resented Brown's clique it was only a sign of how much they desired to be immersed in the programme of a new government, which was manifested in an incongruously effusive welcome that they gave to Brown when he arrived on Friday, May 2, 1997. They filled the entrance hall and lined the corridors to applaud his accession, in their yearning to make a definitive break with the awful mess that the Treasury had found itself in during the early 1990s.

The orthodox view, held by the more senior mandarins, is that most officials were deeply depressed at the humiliating failure of the Treasury's stewardship of the economy – the combination of accelerating inflation and sharp recession – six years before. And they were supposedly suicidal after the great adventure of joining the European Exchange Rate Mechanism turned out to be a disaster (see pages 183-4). "The Treasury was thoroughly demoralised by the whole thing," says a senior Treasury veteran. "We were being attacked right, left and centre. People don't like working for an institution that's being attacked. The people at the top may have pretty thick skins, but at the bottom when they hear negative things on the radio, it's not nice."

However, in fact there was a sharp difference of view between top management and the younger staff. An official, who is now well up the hierarchy but was a fast-track youngster during the ERM crisis of 1992, explains:

In 1990 to 1992, it was obvious that conditions in the Treasury had to change. Everything was going wrong, though the traditional Treasury did not realise how bad it was. There was a loss of control of public spending, there was a house price explosion, interest rates were going up to record levels, companies were going bust. It was terrible.

However, it was a myth that this was all bad for Treasury morale. If you were relatively young, it was hugely entertaining. There was a feeling in the younger parts of the Treasury that the government was getting its well-deserved come-uppance.

At the time, the most important official was Terry Burns (now Lord Burns) who was the Chief Economic Adviser and – from May 1991 – the Permanent Secretary. He still felt the wounds of the ERM disaster in February 2002, when he was beginning a new life as Chairman of Abbey

National, the mortgage bank. This is what he said to me in an interview:

> By a long way it was the worst experience I have been through profes-
> sionally. It was weeks and weeks of difficulty, where you can see a loom-
> ing disaster, you keep trying to do things about it but you just cannot
> relieve the pressure. To be forced out so soon after we joined felt like a
> major setback – and you don't like to be part of that.
>
> The day (when sterling left the ERM) and the previous day were
> extremely terrible. I had been Permanent Secretary for about 15 months.
> It was a very difficult period. In that world, there are many times you
> come across problems, and you think they are going to cause you huge
> difficulty, but with patience and clever footwork you get your way
> through them. On that occasion, there was no way through. We had to
> leave and there was no easy way of leaving. So that was not a nice time.
> But there we were… My task was to improve management of the
> Treasury and rebuild economic policy.

Out of this morass, Burns took the important first steps towards re-
establishing the Treasury's reputation and modernising both its internal
workings and its approach to managing the economy. Although Balls and
Brown have a slight temptation to regard 1997 as Year Zero for the rehabilitation of this great institution, that's unfair – just as its equally unfair
to imply, as Burns occasionally does, that their valuable reforms were no
more than the logical conclusion of what he started.

As I discuss in the chapter on the Bank of England (see page 122),
Burns put in place a more sensible approach to combating inflation,
which can now be seen as a useful precursor to Brown's historic decision
to transfer control of interest rates to the Bank. And Burns – helped by
like-minded officials, such as Paul Gray, who was the personnel director
in the mid-1990s – began to modernise the management structure of the
Treasury.

Indeed Burns, Brown and Balls have many interests in common, both
professional and personal. They have similar views about how to manage

the economy. They were all committed to learning the lessons of the Treasury's past failures. And they are all obsessed with football. But their early relationship in government was appallingly bad – and in spite of Brown's visceral dislike of conflict and Burns's emollient character, their differences came close on a number of occasions to prompting a public conflict which would have damaged both men.

There was misunderstanding, wilful and accidental, on both sides. However, in the year before the general election of 1997, Balls and Burns went through the motions of putting in place a sensible working relationship. Burns took advantage of permission granted by the then Prime Minister, John Major, for senior officials to liaise with the opposition. He met Balls around 20 times in this period. Brown kept his distance – he met Burns once in the House of Commons and possibly on one other occasion – but at the beginning of the general election campaign, when a Labour victory seemed inevitable, Balls gave Burns copies of secret policy documents on proposed reforms of capital gains tax and corporation tax and on the imposition of a climate change levy, which was designed to reduce the emission of greenhouse gases through penalising polluters. A senior Treasury official says: "I really don't think we could have been better prepared for Labour in policy terms."

The policy gap between the Treasury and the New Labour government was certainly a fraction of what it had been 18 years before when the Tory government of Margaret Thatcher was elected. "Back in 1979, there was a far bigger gulf between the Treasury and the in-coming government on issues of substance," says an official who witnessed at close quarters both watersheds in British political history. "It's important to remember that in 1978 Wass (Sir Douglas Wass, then Permanent Secretary) had made a speech which appeared to say that monetary targets were a bad idea." Wass, on behalf of the Treasury, had attacked the very kernel of the new Thatcher government's anti-inflation approach immediately before he won the 1979 general election. There was no welcome mat, no cheering from the rafters, for her and her first Chancellor, Sir Geoffrey Howe.

Another official recalls just how traumatic it had been for the Treasury to adjust to this monetarist Tory government, after decades of various shades of Keynesian administration, both in Labour and Conservative guise:

In 1997, there was a small group of us at senior level who could remember what it was like in 1979. The real memory of 1979 was how badly the Treasury served the Thatcher government for the first two years in power. And the reason is that we failed to understand the magnitude of the shift in policy-making. The changes they tried to do from the word go were pretty radical: a switch from direct to indirect taxation; huge changes to industrial relations legislation, which went through far slower than was needed; and so on.

We swore we would not make the same mistakes again when Labour came in. So we read everything that Ed and Gordon had written or said. And we set up teams to come up with plans to implement what we thought they would do.

In other words, the change of government should have gone well for both the Treasury and Labour. And the weekend after the election, Brown broke the habits of a lifetime by creating the impression that he was comfortable with the idea of sharing all his ideas and plans with people whom he had never met before.

"The first weekend after the election lulled us into a false sense of security," says an official. "On the Saturday and Sunday, there were meetings all through the weekend and we talked with Gordon, Ed (Balls) and Geoffrey (Robinson) about independence for the Bank of England, the windfall tax, the New Deal. There were about 15 senior officials around the table. But this was the one and only policy discussion of this sort that we ever saw. After that, Gordon reverted to his accustomed working method. Gordon only worked with people he trusted, principally Ed (Balls)." The challenge for Treasury officials was to become trusted and for Brown and Balls to become more trusting. It would happen eventually, but the mutual courtship was traumatic. Predictably, the Treasury had learned the wrong lesson from 1979. Rather than preparing itself in policy terms, it should have thought more about Brown's method of working, his modus operandi. An official explains:

There was an enormous change which we did not anticipate. The people who came to power in 1979 were seasoned government ministers: they had been in the Heath government of the early 1970s. They knew about the normal relationship between civil servants and ministers. Under this traditional model, civil servants served up papers, ministers read them, there were meetings. Civil servants might rework part of the proposal. But ministers usually implemented the policy and usually did what civil servants had recommended.

Gordon knew none of this. He had no experience of any of it. And we had not thought about the implications of his inexperience. It was an amazing oversight by us.

In fact, it was worse than that. Not only did Brown have no experience of working in government, he had no desire to adjust his working habits. "It never occurred to Gordon to consider how he should adapt," says a highly placed mandarin. "That is not the way he thinks at all. He took the view this is how I do things – and he refused to change."

In the Treasury before Brown, Chancellors had traditionally sent reams of letters to colleagues instructing them to do this or that, or raising problems with the way they were doing things. Not all Chancellors liked this system: in the early 1990s, correspondence piled up under Norman Lamont, so his high-flying Private Secretary, Jeremy Heywood (who became Tony Blair's Principal Private Secretary), somehow had to keep the machine functioning. But Lamont was a relatively short-lived exception. His successor, Ken Clarke, may have maddened his officials by failing to read important documents until the very last moment, but he was a classic man of action, taking decisions very rapidly when they needed to be taken.

As for Brown, he was a contrast with Lamont in that it was not poor time-management that stopped him signing letters. Rather, it was a simple matter of principle that he would not append his moniker to anything that could come back to haunt him at a future date. "I think it all stems from his experience in opposition, when he caused great embarrassment to the Tories as a recipient of leaked government documents," says an official. "So as Chancellor, he was particularly wary of furnishing pieces of paper, even to his supposed friends. Gordon did not want any papers containing his signature that his colleagues could use against him. By contrast, Clarke would send eight of these missives in one go, to Health, Education and so on."

Brown's behaviour was very unsettling for the mandarin class, as one of his cohort recalls:

> The mindset was, 'If we don't put something down on paper, pre-emptively, then the decision will be taken in Number 10 without us having our say.' We would say, 'Of course they won't, they're bound to do what we suggest.' Even so, there was a long period when the Treasury was obsessed about getting Gordon to send a letter relating to the five tests (of whether to join the euro) in May and June (1997). But he just didn't want to send it.

Ultimately, a new working method was established, which largely obviated the need for letter-writing. When cross-departmental issues needed sorting out, Balls acted as fixer: he would smooth things over with other special advisers or officials in Number 10, or the Department for Education, or wherever there was a problem to be resolved. A particularly important relationship for Balls was that with Heywood, the former Treasury official of a similar age to him who moved to the Prime Minister's private office in 1998 and became Blair's Principal Private Secretary (PPS) in 1999. Balls and Heywood also worked closely with Brown's Private Secretaries, Tom Scholar and Mark Bowman. Balls therefore created the space for Brown to carry on in government more or less as he had in opposition, which was to concentrate on just one big issue at a time, analysing it to death until implementing it. Brown made sure he got his way on this big initiative, whatever it might be, by seeing any affected minister outside the Treasury at the last possible moment – which could be Blair or Blunkett at Education for example – and then bludgeoning him or her into submission with the force of his arguments.

The relationship between Brown and career civil servants was initially most fraught in the area of relations with the media. Brown brought his personal Press Secretary, Charlie Whelan, into government as a special adviser. Whelan was close to Brown, he had a big personality and he was well-known to most political journalists. The consequence was that the Treasury's head of communications, Jill Rutter, felt marginalised – even though Whelan, as a political appointee, did not have the formal authority to run the whole of the department's media operation. In these circumstances, Rutter – a bright, dedicated career civil servant – really should have been moved to another job. But Burns asked her to tough it out "for the good of the Treasury" and to preserve the integrity of the press operation – which was a laudable if naïve ambition. Rutter ultimately felt isolated from the new political masters and let down by her more longstanding Treasury friends and colleagues. Before 1997 was out, she had left the Treasury for BP – which for several years deprived Whitehall of a talented public servant and the Treasury of a rare female high-flyer (she returned to the civil service in 2004, as Director of Strategy and Sustainable Development at the Department of Environment, Food and Rural Affairs).

Whelan himself quit at the beginning of 1999, after he became a public figure in his own right – the putative leader of Brown's allies in a long-running conflict with 10 Downing Street – rather than simply a messenger for the Chancellor. When spokesmen become as famous as the people they represent, it's time for them to go. And with his passing, Brown adopted a less divisive approach to media relations. The Treasury's Director of Communications – always a career civil servant, rather than a political appointee – once again became his principal intermediary with newspapers and television, in a shift of power back to the mainstream civil service. However, Brown and Balls took great pains to ensure that appointees to this job were ambitious, were enthusiastic about promoting the Treasury's cause 24 hours a day and were sympathetic to their agenda.

Another of Brown's breaks with tradition – which upset Burns – was in respect of meetings with the Prime Minister. Traditionally, when Chancellors went to 10 Downing Street for meetings, the Prime Minister's Principal Private Secretary would be present and would take notes for circulating to relevant people. And this system continued for a short while after Labour's election victory. However, Brown felt the records of these chats "misrepresented what had gone on", according to an official, and asked Blair to "chuck this guy out". The Prime Minister agreed, presumably because he had been dealing with Brown on a one-to-one basis – with no one else in the room – for years and saw no reason to change.

But the mandarins hated being shut out, as one makes clear: "Tony and Gordon excluded everyone. They are both bad at debriefing, and said contradictory things about what had been agreed. This is wrong. The Private Secretary should know everything, should listen to everything. There were moments when the right hand did not know what the left hand was doing."

There are many examples of Brown and Blair having a different recollection of what they had agreed in their meetings, which caused inefficiencies and tensions at the top of government – such as when they discussed the deliberate leaking to the *Times* of a new policy towards British membership of the European single currency in the autumn of 1997 (see pages 208-11). So it was subsequently decided that Heywood, Blair's Private Secretary, would be admitted to the tête à têtes and that Balls should come too, as the representative of Brown (to make doubly sure that official notes of what had been negotiated reflected Brown's point of view).

Balls's status within the Treasury was now enhanced even more by his proximity to the odd couple. "Often, our only knowledge of what Gordon and Tony had agreed would come from what Ed chose to tell us," says a Treasury official. Balls and Heywood also borrowed the powers of their respective political masters and made significant political decisions. "As early as 1998, the spending review was sorted out by them," an official says.

Inevitably, many civil servants felt bewildered by the new modus operandi and disenfranchised by the upstart Balls, of whom they were both fearful and resentful. Some made no effort to adapt and were forever outside the circle of power under Brown. Burns himself found the new world profoundly uncomfortable. His attitude, according to a senior official, was: "It is not easy (for new ministers) to fit in to the machine. But ministers have to work with the machine. Eventually we tend to drag them into the normal way of doing things." But that's not how it worked with Brown. The Treasury would have to fit in with him.

***

Burns had and has admiration for Brown's ability to think and act strategically, his ability to avoid distraction by the political noise on any particular day. But from the start, the Permanent Secretary managed to rub his new colleagues up the wrong way. They regarded him, for example, as responsible for the potentially lethal misunderstanding that arose between Brown and the governor of the Bank of England, Eddie George, within days of the general election over Brown's plans to reorganise the Bank (see pages 138-42). Geoffrey Robinson, in particular, took a dislike to Burns, whom he felt was trying to delay this most vital of the new government's proposed reforms, as he made clear in his political memoirs:

What Terry (Burns) was unhappy about was the sheer speed and scale of the changes proposed for the Bank – notably the removal of its regulatory functions. It was this that he wanted to delay... He was wrong, of course, but it was one of the few points on which the Permanent Secretary took a definite position. [*The Unconventional Minister*, 2000].

Alienating Robinson was dangerous for Burns, because the new paymaster general was one of a trio of individuals – along with Balls and Whelan – with whom Brown felt comfortable.

For months, the concern among many Treasury officials was that Brown's important decisions were taken in Robinson's Park Lane apartment, rather in Whitehall – which was partly true. It took Brown around 18 months to slough off many of the habits and practices of opposition. One of these was to meet almost every night in Robinson's flat, as had happened in the year or so before the general election. Slightly obtusely, Brown and Balls failed to recognise the message they were sending by continuing to do so after May 1, especially in the run-up to the Chancellor's important first budget of July 1997. "Terry felt that discussions that ought to have been happening in the Treasury with him were happening without him," says an official.

The Treasury tradition was for a Chancellor to thrash out tricky issues with his Permanent Secretary, which is what Burns had understandably been expecting. But this was not how Brown had ever worked. His style was to kick issues around with Balls and – for quite some time to come – almost no one else. So it was Balls who gradually recruited the Treasury's career civil servants into these deliberations. He had regular meetings with senior officials such as Steve Robson, Robert Culpin, John Gieve and Gus O'Donnell. But Burns chose not to attend these sessions – which was interpreted by officials as a statement that it would be *infra dig* for a Permanent Secretary to consort freely with a special adviser.

Some of the tension that arose between Burns and Balls stemmed from a rivalry and absence of mutual respect, which derived in part from their similar career histories. Burns had been brought into the Treasury from the London Business School in order to give intellectual credibility to a monetarist approach to the control of inflation that the then

Chancellor, Geoffrey Howe, wanted to pursue. And at the remarkably young age of 36, he was made Chief Economic Adviser to the Treasury.

Balls, too, was a technocrat, who had studied at Oxford and Harvard's Kennedy School. If anything, he was even more precocious and well-connected than Burns had been. At Harvard, he had caught the attention of the distinguished economist Larry Summers, who went on to become Clinton's Treasury Secretary and is now the president of the Ivy League university. At a seminar I attended at Number 11 Downing Street in the dying days of the Clinton administration, Summers warmed up his audience by quipping that it was a privilege be in the presence of the real power in the land, Mr Balls. Like Burns, Balls was also to become Chief Economic Adviser to the Treasury – in 1999, when only 32 years old.

There was, however, one seemingly significant difference between Burns and Balls. Although Burns had been chosen by Howe because his views on economics were regarded as in tune with those of the new Tory government – he was a proponent of controlling the money supply as a bulwark against inflation, in place of the discredited "incomes policies" of the Labour government of the mid-1970s – he was not a special adviser, not an official Tory representative in government. By contrast, Balls – a Labour member since his teens – was an avowedly Labour-supporting special adviser. However, Burns, just like Balls, was brought in to the civil service to give intellectual support to a massive policy shift desired by a new government wanting to make a break with its allegedly failed predecessor. In that sense, he could be *seen* as a political appointment, even if he had no role in the Tory Party machine. So what added a frisson to the relationship between Burns and Balls was that Burns had infiltrated the Treasury and been accepted as one of its own, whereas Balls felt he was being treated by Burns as a dangerous outsider.

Did Balls's party-political taint undermine the objectivity of his economic advice, thus making it a constitutional outrage that Sir Andrew Turnbull – who succeeded Burns as Permanent Secretary – would later give him the title of Chief Economic Adviser? Balls was sure it did not – and there has been no discernible worsening in the Treasury's judgements on the economy over the past few years, even if it has become a little more prone to presenting statistics in a way that exaggerated the government's achievement. Paradoxically, what has probably protected the integrity of the mandarinate is that Balls – unlike Burns – had no desire to become a career civil servant; he never had ambitions to become Permanent Secretary. His desire for the title of Chief Economic Adviser was as much vanity as anything else, a need to be seen as a cut above previous special advisers – which was no more than a reflection of reality. What's more, there was never any muddying of who did what: Balls never pretended to be a neutral official.

Even so, it's slightly odd that Balls faced very little criticism – from journalists or MPs – that he was politicising Whitehall, even though he was just as powerful as Alastair Campbell and Jonathan Powell, the Prime Minister's most influential political advisers, who were constantly having to defend themselves against that charge. The probable explanation is that, unlike them, Balls never sought direct management responsibility for civil servants. Powell and Campbell acquired the formal ability to direct career civil servants through an Order in Council, shortly after the general election. But this power eventually became more of a hindrance than a help to them. Campbell, in particular, received so much flak for allegedly subverting the priceless neutrality of the civil service that when he quit the government in 2003, Blair did not transfer his formal authority over neutral officials to another political appointee.

Balls, however, was largely ignored during the furore over whether Blair's appointees were riding roughshod over the constitution, even though he was arguably more powerful than his own Permanent Secretary. He was lucky: his appointment in 2002 as chairman of the IMFC Deputies Committee – which establishes the priorities for the IMFC, which in turn sets the agenda for the International Monetary Fund – shocked Whitehall traditionalists, who believe this role of standing in for the Chancellor on the international stage should never have been taken by a political appointee. But they kept their concerns to themselves.

Also the 2004 Treasury departmental report lists Balls as a full member of its governing body, the Treasury Management Board or TMB (he had earlier been appointed to a special strategy committee of the management board and attended TMB to discuss "strategy on future government policy"). So in a very formal sense, he was now at the pinnacle of the Treasury hierarchy, even if he did not receive executive powers. He says that he never requested this position, that it was thrust on him following a review carried out for Sir Andrew Turnbull, who was the Permanent Secretary until 2002. And he also says that officials could in theory have ignored everything he said. So why did they never ignore him? Because Balls always spoke with the full authority of the Chancellor: he was, to employ the sobriquet that was eventually given to him, the "Deputy Chancellor".

***

An early spat between Burns and Balls was precipitated by a series of scoops that I had written for the *Financial Times* on the contents of Brown's first budget on July 2. They included Brown's plans to raise billions in new tax revenues by abolishing the tax credit on company dividends and to set a "symmetrical" inflation target for the Bank of England of $2^{1}/_{2}$ per cent (which meant that the Bank should work to ensure that inflation should neither be below or above that target: see pages 144-6). When on July 2 itself, the day of the budget, I wrote that Brown was to announce a "deficit reduction plan", Burns had a blazing row with Balls, accusing him of leaking price sensitive information to me. It was slightly odd that this was the story which Burns blew up over, since the idea of a Chancellor announcing an intention to cut the national debt was considerably less sensitive than the other information I had been divulging in my reports. However, there was a bit of a stink in the Commons about it, with the opposition leader, William Hague, calling for a police enquiry.

Burns believed that Balls and Whelan were breaking the venerable and sacrosanct prohibition on budget leaks and he wanted to nail them (Hugh Dalton famously resigned as Chancellor in 1947 when he leaked some of his budget to a journalist, just a few minutes before addressing the Commons). Anyway, I know that it sounds pompous, but even now it would be wrong for me to say whether Burns was right or wrong in his suspicions about my sources. But Brown decided that the only way to reassure the Permanent Secretary was to encourage him to hold a leak enquiry, in collaboration with Robin Butler, the head of the home civil service. Treasury phone records were examined, to see if anyone rang me. And Burns spoke to one of my less loyal colleagues, who told him that he did not think that the leak came from a career civil servant (although no one on the *FT*, apart from me, could possibly have known the origin of the article). All this was set down in a memo by Burns on July 11. However, the issue faded away after Brown – in a mischievous mood – called Burns's bluff by saying that Balls really ought to be sacked if it was clear that he was the leaker.

None of this made Balls any more emollient towards the Permanent Secretary. Apart from anything else, he was – and is – a vocal critic of the Treasury's performance as manager of the economy in the previous two decades, which was painful for Burns since he was at or near the helm of the Treasury for much of that period. Balls summarised his critique, which is that the Treasury is only really happy during a crisis, when I interviewed him in 2001 (*Sunday Times*, September 30):

> The old idea that the Treasury is at its strongest and most powerful when there's a short-term crisis and therefore you sit back and wait for that moment before you act, that's not the way we do things in monetary and fiscal policy any more.

One of Balls's very first initiatives was to encourage the Treasury to own up in public to its past errors in a cathartic act of atonement. This took the form of a paper, "Fiscal Policy: Lessons from the last Economic Cycle", published in November 1997 in conjunction with the

Chancellor's autumn statement (which had been renamed the Pre-Budget Report). Balls could have written it himself, but he felt that would not have achieved his purpose of communicating throughout the Treasury what it was that he wanted the department to become. And simply ordering officials to write the paper (which in theory he could not do anyway) would not have won hearts and minds: it would have become a "political" document, rather than the Treasury's "objective" assessment of its past failures. So he had an informal chat with the departments' economists, who turned out to be enthusiastic about what Balls had in mind, presumably because most of them were not old enough to be implicated in the Treasury's past errors. Under Joe Grice, they went off to write the paper, which did not disappoint Balls.

Its thrust was that the Treasury under Lawson in the mid 1980s had made a dreadful error by assuming that a swing from public borrowing to healthy surpluses at the peak of the economic cycle would not evaporate. And the paper points to two lessons: when planning future spending and revenues, "adjust for the economic cycle and build in a margin for uncertainty"; and publish all relevant forecasts and economic data, so that outside observers can evaluate whether the Treasury's plans make sense.

Owning up to mistakes is not necessarily a bad thing for institutions. In time, it can be a spur to renewed success. However, the Treasury's self-flagellation was particularly humiliating for Burns, since it was tantamount to his colleagues repudiating his performance as Chief Economic Adviser. "Terry completely freaked out," says an official. Burns, understandably, felt that Balls was out to get him. "It doesn't help when you keep reading in the newspapers that people hold you responsible to some degree for these events," he told me in 2002.

Burns stormed over to see Balls, who – somewhat disingenuously – said he could not see what the fuss was about, since the document had been drafted by Burns's officials. And when Burns asked the authors who had ordered them to prepare the thesis, they replied that it was all their own work. Finally, Burns went to Brown's office, to ask the Chancellor to intervene. But Brown's Private Secretary sent Burns an email saying the Chancellor had read the paper and was very happy with it, because it set the way forward for policy (it's plausible that Balls drafted this email, such was Brown's confidence in him). Either way, Burns could not prevent publication.

In fact, the public act of contrition became an annual event. The following year – in "Delivering Economic Stability: Lessons from Macro-economic Policy Experience" – the Treasury effectively apologised for creating a "boom and bust" culture in the UK through failing to sensibly coordinate fiscal policy (taxing and spending) with monetary policy (the setting of interest rates). And in the autumn of 2000 – in "Planning Sustainable Pubic Spending: Lessons from Previous Policy Experience" – it said sorry for its "short-termism" in the way it allocated funds for public services. This was catharsis with a capital "C".

***

The Hotel Group had a gang mentality, both before and after its extraordinary year-long battle from the end of 1997 with Alastair Campbell's 10 Downing Street mob – which was a great spectator event, especially for political journalists. However, whoever is in power, there's always rivalry between those who serve the Prime Minister and those working for a Chancellor. Treasury officials are never really happy unless they are getting one over on the self-regarding chaps down the road in Downing Street, and the Prime Minister's team are usually jealous of the Treasury's control of the purse. Even so, Whitehall had rarely seen a government civil war quite as intense as this one, as Brown insisted on exercising the unprecedented powers promised him by Blair at Granita in 1994 while the Prime Minister's team tried (in vain) to rein him in.

One respect in which Brown exploited the Granita licence was by withholding information from Blair and his officials. He felt fully justified doing this, by what he perceived as a breach of trust by Blair in June 1997, shortly before his first budget. On June 26, he and the Prime Minister had agreed that mortgage interest tax relief, a tax break for homeowners, should be cut, in order to dampen a booming housing market (and raise useful revenue). The decision to cut MIRAS was then leaked to the press. And – horror of horrors – it wasn't the Treasury doing the leaking. "We had a huge row because we were convinced that Mandelson leaked the mortgage interest rate stuff," says a colleague of Brown. "From that moment on, Gordon thought, 'Well, I'm not going to tell you anything'."

A pattern was then set of Brown withholding from Blair information about what would be in his budgets, his biennial spending reviews, and his Pre-Budget Reports (which take place every autumn and are mini-budgets in their own right) until the last possible moment. The Prime Minister would routinely ask the Chancellor to tell him what he was planning for taxes and expenditure. And occasionally the Chancellor would divulge one or two precious nuggets of information.

Blair gradually acquired the slightly demeaning role of supplicant on behalf of departments which felt they were not being given sufficient resources by the Treasury. "Blair never ever thought there was any purpose engaging in some rational debate," says a Treasury official. "In the spending review, he would make outrageous demands like, 'I've got to have this for defence, this for the Home Office, this for education.' And you'd look at it and say, 'That doesn't add up'... The way he came to deal with the Treasury was that he always thought we had some hidden plan, some back pocket."

Anyway, in the early days of government, this tendency of Brown and his chums to see opponents all around – certainly in Downing Street and even in the Treasury – probably meant that they executed their policies far more effectively and ruthlessly than would have been the case if they had been more relaxed. Everything had to be done quickly, because they never knew when the enemy would strike. This was not altogether a bad thing, although it was unsustainable, because it made them impervious to policy ideas and suggestions emanating from outside their closed circle. It was eventually replaced by a more consensual approach within the Treasury – if not with Downing Street – when Brown became convinced that his own department could be trusted.

Burns himself was viewed by the Hotel Group as a member of a potentially hostile cabal, a putative mandarinate freemasonry – whose other alleged members were Robin Butler, the head of the home civil service at the time, and Sir John Birt, former Director General of the BBC. Early in the life of the government, when one of Brown's circle described this enemy within to me, my reaction was that he was not getting enough sleep (which is probably true, since this chap now claims never to have been a proponent of this conspiracy theory). Geoffrey Robinson actually confided his suspicions to Birt, who passed them back to Burns.

And what was the alleged crime of Burns and his pals (apart from the fact that they play golf together)? Well, they were apparently too wedded to the status quo in government, they were too resistant to radical institutional change – and Burns inadvertently confirmed Brown's worst fears about all this when he delayed the hiving off of the Bank of England's regulatory functions in May 1997 (see page 139). Also they put themselves in the wrong camp by being chummy with Peter Mandelson – and since 1997, they've been taken up by Blair (Burns led an enquiry into hunting with hounds which took some of the heat out of the foxhunting debate, Butler reviewed the conduct of the security services in the run-up to the Iraq war, and Birt is an adviser to the Prime Minister).

In fact, they are not opposed to change *per se*; they just like to take it carefully, one step at a time – which can be maddening for a new government (as it was in 1979 for Margaret Thatcher and Geoffrey Howe, when Treasury conservatism delayed the implementation of the new Tory administration's radical programme). I'm sure that Burns's intentions were honourable. He's not a schemer or a wrecker. But, having run the Treasury for a long time, he may not have been as tolerant of Brown's new way as he should have been.

Burns also made one startling misjudgement: he recommended to Brown that the Treasury move out of Whitehall to Vauxhall during a proposed redevelopment of its headquarters in Whitehall. One senior civil servant explains why this was a mistake:

> Terry's recommendation to relocate the whole of the Treasury away from Whitehall, while the building was being redeveloped, was a disaster. He failed to understand that Gordon would never move away from close proximity to the Prime Minister. There was simply no possibility of Gordon moving away.
>
> But Gordon would never say this to Terry for obvious reasons. He would only complain about the cost of moving away – which of course he did. And Terry just did not see that the issue was not really the cost, so he continued to argue for the move. It was appalling, but Terry seemed to have no understanding of how important it was for Gordon, Ed and Geoffrey not to move out. Anyway all of this got us off on exactly the wrong foot.

Robinson was mandated by Brown to come up with a scheme that would allow him to stay put – which Robinson duly did (the expensive and horrendously noisy removal of a thick concrete layer above the Cabinet War Rooms at the back of the Treasury's Victorian edifice was abandoned and the redevelopment was carried out in two phases, allowing Brown and the officials to relocate from the front to the back of the building as the refurbishment progressed). But with this kind of disagreement constantly bubbling up, Burns and Brown's circle found it impossible to build an entente.

Burns had particular difficulties with Robinson, who was a wealthy businessman and long-serving Labour MP. He was the government's self-styled entrepreneur in residence, which meant he was given free rein to broker deals between departments, or with the private sector. Having been given the old but comparatively meaningless title of Paymaster General, he was not in the Cabinet. But for a while he was more powerful than many ministers of cabinet rank, simply because he was in the unusual position of having the trust and support of Brown and Blair – although eventually, when hostilities between the Treasury and 10

Downing Street intensified, he sided with Brown against Blair.

Robinson had forged his relationships with Brown and Blair in the mid-1990s. They both needed funding for their private offices and the expensive work of creating detailed policies fit for government. Robinson seemed to be the perfect donor: as a well-heeled Labour MP, the media would find it difficult to impugn him (or so Brown and Blair naively believed). Anyway, while in opposition, Robinson contributed a generous £208,455 to pay for the tax, legal and other specialist professional advice that Brown needed when formulating his policies, including the windfall tax on the privatised utilities and the use of the tax system to boost the earnings of the low paid through tax credits (the money is shown as "donations received" in the 1996-7 accounts of a specially created research business called the Smith Political Economy Unit Limit).

Robinson also gave donations to finance Blair's office. And Blair and his family borrowed Robinson's Tuscan villa near San Gimignano in the summers of 1996 and 1997. Such was Robinson's generosity, he installed a brand new kitchen in anticipation of the arrival of Cherie Blair in 1996, because he had been mortified to learn that she had been scathing about the state of the cooking equipment she had found when borrowing a house belonging to another New Labour friend.

As a multi-millionaire, Robinson seemed to be symbolically valuable to Blair and Brown. The New Labour vanguard was obsessed with recruiting business people to their cause, because they believed that one of their party's serious weaknesses was the perception that it did not understand wealth-creation (Jonathan Powell, Blair's Chief of Staff, evinced a conviction in the mid-1990s that only a public endorsement for Blair from Richard Branson could secure the 1997 general election – which Branson never quite delivered). So it was hip hip hooray that a fabulously wealthy businessman like Robinson was putting his cash behind them.

In fact, their enthusiastic adoption of Robinson showed quite how little Brown and Blair really knew about business, because in the City he was regarded as just a little too sharp. His Transtec conglomerate had a mixed reputation. And it later turned out that a sizeable part of his vast fortune was a bequest from a remarkable business woman, the Belgian car importer, Joska Bourgeois, whom Robinson had befriended.

What particularly riled Burns about Robinson was that – perhaps taking a leaf out of the book of the Prime Minister and Chancellor – he didn't follow the convention of making sure detailed notes were taken of all his discussions as a minister. These covered such diverse subjects as whether a private finance deal could be arranged to allow the Royal Family to keep the Royal Yacht (Robinson decided against in the end, though he worked hard in 1997 to find a well-heeled company or individual prepared to stump up tens of millions of pounds) and whether coal mines should be kept open in the face of falling demand from power companies. One senior official recalls:

When Robinson talked to people there were no records taken. We had no way of knowing what he had promised to whom. In terms of the machinery (of government), this was very difficult. It was dangerous. He was trying to arrange deals, for the Royal Yacht or wherever. There was an inadequate paper trail, which is important. The UK system of government is relatively insulated from criticism because of the safeguards that are in place, because of the paper trail.

Brown presumably regarded such concerns, if he was aware of them, as needless fussing. He liked Robinson's can-do approach – as did the Treasury's more entrepreneurial officials, such as Steve Robson – which was gleaned partly from his life in business and partly from having been on the margins of government since the 1960s (when he was a researcher at Labour's then headquarters at Transport House in south London). When Balls or Brown were having doubts about whether to press ahead with a controversial reform, Robinson put fire in their belly. And, because he knew his way around the City, he could take one of their ideas – for a windfall tax on the privatised utilities, or for a reform of corporation tax – and obtain the relevant external help to transform it into a practical measure. "The windfall tax wasn't Geoffrey's idea, but we'd have never done it in the way we did without him," says one of his colleagues.

In the end, Robinson's overall record in government was mixed. His rescue of Britain's coalmines could only ever be a short-term fix; pit closures were delayed rather than abandoned forever, at some economic and environmental cost. And the abolition in 1997 of the tax credit on dividends and an associated reconstruction of the corporation tax system – which raised some £5bn each and every year and which Robinson helped to drive through – has implicated the government in the financial crisis currently afflicting pension funds, by reducing the cash flow of these funds (a confidential document on all this drawn up for Brown in opposition, with the title "Cascade", was too sanguine about this risk). However those who say that Brown and Robinson have sole responsibility for the hole in many company pension schemes are wrong: companies themselves share part of the burden of guilt, for effectively skimming off surpluses from the funds when the going was good in the 1990s; and, as germanely, there was a lobby of senior business people who, shortly before the 1997 general election, pressed for the dividend tax credit to be abolished because they thought it put too much pressure on companies to pay dividends rather than investing for the long-term growth of their businesses.

On a more positive note, the £5bn windfall tax on privatised utilities was a relatively painless way of raising valuable revenue for employment creation. Also Robinson was involved in the tortuous process of reducing capital gains tax, which – through various complicated reforms – has created a system that provides superior incentives for wealth-creation and risk-taking by entrepreneurs, though it also gives substantial rewards to those with inherited assets who did not need them (see page 286).

Now, the counterweight to Robinson's drive and energy was that his personal financial affairs appeared ferociously complicated and always seemed to be throwing up a mini-crisis of some sort. One, that occurred towards the end of 1997, was the disclosure that he had an interest in a substantial offshore trust. There was nothing intrinsically wrong in this, except it was a bit embarrassing because Brown had made a big thing of cracking down on such tax avoidance. Here is Burns's account of what happened:

> The *Independent on Sunday* discovered that Geoffrey was a beneficiary of an offshore trust. He put out a press statement explaining this. And he wanted to put in it that I had approved his arrangements, that he had shown me all his arrangements and that I had approved them. I knew nothing about it (the trust). But it did not fall to me to approve it. The job of the Permanent Secretary is not to approve or not. Ministers take decisions about how they deal with their personal financial affairs. They are supposed to take advice from the Permanent Secretary.
>
> I had had a meeting with him about some aspects of his business. He clearly came to think that he had told me he had an offshore trust. When he told me this journalist was on to the story, I certainly had no recollection of having been told about it. So we had a long and tortuous business of negotiating a statement that he made on a Saturday night.
>
> He felt basically I should be giving him more support. My view was that it was an illusion to think I could give him support. But everyone at that stage was dead keen on protecting Geoffrey and it was seen that my role was being awkward and unnecessary.

Robinson's memory of all this is different. He insists that the offshore trust was discussed with Burns in a meeting on May 21, 1997. "I informed the Permanent Secretary of the existence of the offshore trust," Robinson says in his political memoirs. "He seemed well satisfied." So when Robinson learned of the planned exposé in the *Independent on Sunday*, he did not believe that he had "much to fear". What's fascinating is that Brown then immersed himself in helping his ministerial friend. "I met Gordon in his office early the next day to discuss how we should handle the matter," Robinson writes. "He stressed that I should get out a complete statement dealing with all aspects of the trust... As was usually the case on matters of this kind, Gordon went to his word processor and pounded out the first draft [*The Unconventional Minister*, 2000]." It was this statement that Burns did not like and would not approve.

Eventually a compromise was agreed – though in difficult circumstances for Burns. He is a devoted supporter of Queens Park Rangers and had travelled to watch his team on Saturday November 29, 1997. With just minutes to go before kick-off, he was telephoned by Whelan and gave his permission for a statement to be given to the *Independent on Sunday* and other Sunday newspapers. The statement concentrated on Robinson's creation, on May 7, 1997, of a so-called "blind trust" – as distinct from the separate offshore trust – into which most of his assets were placed, in accordance with official guidelines on what ministers should do with their investments and business interests (when a minister puts his assets into a blind trust, he has no control over them or even the ability to see what happens to them). Robinson's statement says:

> I informed him (Burns) that I was a discretionary beneficiary under a trust established for my family (the offshore trust). After advice from the Permanent Secretary and Titmuss Sainer Dechert [Robinson's lawyers], I decided in accordance with their advice that there was no need to include this in the blind-trust arrangements, since I was a discretionary beneficiary [with no control over the offshore trust].

Now, anyone reading this might conclude that Burns had approved Robinson's offshore trust arrangements. However, the statement does not quite say that: it was a triumph of official obfuscation.

Both Robinson and Burns were becoming thoroughly miserable as 1997 drew to a close. Robinson was under attack by the Tories and in the press for his alleged hypocrisy in having an estimated £12.75m held in the controversial offshore trust domiciled in the tax haven of Guernsey. And the charge of double-standards only intensified days later, when Robinson announced a radical overhaul of tax breaks for savers. Personal Equity Plans (or PEPs) – a successful Tory initiative to encourage investment in shares and gilts – were to be scrapped and replaced by so-called

Individual Savings Accounts (ISAs). In the process, there was to be a scaling back of tax exemptions available on such investments – which made sense, because there was compelling evidence that the tax benefits were being reaped by those on higher incomes, who would have saved even without them, and that the tax breaks were doing little to stimulate savings among the less prosperous. However, because of the disclosure that Robinson was not paying British tax on millions held in trust for him, there was an outcry that he was abolishing some measly perks enjoyed by the middle classes.

The protests from the *Daily Mail* et al were so noisy that they forced a spectacular U-turn on the Treasury. When the ISAs were finally made available, the middle-class tax breaks were largely preserved – which made a dreadful nonsense of the entire reform. It ended up being an expensive failure.

Robinson was damaged, though he clung on in post for another year through a succession of scrapes: the Tories attacked him for failing to register one of his business interests in the Commons register of members interests; and embarrassing links to the late Robert Maxwell, the corrupt deceased media magnate, were disclosed. As each little drama ran its course, it became progressively more difficult for Brown and Blair to sustain a protective and indulgent attitude to their friend. And when the government was rocked by the revelation that Robinson had lent £373,000 to Mandelson to buy a house in Notting Hill, both Robinson and Blair's favourite minister departed for the backbenches, on December 23, 1998.

As for Burns, he had already jumped ship. After Christmas of 1997, the early squalls were over. Burns had worked hard to rebuild Brown's relationship with the Bank governor, Eddie George, following the uncomfortable start of their relationship (see page 142). And the Treasury itself was beginning to adjust to the new regime. "If you find yourself as Permanent Secretary in the role where the major impact you are having on people's lives is to be seen to be awkward and to be stopping them doing things they want to do, it isn't comfortable," Burns recalls. "It was more sensible all round, for everybody, that I should go...

I had some discussions with Richard Wilson who had just become Cabinet Secretary and with Number 10 about whether I should go and do something there. But I came to the view I needed a clean break. By then, I was limited in terms of what I could do (at the Treasury) and it was better that somebody else should take it on... We had done all the early moves. The place was beginning to settle down."

***

Burns left in the middle of 1998. Gradually, under the new Permanent Secretary, Sir Andrew Turnbull (who is now head of the entire home civil service), the two Treasuries – the Treasury of Brown, Balls and the tiny number of officials they trusted, and the Treasury of the hundreds of other officials – became one. As much as anything else, Balls's budget and public spending advice won round doubters among the career civil servants. The Tories sustained a noisy campaign that Brown was squandering the golden inheritance he had received from them (and in fairness to his predecessor, Ken Clarke, the inheritance was pretty good), but the economy sailed through the international squalls of 1998, growth accelerated and the national debt was steadily reduced. For the first time in decades, the Treasury did not have to feel embarrassed about its economic record. And anyway, the Oxbridge males who throng it tend to have a grudging admiration for intellectually able loudmouths (Balls therefore has something in common with Nigel Lawson).

The Treasury itself signalled the end of its internal strife in a *Guardian* feature-article on the department in November 1999, which was published on the eve of Brown's Pre-Budget Report of that year. After showing initial reservations about granting access to the relevant journalists, Turnbull agreed to be interviewed and then gave a big and public hug to Balls and the other special advisers, including Ed Miliband, Spencer Livermore (who has specialised in employment-creation initiatives since 2001) and Ian Austin, who has been a shrewd and effective successor to Charlie Whelan. Turnbull said: "The special advisers play a much bigger role than in the past, but that's partly because the special advisers are of such a high calibre." And he added: "The idea that they (the advisers) don't work with Treasury officials is complete bunkum."

It was also Turnbull who drove through the remodelling of the Treasury's building that has been so important in opening up its culture. However, the Treasury only became truly Brown's when Gus O'Donnell became Permanent Secretary in 2002. This is not to say that they could not possibly fall out. It is simply that Brown and Balls trust O'Donnell implicitly.

O'Donnell never manifested qualms about Balls's sway in the Treasury in the way that Burns did. And so Balls went from strength to strength, as his office and that of Brown's private office worked hand in glove. He and the Chancellor were in contact by phone around the clock, wherever they were in the world. However, after seven years as the senior consigliere, Balls wanted to leave the backroom and become a visible, accountable political player. On June 30, 2004, he became the Labour candidate for the safe Labour seat of Normanton, at which point he was forced to quit his Treasury post (though he remains, on an informal basis, a close adviser to Brown). His departure is the most tangible sign that Brown no longer has the slightest doubt that the career civil servants are there to serve him.

Meanwhile, the reputation of the Treasury as a whole has rarely been higher – in part because the economic performance of the UK has been good by most standards. Since the recession of the early 1990s, or more precisely since the second quarter of 1992, the British economy has expanded at a compound rate of around 3 per cent a year, without a single quarter of negative growth. Of the major global economies, only the US and Canada have expanded faster: our growth rate has been more than double that enjoyed by Japan and Germany. The UK's inflation rate, too, has been remarkably low and stable.

It would be absurd to give all the credit to the reconstructed Treasury. Praise is due to Thatcher, Howe and Lawson, and their 1980s programme of deregulating swathes of the economy, privatising state-owned utilities, reducing taxes and limiting trade union power. Also, Brown has had his share of setbacks and failures. As a nation, we are not saving nearly enough for retirement – and the Treasury can be accused of meddling in this sphere, rather than coming up with a strategic solution. As for Brown's ambition to boost the productivity of British companies to levels that compare with the US, that remains a beautiful dream. Meanwhile, inflation in the residential housing market has been excessive, there has been a rising trend to government borrowing, and the British taxation system has become more complex (perhaps to a degree that has a negative impact on the competitiveness of the economy).

But as yet, and for the first time in living memory, the Treasury hasn't mucked it up: it has not transformed a period of growth into boom and then bust. Even the relatively impressive economic record of the Thatcher administration was undermined by the misguided stimulus engineered by Lawson as Chancellor in 1987.

And what about the charge that Brown has politicised the Treasury in a way that impugns British constitutional custom and practice? One official says: "I really don't buy this argument about the politicisation of the civil service. Under Lawson and Lamont [two recent Tory Chancellors], mainstream civil servants were asked to write political speeches. The relationship between Whitehall and ministers back then was too cosy." And there's also a more positive case for what Brown has done, made by another official:

In many ways the change in the relationship between Chancellor and officials should have been welcomed by democrats. Under Brown, the balance of power between civil servants and ministers changed, with the Chancellor and his allies the dominant factor in determining policy. Amazing as this may seem, that's not how it was before

In the late 1970s, when Denis Healey was Chancellor, most policy initiatives were from the Treasury machine, not from ministers. And I never once saw Healey overturn official advice. It was also rare for ministers to overturn civil service advice, even under Thatcher.

But who's the real power: Brown or Balls? Brown has respect for Balls, but the Chancellor is the senior partner. "Gordon is his own person," says one of their colleagues. "Those who criticise him for deferring too much to Balls have got it wrong. He sensibly does not get drowned in detail; he thinks strategically. The technical stuff is for Balls. Ed takes the nitty-gritty off him, relieves him of the minutiae."

However, Balls is not simply a technocrat. "I don't under-estimate the debates that go on behind closed doors when no officials are present," says a mandarin. "I'm sure Brown and Balls don't always agree. Balls's strength is the quality of the relationship forged in opposition. And he is not a sycophant."

Or as another official puts it: "It has been an unprecedented partnership. Heaven help the government if Balls ever stops working with Brown in some capacity. There is no one else capable of standing up to him."

CHAPTER FOUR

How the Bank of England made a credible
socialist of Gordon Brown

T he single most important reform to the machinery of government carried out by New Labour was probably its first: the
transfer of control over interest rates from the Treasury to the
Bank of England, which was announced on May 6, 1997, five days after
the general election. Gordon Brown was conspicuously aware that this
was history (his moment, decidedly not Blair's) – and since it was economic history, he invited a quartet of *FT* editors and writers in to interview him about it that morning (Richard Lambert, the editor, Martin
Wolf, chief leader writer, Philip Stephens, political commentator, and
me, the political editor). This was an *FT* event, *par excellence* (there were
25 separate articles about it in the following day's edition of that newspaper). But less orthodox and hideously post-modern was that a Scottish
television crew was filming him in conversation with us (we should, in
retrospect, have refused to participate in this Soviet-style, image-building
exercise, arranged by Charlie Whelan, his irrepressible press aide). As we
settled into the armchairs, redolent of a gentleman's club, at one end of a
sombre boardroom that then served as the Chancellor's office in the
Treasury (which Brown has since vacated for smaller, brighter and less
oppressive quarters on the St James's Park side of the monolith), we did
our best to ask challenging questions. Why, for example, was there no
reference to this substantial constitutional change in the Party's election

112

manifesto? Well, Brown's unsatisfactory answer was that there was a "hint" of it and it was just unfortunate that no probing journalist had asked him about his plans for the Bank of England in the press conferences that preceded the election – which showed New Labour's slightly unfortunate tendency to be less than straightforward in the way it communicates with voters (and which Brown would these days recognise has contributed to the mistrust felt by much of the electorate for politicians).

But, to be frank, the *FT* rather pulled its punches and was swept up in the excitement of the moment. It was impossible to deny that Brown had pulled off a brilliant coup. This party, which had been in the wilderness for almost 20 years, suddenly acquired the economic credibility lacked by its "old" Labour predecessors. And, if political power is rarely lost until the governing party proves its economic incompetence, this single initiative gave Blair and Brown a firm grip on power that Attlee in the 1940s and Wilson in the 1960s and 1970s never possessed.

For Brown and Balls, there was an immediate demonstration of why giving up the right to set interest rates was absolutely the soundest way to go. Although he had announced that he was transferring the power to set interest rates to the Bank, it would take a few weeks to make the necessary arrangements. So for the first and last time, Brown had to decide what to do with interest rates, having consulted with the Bank's Governor, Eddie George. He and Balls wanted to raise them by $1/_2$ per cent, to choke off any inflationary pressures building in the economy. George – who received strong support on this from Derek Scott, Blair's Economic Adviser at the time – felt $1/_2$ per cent was too much and could be destabilising to financial markets, when combined with the shock of the decision to create an independent central bank. Blair intervened and said to Brown: "I'm very worried about going for a half, we should go for a quarter." On almost any other issue, Brown would have ignored the Prime Minister. But he decided there was no point in having an argument with him, when he had already decided to give up the government's right to have any say over interest rates. On the other hand, here was his first-hand proof of one of the great flaws with the system he had inherited and was disbanding: Prime Ministers never like to raise interest rates for fear of alienating voters.

By making it impossible for Prime Ministers – or Chancellors – to muck things up by setting the wrong interest rate, Brown also destroyed the Tories' legitimate claim to be the natural party of government. Collective anxiety about Labour's capacity to wreck the economy had kept it out of office for most of the 20th century. And on the rare occasions when Labour governments were elected, their respective ministers suffered from the constant worry that some kind of exchange rate or borrowing crisis was just around the corner. But Brown's ceding of the personal ability as Chancellor to set interest rates (an intoxicating power) created more stable economic conditions – and also distanced him from the full political consequences should the economy ever turn down sharply (which astonishingly – and almost without precedent for 100 years – it hasn't done so far).

By way of corroboration, a senior official at the very pinnacle of government vouchsafes that the main reason why Margaret Thatcher in the late 1980s resisted the urging of her Chancellor, Nigel Lawson, to hand sole responsibility for fighting inflation to the Bank of England was that she recognised that such a move would reduce the electorate's fear of a Labour government. If Labour had become unable to undermine prosperity by setting interest rates at the wrong level, then you and I could have voted with our consciences rather than with an eye on our mortgages and wallets. And that would have been to the detriment of the Conservatives who were – probably wrongly in the light of post-war experience – viewed as the sounder stewards of the economy. This was the official's analysis:

Thatcher's argument against giving independence to the Bank was that people would believe it would constrain Labour and therefore they would not be worried by Labour's recklessness. But the Tories took a big gamble, because that argument is true only for a long as Labour continues to be reckless. As soon as Labour decided to trump the Tories by saying, 'If you won't play the independence card we will', the Tories lost. It was a masterstroke.

Now, one salient characteristic of this reform is that Blair played almost no role in its development or implementation. Between 1994 and 1997, this was all the handiwork of Brown and – especially – Ed Balls. Such was the detail of their preparations that the changes could be announced within less than a week of taking office. Which is not to say there were no hitches: in fact, Brown came close to fomenting a full-scale City crisis shortly afterwards, when the governor of the Bank of England was on the verge of quitting (however powerful Brown was, he would have been wounded forever if he had lost a governor so quickly). But the essence of the Brown/Balls design for the new monetary policy system has withstood all tests to date – and is now regarded by the three major political parties as the bedrock of the British system for economic management (although, paradoxically, one that Brown would be willing to drop, if he ever thinks the time is right to join the euro, which is probably a marginally less remote prospect than most commentators believe).

Apart from anything else, the stability of the inflation rate in a narrow range around $2^{1}/_{2}$ per cent on the discontinued RPIX measure (replaced by a euro hybrid called the Consumer Price Index) has been a boon to businesses in helping them to plan their budgets and to investors in forecasting the long-term returns of their savings and investments. And a sharp drop in interest rates has benefited borrowers (although one consequence has been to pump up a housing boom to a dangerous extent). Anyway, in part because of the Granita deal on the division of functions between him and Brown, throughout the development of the policy in opposition Blair was kept informed though rarely consulted.

***

The creation of the Bank of England's Monetary Policy Committee, with its power to set interest rates, was not an idea plucked out of nowhere by Brown and Balls. Although the Tories never had the good sense to do it themselves, in some ways it was the natural culmination of a series of reforms implemented after the UK's humiliating exit from the European Exchange Rate mechanism on September 16, 1992. The ERM debacle was a once-in-a-generation turning point in British politics. And Brown spotted this at the very moment of crisis, according to Lord Elder, who was then Chief of Staff for the Labour leader of the time, John Smith. "John and I were in Berlin at a Socialist International event," says Elder. "Gordon rang up, when we were ejected from the ERM. He kept saying, 'You have no idea how important this is – we were always the Party of devaluation.' He kept saying it over and over again."

Hitherto it had always been Labour that was castigated as the Party unable to maintain a sound currency. Labour Chancellors devalued the pound in 1949 and again in 1967. Labour had been in office when there was a run on the pound in 1976. And the Party had been in power when the policy of pegging the pound to the gold price – the so-called Gold Standard – was abandoned in 1931.

To make matters worse for John Major's government, membership of the ERM was the centrepiece of the Tories' anti-inflationary policy. The UK had joined the Exchange Rate Mechanism of the European Monetary System in October 1990, after a decade of turmoil in the way that the government attempted to control inflation. First, after Thatcher took office in 1979, the Tories tried to limit the growth of a broad measure of money, called £M3. When that didn't work terribly well in reining back price rises, a narrower money measure, M0, was also targeted. But through it all, British inflation remained high and volatile by international standards. Indeed, from 1980 to 1998, the UK had the second highest inflation rate of the Group of Seven leading industrial countries and the third most variable and unpredictable rate (Italy was the worst performer on both counts). Even so, the ERM had promised a rather more effective anti-inflationary discipline.

Membership of the currency system bore down on the rate of price rises in Britain because a British Chancellor was obliged to set interest rates at a relatively high level, in order to prevent the sterling exchange rate falling through a floor set by the system. There was only one problem. Perceptive international investors, led by the influential speculator and international political activist, George Soros, calculated that the British economy was not strong enough to cope with such powerful deflationary medicine. And they tested their theory by selling sterling and presenting the government with two equally unpalatable choices: raise interest rates to crippling levels or withdraw from the ERM.

On September 16, 1992, John Major as Prime Minister and Norman Lamont as Chancellor led a humiliating exit from the ERM – and bang went all their anti-inflationary credibility in the financial markets. But if the Tories were now bereft of a policy to combat inflation, so too was Labour. It had provided cross-party support for the ERM adventure, to prove to the City that it too was serious about squeezing inflation out of the British economy (one of the very few senior Labour frontbenchers who opposed support for the ERM in the late 1980s was Brian Gould, an irascible New Zealander who quit British politics more than a decade ago). But, without the ERM bulwark, Labour was bad old, inflation-loving Labour once again – or at least it would be in the eyes of many voters.

The scale of the jolt given to Brown by the ERM debacle can be seen in a speech, given before the crisis on February 17, 1992 to Labour's Finance and Industry Study Group, a group of trade unionists, economists and Labour-supporting business people (a rare species back then). It was about the need to boost investment, in order to increase the capacity of the economy to growth faster. Some of his rhetoric, and a small number of policies he describes in this and other speeches of the time, survived. But mostly it's redolent of a less sharp-edged Brown. There's none of the talk of prudence and tough choices which defined his early years as Chancellor, but there are lots of references to creating "fulfilling" employment, ending the supposedly unnatural barriers between managers and workers and forming partnerships for long term investment between City institutions and companies. Anyway, this is almost the last sighting of a softer, almost utopian Brown. This Brown had placed too much faith in the ability of the ERM to create stable economic conditions.

Brown's economic education throughout the 1990s took him from "all we need to do is persuade companies to invest more to save the British economy" to "there will be no meaningful investment unless we bring stability to inflation and the public finances". His intellectual companion along the way (periodically his tutor) was Ed Balls. Through late 1992 and 1993, Balls had worked in an informal capacity with Brown and John Smith. And he also produced a discussion paper for the soft-left think tank, the Fabian Society, called "Euro-Monetarism – why Britain was ensnared and how it could escape", which he discussed with Brown while it was in preparation (see page 186). It is this essential early tract, mapping out an approach for a Labour government to monetary policy that – although different from what ultimately happened in 1997 in some respects – lays down the big principles that were ultimately adopted.

The young Balls deserves as much credit – probably more – than anyone else for the creation of the modern Bank of England. Along the way he had useful informal conversations with Mervyn King – who was in charge of economics at the Bank, became deputy governor after Labour took office and is now the Governor. Balls would bounce ideas off him and seek his views on the way that different central banks around the world operate. But he did not communicate to King his blueprint for a reformed Bank of England. And liaison with the Bank more widely was fairly limited: there was one meeting between Brown and Sir Edward George, Governor of the Bank, in early 1997, to discuss technical issues, but no hint was given by Brown of the coup he planned.

Funnily enough, it's one of those reforms that everyone wants to claim for themselves. Senior Treasury mandarins have told me that there was a "historical inevitability" about the decision to give control of interest rates to the Bank, following changes to the system of monetary control that were initiated in phases after the ERM debacle (there's more on this below). And close friends of Brown have told me that he was clear it was the right way to go a good ten years ago (though there's little evidence for this). Others have pointed me to a compelling article written for Brown in the spring of 1997 by Gavyn Davies, who at the time was an influential economist at the investment bank Goldman Sachs and has since been and gone as Chairman of the BBC (a version of this paper was published in the *FT* on April 1 1997). But the reality is that Brown and Balls had made all the relevant decisions on the structure and powers of the new Bank by 1996. Anyway, the nub of Balls's Fabian pamphlet was this:

> The macroeconomic role of government should be to construct a stable and predictable monetary framework, a platform on which sustainable growth can be built...
>
> Across the world the evidence is clear: if politicians and their civil servants control interest rates, then the temptation to manipulate the economy for short term electoral advantage is likely to result in higher inflation and more variable inflation with no long term return in terms of higher growth or lower employment.

In other words, nothing but economic ill came from politicians controlling interest rates. Meanwhile the arguments for giving control of interest rates to the Bank were also political:

> Labour government ministers have little to gain and a great deal to lose from trying to run monetary policy themselves... Successful developed economies – including left of centre governments such as Australia – have realised that an independent central bank, charged to deliver low and stable inflation, is a better way to achieve macroeconomic stability.

Balls's strong conviction was that there was no over-riding reason why a Labour Chancellor should wish to retain the power to manipulate base interest rates. In fact, the reverse was true. Markets were likely to regard the anti-inflationary zeal of an independent central bank as more credible than that of a Chancellor, who would always be under intense political pressure to cut interest rates.

And if interest rate decisions were depoliticised in this way, interest rates in general would – paradoxically – be lower over the long term, because investors in sterling assets could be more confident that their returns would not be whittled away by inflation. So by giving up a set of important economic powers, a government's reputation and popularity would probably be enhanced over the medium term. Balls continues:

> The advantage of such an independent central bank to the UK economy would be a transparent, accountable and predictable monetary policy... It would become an important bulwark against short-termism... The economy would no longer be controlled by a secretive Treasury. Interest rates could no longer be manipulated for short-term political reasons without any public scrutiny or control... The advantage of an independent central bank for the Chancellor is credibility... This would strengthen and not weaken the hand of a Labour government."

Moving from the general case to the particular, Balls could not resist a dig at the Treasury, launching a broadside at its long-term performance: "No one has mastered the art of boom-bust economics better than the British Treasury... Power to set monetary policy remains in the hands of government ministers and unaccountable Treasury civil servants who seem able to live on despite their errors, while hapless Chancellors take the blame."

One of the "unaccountable" civil servants Balls had in mind was Sir Terry Burns (now Lord Burns) who had been the Chief Economic Adviser to the Treasury through the inflationary ups and downs of the 1980s and was the Permanent Secretary in overall charge of the department during the 1992 sterling disaster. And who, of course, was still running the Treasury in 1997, when Balls and Brown took up residence there after the landslide general election victory. Unsurprisingly, the working relationship between Burns and Balls would be uncomfortable.

The Fabian paper is redolent of an angry young economist in one other respect. Balls is scathing about the governance of the Bank of England – and his hostility foreshadows a period of tumult in the relationship between Brown and the Bank for just a few weeks in the spring and summer of 1997. Balls called for sweeping reform of the Bank, the removal of one of its most important functions in the City, as a watchdog of the commercial banks, if it were to be endowed with new monetary policy powers. He says:

This would have to be a very different institution from the Bank of England, which currently runs monetary policy on the Treasury's behalf, and whose credibility has been undermined by recent regulatory failures... An independent British central bank would perform its macroeconomic task better if it were not also responsible for City supervision, and if it were staffed by outsiders with proven track-records in economic or financial management.

***

Brown in the early 1990s could be as cruel as any politician about the economic record of John Major and his hapless Chancellor, Norman (now Lord) Lamont. But he owes them a debt, because in their act of political suicide – the forced exit from the ERM – they were bequeathing to Brown and Blair an economy from which many of the inflationary pressures had been squeezed. During the UK's painful two-year stint in the ERM, interest rates were kept at high levels while economic growth was sluggish. And tax increases announced in successive budgets in 1993 took even more oomph out of the economy. This was anti-inflationary shock-treatment that had an enduring effect. Lord Burns, who had only recently been promoted to the post of Treasury Permanent Secretary when the ERM crisis erupted, described it like this to me: "It was a decisive moment because it got the whole level of the inflation rate down and to a much lower level. If it had been left to a conscious choice, we might not have taken the (deflationary) decision. So it became a major force for aligning our inflation rate with everyone else's inflation rate."

After the ERM ejection, Burns, Lamont and Major reinforced the squeeze on inflation with a new system of "targeting" the inflation rate, which for the first time told consumers and businesses what level of inflation the government wanted to achieve. And there were further reforms after Ken Clarke replaced Lamont as Chancellor in 1993. So when Brown eventually captured the Treasury's Victorian citadel in May 1997, his scope to meddle with interest rates had already been constrained to an extent.

The new system became characterised as the "Ken and Eddie show" (after its leading players, Ken Clarke – Chancellor until 1997 – and Sir Edward George, the Bank Governor from 1993 to 2003). It included a public commitment by the government to reduce inflation to less than $2^{1}/_{2}$ per cent by the end of the parliament. And to help achieve this, the Bank started publishing a more rigorous quarterly assessment of the UK's inflation outlook. There was also an attempt to help markets understand how interest rate decisions were made, through the publication of the minutes of the monthly meetings between the Chancellor and the Governor of the Bank of England, after a six-week delay. These changes were not trivial. They helped to bring inflation down and – just as important – they were viewed as positive reforms in the City.

The system would have flopped if the Chancellor had lacked the backbone to raise rates when necessary. However, Ken Clarke was a formidable Chancellor – which he proved in September 1994, when the painful early 1990s recession was still fresh in memories, by pushing up interest rates. It was Labour's reaction – in the form of an article published by the *FT* under the by-line of Tony Blair, who had at that time only recently assumed the leadership – which was perhaps more significant (the article was in fact written by Balls, who had been working for Brown for six months, not long enough to understand that Brown wouldn't be overjoyed that Balls was moonlighting for Blair; Brown, who was in Portugal, gritted his teeth and let it pass). For possibly the first time in its history,

Labour distanced itself from the inevitable clamour of complaint about the interest rate rise from trade unions and manufacturers by failing to dispute that the rate rise was necessary. Instead Balls – in Blair's clothing – attacked the government for failing "to create the conditions necessary for sustained growth without accelerating inflation".

Balls and Brown were not yet highlighting what they perceived as the main defect in the Tories' new anti-inflationary approach, that the ultimate decision on whether to raise or lower rates still resided with the Chancellor. They edged in that direction in the spring of 1995, when it was widely believed that Eddie George had recommended an interest rate rise, on fears that inflation was bubbling up, but that Clarke had over-ruled him (this was shown to be so, when minutes of their discussion were published in June of that year). Investors will tend to believe that a professional such as George would be more likely to get it right than even a politician as persuasive as Clarke. As it happens, on this occasion, Clarke was probably the more acute judge and George was wrong – though few investors thought so at the time, which is what matters in a world where trillions can flow across borders if changes to interest rates are even fractionally different from what the markets expect. Mistrust of Clarke's motives was heightened by the proximity of local elections, when a mortgage rate rise would have been a disaster for the Conservatives. Confidence in the system wasn't helped when the meeting between Clarke and George was delayed by a couple of days, until after the polling day of May 4, 1995.

Here was a big political opportunity for Brown to send out a message that he was in a different mould from his Labour antecedents. The normal approach of a shadow Chancellor would have been to attack the deflationary central banker, George, for wanting to impose punitive interest rates that would put jobs at risk. But Brown, in a speech on Labour's macroeconomic framework (delivered on May 17, 1995), in effect sided with the Governor by saying that "the underlying problem… is that the Conservatives have failed to take the medium-term action to ensure that their inflation target is met." In other words, Labour was claiming to be tougher on inflation than the Tories – which was not the way the world was supposed to be.

***

Another vital staging post on Brown's road to the granting of Bank independence had taken place earlier in the spring, on March 3, 1995. It was an all-day meeting of New Labour's vanguard, including Blair and Brown, at the Hampshire home – a 1635 hunting lodge in Fritham – of the Labour-supporting advertising executive, Chris Powell (brother of the more famous Jonathan and of Sir Charles: Jonathan is Blair's Chief of Staff; Charles Powell was one of Thatcher's most trusted aides). John Prescott – Labour's deputy leader and putative figurehead of the traditional wing of the Party – was excluded, which he was not at all happy about (Philip Gould, *The Unfinished Revolution*, 1998).

Balls gave a talk to Labour's new leader, Blair, and his assembled aides about a 22-page policy paper he had drafted under the unappetising title, "The Macroeconomic Framework". It was about how to reinforce the perception of Labour as a competent manager of the economy. The challenge, said Balls, was "to avoid the impression that we will be less tough on inflation than the government".

Philip Gould, Blair's adviser on opinion polls, concurred. He told the Fritham convocation that "Labour is highly susceptible to negative campaigning... Deep down people do not really trust Labour on the economy." So what could Brown do to win that trust and hold it? Well, ceding power to manipulate interest rates – or giving up the illusion that it was somehow vital for a Chancellor to be able to pump up short-term growth through cutting rates – would probably help. "It is important to kill off the view – which already has some credibility in the City and elsewhere – that Labour cannot afford to meddle with the current relationship between the Governor of the Bank of England and the Chancellor," said Balls. And the heart of his argument was that the sacrifice for Brown would be trivial in practice:

In a global and integrated capital market, there is little that any national government – and particularly a Labour government in a small country like Britain – can achieve by manipulating interest rates or exchange rates in the short or medium term. Stability and credibility are all.

This analysis represents a fundamental break with the past. All previous Labour governments had been damaged fatally by their excessive confidence in their ability to manage short-term growth, which in practice led to sharp and deep cycles of economic boom and bust. Balls's recommendation was to let the short term look after itself, by building a stable framework for the control of inflation and public borrowing (see pages 160-2). His specific proposal was for "'operational control' over interest rates being transferred to a re-structured and accountable Bank of England, which would be charged with pursuing government-determined targets".

In other words, the Treasury would set the inflation target and an overhauled Bank of England would have discretion to achieve the target. And lest anyone should believe that Balls was motivated exclusively by pure economic theory, he also appealed to the cruder instincts of his audience:

This loss of operating freedom could bring substantial benefits as well as a credibility boost. It would allow a Labour government the political freedom to criticise or express doubts about interest rate increases even when there is clearly little option but to raise them – just as Clinton has been able to express public misgivings about the Greenspan rate increases while privately supporting them...

Most important, independence means there is someone else to blame/be blamed if things go wrong for reasons which no central banker or politician could either anticipate or control; ie some freak domestic event or an international disruption in what are increasingly volatile world financial markets. British Chancellors, especially Labour

Chancellors, have been repeatedly impaled on stakes over the past 40 years, not all of which were of their own making.

In fact, those narrow party political arguments were slightly naïve – and, when it came to it, Brown took pains not to criticise the MPC, even on the rare occasions when its members behaved eccentrically. The only way for a Chancellor to ensure that markets don't harbour doubts about the independence of a central bank is for the government neither to praise it when things are going well or blame it when the going gets tough. And – to his credit – Brown's relationship with the Bank since taking office has on the whole been a disinterested one. By contrast, Blair has been unable to resist trying to take credit for the Bank's cuts in interest rates – which makes him vulnerable to attack when the interest rate cycle moves in the other direction. Also Balls, in February 2004, seemed to rile the latest Governor, Mervyn King, by calling for an interest rate rise before the decision had been taken, a statement which could have been interpreted as the exertion of government pressure on the Bank (although, in the history of the Labour Party, it's little short of extraordinary that one of its senior members should be attacked for a demand that interest rates should be increased).

Balls had one more reason for why giving some form of independence to the Bank would be good for Labour's reputation: it would help to persuade the City and other EU governments that it was serious about participating in economic and monetary union (see page 187). In fact, when it came to the crunch in 1997, Balls and Brown turned this argument on its head and went for a form of Bank independence which was not in fact compatible with the Maastricht Treaty that would create the euro. But it is striking that two years earlier, the pro-euro symbolism of their proposed Bank reform should have been a positive factor.

But were there no serious costs from giving up the power to set interest rates? Balls fixes on just one: "Critics will say that we have capitulated in the face of the forces of international finance." Those critics would be right, but fighting those forces – in a "globalised" world without barriers to flows of capital – was about as sensible as commanding the tide not to rise.

If it was clear to Balls and Brown that creating an independent central bank was the right way to go, Brown was still some way from deciding precisely when such a bold initiative should be taken. Some of what Balls had said to the Hampshire group in March was repeated in that speech given by Brown on May 17 1995, which sided with Eddie George in his tussle with Ken Clarke. But Brown made no commitment to give autonomous powers over interest rates to the Bank.

Strangely, this important speech – which mapped out much of Labour's future macro-economic approach – attracted little attention or comment at the time. Brown said that he wanted to "remove the suspicion that short-term party political considerations are influencing the setting of interest rates" and to that end he would "consider whether the operational role of the Bank of England should be extended beyond its current advisory role in monetary policymaking". And if the Bank were to be re-made in this way, it would have the "openness of debate and decision-making which occurs in the United States", the "internal democracy of decision-making" of Germany's Bundesbank, and targets set by government as happened in the New Zealand system. He also gave a detailed account of institutional reforms at the Bank which he later implemented, including the creation of a "Monetary Policy Committee" consisting of "the Governor and Deputy Governor, both appointed by the government, and six directors, also appointed by government in consultation with the Governor and Deputy Governor". It is this MPC (with the addition of a second deputy governor) that now controls the setting of interest rates. Anyway, the *Times* noted this nod towards independence for the Bank, but the Treasury did not wake up to what Brown was planning for many more months.

The policy was more-or-less all there and Balls was gung-ho to unveil the last element, that the Treasury would lose control of interest rates. But this was one of those rare times when he was over-ruled by Brown, who was worried that the Bank would do something stupid to undermine its reputation before the general election. Also, empowering the Bank in this way might have been seen as a promise of higher interest rates, since the Bank's governor, George, was famously keener to raise rates than was the Tory Chancellor, Clarke. Brown worried that he and Labour would be attacked during a general election campaign for wanting to raise voters' mortgage rates and borrowing costs. So he became coy about his intentions and seemed to go into reverse in respect of his enthusiasm for Bank independence. On April 29, 1996, he said: "Further reforms of the relationship between the Treasury and the Bank will be considered only after our current proposals for reform are properly enacted and the Bank demonstrates an acceptable track record of advice." There was a clear implication – reinforced in briefings given by Balls – that it would be months or years after a general election before the Bank became truly independent. When I look back at my conversations on this subject with Balls and Brown at the time, I have a powerful recollection of evasive answering.

In September 1996, Brown finally made up his mind to legislate fairly early in the parliament for a handover of these new powers to the Bank. "From that September, Brown thought about it a lot, trying to work out what the case should be," says the official. His determination to press ahead with the reform was reinforced by a conversation he had with Alan Greenspan, the legendary Chairman of the US central bank, the Federal Reserve, on February 20, 1997. And the decision to announce it within days of the May 1 general election was taken on Monday April 28, just three days before polling day.

A description of the "let's go for it" moment – in all its inevitable banality – is given by Geoffrey Robinson, Brown's close ally, whose Park Lane apartment was home from home for the then Shadow Chancellor and his team:

He [Brown] was obviously very preoccupied when he walked into the flat and came straight to the point: 'Look it's the Bank independence [sic],' he said. 'I've come to the conclusion that we should do it straight away.

Immediately on taking office. The first thing we should do – can you get your paper out, Ed, and get it properly written up?' [*The Unconventional Minister*, 2000].

According to Robinson, Balls's response after Brown left the room was a tantalisingly incomprehensible one: "We now know he still wants to be leader." Robinson records the future Chief Economic Adviser to the Treasury as adding: "I've always wanted to sort the Bank out" – which was a characteristically Ballsian threat.

***

In the final week of opposition, Balls had two meetings with Lord Burns (then Sir Terry Burns) who was the Treasury's Permanent Secretary. By this stage, Brown and Balls took for granted that Labour would win the election, so they needed to arrange the logistics of his early days as Chancellor. Balls asked Burns to bring forward the scheduled, regular meeting between the Chancellor and the Bank Governor – the meeting which sets interest rates – by 24 hours to the following Tuesday morning at 8am. "Terry was in a state because it was very disorderly to change the time of the meeting," says a government official. But Balls thought it was essential, because he did not want Brown's early days in office marred by market volatility stemming from uncertainty about what would happen to interest rates (markets were closed on the Monday, which was a bank holiday).

Balls saw Burns again on the Thursday, election day itself, and told him that Brown was planning something big, although Balls would not yet say what that was. Was it still too risky for Brown to show his hand on Bank independence, even to the Treasury's Permanent Secretary, the most important official at the Treasury, with whom he would have to work in close proximity?

Well, Balls did not wholly trust Burns on the sensitive issue of what should happen to the Bank. His wariness stemmed from meetings he had held with Burns and with Sir Howard Davies (who by then had moved from the CBI to become deputy governor of the Bank) earlier in the year.

At the beginning of 1997, Balls had lunch with Davies at the Bank and held a meeting with Burns at 5 o'clock on the same day. At these meetings, they both tried to persuade Balls to hand over control of interest rates to the Bank as it was then constituted, without going through the bother of passing a new law. Balls came away convinced that they had both assumed – wrongly – that Brown would only wish to change the statutory underpinning of the Bank's role as part of wider legislation for joining the euro. He also concluded that they were motivated by a desire to ward off the kind of radical institutional change – such as importing a new group of economists and monetary experts into the process of setting interest rates – which he and Brown regarded as vital. With power almost within their grasp, Brown and Balls were both acutely wary – probably too wary – of the possibility that officials who had served Thatcher and Major for almost two decades might try to preserve the status quo and entrench their own power.

Meanwhile, it's striking that the Bank of England and the Treasury seemed to believe that Labour's plans for the Bank were subsidiary to its ambitions to take the UK into the euro. Officials had apparently ignored the clues in Brown's speeches indicating his interest in carrying out a very British reform of the central bank. On election day itself, Burns came away from his meeting with Balls feeling sure that there was a plan afoot to do something to the Bank of England and sensing that it might well be some kind of preparation for joining the European single currency.

In these very last minutes of the Tory government, Burns commissioned a paper setting out the Treasury's thoughts on how the Bank could be made more independent as a precursor to joining the euro and also what kind of powers the Bank should be given if the UK stayed outside the euro zone. This urgent task was given to Tom Scholar – a bright, terrier-like young Treasury official – at 6pm that evening, just hours before the polls closed. The document was to be a welcoming gift for the new ministerial team. Scholar researched and wrote through the night, culling information from unpublished work the Treasury had done years before. He sent his paper to Burns at 5pm the next day, hoping to escape to the pub. It was not to be. An hour later Burns summoned him again, this time to a meeting with Sir Nigel Wicks (the Second Permanent Secretary, or number two in the Treasury) and Sir Alan Budd (the Treasury's Chief Economic Adviser). They were in a state of some excitement.

If you want a mental image of this gathering, Burns – with his flat vowels – is like a dour, unflappable football manager (which, given his obsessive passion for Queens Park Rangers, may be his vocation manqué). Wicks – who is slightly reminiscent of the white rabbit in *Alice* – is much more the identikit mandarin, with clipped vowels and an obsession with convention and propriety. Budd looks like a bearded resident of Middle Earth.

Brown, now formally Chancellor, had just given Burns a copy of a letter that he was proposing to hand to Eddie George, Governor of the Bank of England (it was dated May 3, but was in fact handed over on Sunday, May 4). The letter – which had been drafted by Balls on his laptop – spelt out the arrangements for giving absolute control over interest rates to the Bank of England. "For those of us who had worked in the Treasury all our lives, this was a very big deal," says a senior official. "As a symbol of the sweeping out of the old guard and the old ways, it was hard to beat."

Burns and his colleagues assumed that they would have to make significant amendments to Brown's plans, which they were sure would be lacking in detail and coherence. "Of course we all thought that Ed's letter would be full of holes," says an official. An exhausted Tom Scholar and a more senior colleague, John Cunliffe, were sent off to work through the night again and go through Balls's epistle line by line. To their surprise, they found little of substance that needed changing in the draft. The original Balls version and the one that was finally handed to George are strikingly similar. In fact, it is amusing to see that the officials were so busy looking for giant lacunae that they failed to pick up a schoolboy error. Balls put the wrong address at the top. He located the

Bank in the EC1 postal district when it's famously in EC2 (which is as bad as locating the Houses of Parliament in W1, instead of SW1). And the Bank was still in EC1 when the finished document was handed to the Governor (it's even been posted on the Bank of England's website with the wrong address at the top – presumably to preserve its historical authenticity).

Treasury officials' recollection of those first hours is of fumbling in the dark, as they tried to understand Brown's and Balls's preferred working methods. "It was quite a complicated process at this point, because none of us knew each other," says one. "Terry knew Ed a bit, but none of us knew Gordon. They didn't know what to expect from the Treasury." Anyway, Burns and his senior colleagues wanted their imprimatur on the letter, so there were amendments.

Most of the changes were stylistic, though one or two were substantial. The original Balls draft defines the reconstituted Bank's purpose like this: "The objectives of the Bank of England will be enshrined in statute. These will be to deliver low and stable inflation as a precondition for high and stable levels of growth and employment and generally to support the government's economic policy." And this is the final version:

> Price stability is a precondition for high and stable levels of growth and employment, which in turn will help to create the conditions for price stability on a sustainable basis. To that end, the monetary policy objective of the Bank of England will be to deliver price stability (as defined by the government's inflation target) and, without prejudice to this objective, to support the government's economic policy, including its objectives for growth and employment.

Now the significant addition to the letter as sent was the phrase "without prejudice to this objective". What this said, explicitly, is that the Bank should put the control of inflation before all other considerations, including the government's determination to encourage economic growth and employment creation. Or, to put it another way, if there were ever any conflict for the Monetary Policy Committee between curbing price rises and supporting "growth and employment", the conquering of inflation was to take precedent.

For the Labour Party, this issue of whether or not the Bank should have an explicit primary responsibility to promote growth is the most explosive. It was the one which troubled Brown himself the most in the run-up to the creation of the MPC. Back in 1993, he didn't think it was necessary to prioritise between a growth target and an inflation one: his speeches implied that it was possible to have both. Then there was a period in the mid-1990s when he considered giving the Bank a target for so-called "nominal GDP", which combines growth and inflation in a single measure (Balls's 1995 presentation to the New Labour vanguard in Hampshire agonises over this). But in the end, he and Balls couldn't come up with a form of words expressing a determination both to limit price rises and create prosperity that wouldn't confuse either the MPC or the markets. Balls persuaded Brown that the MPC's job would be far more difficult if more than one principal aim was enshrined in statute: constraining inflation would be the priority.

This exalting of central bankers – the servants of capital, prepared to sacrifice the prosperity of the many in the cause of sound money – upset and alienated many on Labour's left. They hated the idea that interest rates would be raised at the slightest smell of incipient inflation, irrespective of the immediate impact on jobs. And they tended to ignore the evidence from countries such as Germany, which indicated that prosperity and long-term growth was correlated with a successful anti-inflation strategy conducted by a powerful independent central bank. At the last, Brown got the point – and the best exposition of how he was converted was given by Balls in a lecture to the Scottish Economic Society on October 22, 1997 and Brown's Mais lecture of 19 October, 1999. Their message was that Brown could in practice pursue a more progressive agenda in many areas of economic policymaking than his Labour predecessors so long as international investors could plainly see that his discretion to wreak havoc – such as by manipulating interest rates or borrowing too much – had been limited or constrained.

This theme, of the freedom to govern that comes from constraining a Chancellor's discretion, is a recurring one during Brown's tenure. The powerful idea, which has proved to be true, is that Brown could only give expression to his socialist instincts after playing the role of über-guardian of the capitalist system.

However, if reinforcing the authority of a historically conservative institution such as the Bank generated inner turmoil for Brown, it's striking how little he worried about giving up the glamour and putative power inherent in the setting of interest rates. This set him apart from previous Chancellors and indeed from the Treasury's senior mandarins. For years, they had recognised the compelling logic of transferring the responsibility for rate-setting to the Bank but could never quite reconcile themselves to the loss of this most visible manifestation of their own importance.

One senior Treasury mandarin believes that Brown demonstrated great personal insight in refusing to star in the "Gordon and Eddie Show" in succession to the "Ken and Eddie Show" – or the monthly pantomime of the mid-1990s when Ken Clarke, the Chancellor, and Eddie George, the Governor, were the Ugly Sisters of monetary policy, squabbling over whether to raise interest rates. "The Ken and Eddie show was completely unsuited to Gordon's character," says the mandarin. "It did not fit with his idea of doing things. Gordon does not like public disputes. And he has great difficulty resolving disputes. It is a process alien to his personality. He would have hated all the commenting in the newspapers about whether he was right or Eddie was right." An ally of Brown agrees that the Gordon and Eddie show would have been "a complete disaster". He says: "From the very beginning we were never ever going to do it. No way. In answer to the question, 'Why did we move so quickly [on giving independence]?', the point is that if we had done one meeting of the Gordon and Eddie show and after that we had announced that we were going for independence, people would have said that Gordon couldn't take the pace. And if we had done one meeting of the Gordon and Eddie show and there had been a disagreement, it would have been a disaster. It was a hideous prospect. So we just wanted to get out of that hideous personalised way of doing things."

***

There would shortly be proof of just what a disaster the Gordon and Eddie Show would have been. In their very first meeting after the general election – during the afternoon of Sunday May 4 – there was a misunderstanding between the new Chancellor and the Governor about an important change to the Bank's responsibilities that Brown regarded as vital. This clash of views about what had been said was so dire that George gave serious thought to resigning – which would have been devastating for the reputation of Brown.

The seeds of this dispute had been sown way back in 1992, when Balls wrote in his "Euro-monetarism" pamphlet that the Bank would fulfil its economic functions far better if it gave up its venerable and important role in monitoring the financial health of banks. By the autumn of 1995, Labour's City spokesman of the time, Alistair Darling, was mooting the creation of a super-regulator for the City and the removal from the Bank of its banking supervisory functions. And – in a general sense – the streamlining of financial regulation was official party policy by the time of the general election. Consistent with this, Balls's original unpublished draft of the letter to the Governor said:

> It is intended that a substantial portion of the Bank's regulatory functions, concerned with the proper conduct of business, will, in due course, be transferred to the Securities and Investment Board as part of the government's review of financial regulation, legislation for which will be published in due course.

It was the one part of the missive which filled Burns with dread. He knew George's fearsome loyalty to the Bank, where he had worked for 35 years (his entire career, having joined straight after graduating with a second-class degree in economics from Emmanuel College, Cambridge).

135

And he knew that George regarded the supervision of commercial banks as a vital part of the Bank's activities, the foundation of its reputation as the most influential institution in the City. The point is that the Bank did not think of itself primarily as an economic institution but as the conscience, policeman and tribal baron of the City. The proverbial twitch of the governor's eyebrow struck fear within the Square Mile only for as long as the Bank had the power of life or death over the City's biggest institutions as their supervisor, charged with making sure that the banks stuck to its rules and didn't take excessive risks. At stake therefore was the Bank's view of itself.

George – who is surprisingly emotional and volatile for a banker – would not give all this up lightly (five years before, the *FT* had invented the sobriquet "Steady Eddie" for George – but it was a misnomer). A senior official explains Burns's fears: "On supervision, the wording was too strong and also too ambiguous on the timing of the change. Eddie would have had difficulty with it. This was an enormous call for Eddie." Burns's caution was not, however, shared throughout the Treasury: there was an influential group, led by Steve Robson (who was in charge of financial regulation and privatisation, *inter alia*), which was keen to see the Bank stripped of its regulatory responsibilities, as soon as possible. Robson was a critic of a regulatory system that saw different kinds of firms – banks, brokers, fund managers, and so on – regulated by different watchdogs. This fragmented structure, in Robson's view, was inefficient and unreliable. He wanted to see all of the watchdogs crunched together to form a City super-regulator – and, what's more, he felt he had been given a commitment by Burns that such an overhaul would take place at the moment that the Bank was ever given control over interest rates.

What added a certain frisson to all this was decades of tension and rivalry between the Treasury and the Bank, between Westminster and the City. Bank officials were particularly wary of Robson. They thought he viewed them, somewhat sniffily, as gentleman amateurs in an increasingly professionalized world: it was not a wholly false reading of Robson.

And the most graphic illustration of George's mistrust of Robson was manifested around this time. In a goodwill gesture, the Governor had invited Balls to lunch at the Bank. Balls did not want to be seen as a one-man team, excluding important officials from big decisions and meetings, so he asked Robson to accompany him. Robson cancelled a lunch to oblige. Burns, who understood the tension between Robson and George, came to see Balls at mid morning that day to say – elliptically – that George would prefer to see him alone. Balls did not take the hint. So the duo went to the Bank, where they were seated in a waiting room by a frock-coated footman, who reported that Robson was not welcome. Balls went into lunch alone and Robson's views on the old Bank never mellowed.

However, Robson's enthusiasm to shake up the Bank was grounded in rigorous analysis. Barriers between historically separate financial markets were breaking down. Banks were diversifying into the sale of every conceivable financial product. Insurers were providing services to companies that had traditionally been the exclusive preserve of banks. And securities houses were getting into insurance and lending. So it was increasingly anomalous and cumbersome to have different regulators overseeing these respective sectors. And it was also dangerous, because a specialist banking regulator at the Bank of England might not understand a bank's new insurance or securities businesses, for example – as was, to some extent, demonstrated by Nick Leeson's bankrupting of the venerable British merchant bank, Barings, in 1995.

But if there was strong logic behind the creation of a single regulator – merging together the separate watchdogs for insurance, fund management, securities trading, banking and so on – why couldn't this new super-regulator have been created within the Bank of England? Well, the theoretical and practical reasons for not doing that, once the Bank had control of interest rates, were compelling. The theoretical argument goes like this. Just say the Bank discovers that a leading bank or insurance company will go bust if economic conditions worsen. But also imagine that inflation is surging. What should the Bank do in those circumstances? Raise interest rates to curb inflation? Or cut them to make life easier for the bank on the verge of collapse? In other words, there is an innate conflict of interest for a central bank that is also directly responsible for monitoring the health of financial firms. In theory, so-called Chinese walls – separating the Bank's interest rate and supervisory responsibilities – could have been created to eliminate the tensions between these two different wings of the Bank. But that would not have remedied the other problem, which is that the Bank would have become too big and too hard to manage.

These days, most Bank officials concede that Robson was right, as one makes clear: "The idea of giving new supervisory powers to the Bank, to supervise more things, would have provoked great concern about the power of the Bank. And I think from an internal point of view, the enlarged bank could have become completely unmanageable. Suppose Barings had gone down on the same day as we were deciding on interest rates. You just can't do that." However, this official also explains why that powerful logic was difficult for George to see: "To a large extent he regarded himself as the Bank's guardian and protector. Also he had lots of friends on the supervisory side of things: saying goodbye to them would not be easy."

Stuck in the middle of the debate was Burns, who understood the reasoning and emotions on both sides – which is one of his great skills, but can periodically lead him to prevaricate. He urged Brown to remove from the draft letter its ninth section, headed "Financial Regulation", on the planned shake-up of financial supervision. Brown was reluctant, but Burns kept up the pressure over the weekend. An official recalls the fraught atmosphere: "Terry was in a state about handling Eddie and in a terrible state about his constitutional role holding this [the reform of the Bank] together." Burns, understandably, did not want such a major reform carried out in haste. "The first thing he tried to do was he begged Gordon not to introduce Bank independence that week" says the official. "He said we needed longer to consult and Eddie would be really upset about it. Gordon kept saying, 'This is ridiculous: we are about to make the Bank of England independent, which is what Eddie has always wanted, so how can he be upset?'"

Adding to the fraught atmosphere was that Brown, Balls and Geoffrey Robinson – who had been appointed to the junior ministerial post of Paymaster General – feared that if they did not announce the Bank reform very speedily, their plan might be buried by officials under a mountain of consultations and reviews. They were probably over-egging it, but senior civil servants found the pace of reform troubling. "Terry [Burns] was very worried about doing it at all" one of his erstwhile colleagues recalls. "And he was then very worried about announcing any of the detail, you know the formation of the Monetary Policy Committee, the reorganisation of how gilts are issued, all that kind of stuff. Debt management [the process of issuing gilt-edged stock] would be a big change institutionally for the Bank [it was to lose responsibility for this]. But Gordon insisted that all the detail should be published".

Finally, Burns pushed home on the point that concerned him most. He urged that the plan to remove banking supervisory responsibilities from the Bank should be kept confidential – for fear of fomenting a row with George. "At that point it was a bit like St Peter: you're Chancellor of the Exchequer, you've only been in the job 24 hours, and your Permanent Secretary has three times tried to advise you to do what you think will be the wrong thing," says an official. "So Gordon really could not say 'no' to him again." Burns got his way and the reference to demerging the regulatory function was excised from the letter.

But Brown did not give in completely. He wrote a second letter to George, which unlike the other, more important one wouldn't be published: it would be kept secret (curiously, the letter is dated May 6, even though it was given to the governor on May 4). It stressed that the government's election manifesto contained a commitment to reorganise financial regulation and that the intention was to do this early in the parliament. The Treasury was considering transferring out of the Bank its supervisory responsibilities to "another statutory board", it says, but adds that there will be consultation with the Bank on this reform. For

Brown, there was no ambiguity in the message: the plan was to strip the Bank of its supervisory function. And when he had his first meeting with George on that fateful Sunday, he emerged absolutely clear in his own mind that he had communicated just as much to the Governor.

Nonetheless, George came away with a subtly different message. He thought that Brown had promised him that the Bank would have an opportunity to lobby on the supervisory change, that the Bank might be able to influence it in some way. Since no one else was with them for this meeting, it's impossible to say which of these interpretations more fairly represented the tenor of what was said. Anyway George returned to Threadneedle Street and told his assembled colleagues that they had won the right to set interest rates – and that was a big hooray. He added that the supervisory role might go, but glossed this by saying that he had the Chancellor's word that nothing would happen until the Bank itself had been able to present its case on any changes.

Then the thunderbolt struck. Less than a fortnight later on May 18, George was made to look a gullible fool in the eye of his own loyal people, when Brown announced the creation of the Financial Service Authority, a new independent regulator for the City. The FSA was to acquire the Bank's regulatory functions. In George's view, Brown had failed to honour his pledge to consult the Bank. An official of the Bank recalls the shocks: "Clearly there were enormous qualms here about the way it was done... We had been promised a period of consultation. There is no doubt Eddie came away with that impression. When that was taken away without any warning, Eddie felt that he had been misled. And what he felt most of all was that he was letting the staff down." What went wrong? A government official explains:

The Treasury knew that to go ahead with an independent Bank of England would require a Bank of England Act immediately. Initially it thought it would come back and have a second piece of legislation to transfer supervision. But then it discovered that it wouldn't get an opportunity for a second bill for some time.

So if Gordon was going to do supervision in the foreseeable future, he would have to bring those plans forward. And in order to set up the Financial Services Authority [the proposed new watchdog], the Treasury had to put stuff about it into this initial Bank of England Act – and that meant telling the world what was going to happen.

Brown presumed that George would understand that – for reasons beyond his control – he had to press ahead with the regulatory reforms faster than he had anticipated. He also hoped that his decision to appoint the Bank's deputy governor, Sir Howard Davies, as the first chairman of the new regulatory body would reassure George that the Bank's supervisory staff would be transferred to a safe new home. Brown was wrong. He misjudged how strongly George would feel, partly because they presumed his annoyance would be trivial compared with his great delight about winning independence. In fact, George came close to resigning – and what was even more remarkable, he went public about it, in a rare Bank press conference on May 21. This was pretty uncomfortable for Brown. George had the respect of the markets, so his departure would have shattered the new government's claim to be more competent than its predecessor. And a reputation for competence was what Brown and Balls were trying to nurture more than anything else. For a Chancellor obsessed with stability, it was appalling.

Nor was there any short-term respite. On May 22, in an article I wrote on why George had been thinking of resigning, I quoted "a member of the government" as saying George had "played into our hands" by kicking up a fuss. I added that Brown might not now re-appoint George for a second term in office, when his tenure came up for renewal the following year (Brown and Balls have told me subsequently that they were furious about this leak). Rubbing further salt into George's wounds, I wrote that Gavyn Davies – the influential economist at the investment bank, Goldman Sachs, who was close to both Brown and Blair – was a frontrunner to succeed him as Governor.

According to Derek Draper, the former aide to Peter Mandelson, the impression had been given that George had been put on 24 hours notice: "A whole host of City figures – including the Chairman of NatWest and the Chief Executive of Abbey National – lined up to condemn the Chancellor," he wrote in his memoir of the first weeks of the Labour government (*Blair's Hundred Days*, 1998). "Mandarins were appalled and more bad press followed." A Brown ally recalls the turmoil: "It was all a bit febrile," he says. However, this official insists that Davies was not in fact a strong contender to be governor – precisely because of his proximity to the Prime Minister and Chancellor – and that Brown was horrified at the destabilisation of George (though I had good reason to think otherwise in the spring of 1997). "The idea that a Labour Chancellor could appoint a supporter (such as Davies) as Governor in the first year of government was not on," he says. "At that stage, it would have undermined the perception of the Bank's independence. To be fair to Gavyn, the only job he would have wanted was Governor, and therefore there was nothing else we could give him."

In the event, George recovered his poise and stayed on. The first year of their relationship was shaky, but he went on to develop a close and warm relationship with George, based around their monthly lunches. That Brown kept up these midday, relatively informal meetings is testament to how much he wanted to keep George on side after the terrible debut, for Brown is that rare politician: one who detests lunch. As soon as George retired, in 2003, Brown instituted regular meetings with the new Governor, Mervyn King, at his preferred hour, early morning breakfast. The rapprochement was confirmed when George finally quit the Bank: he gave Brown a so-called "open" letter – a corny reference to one of Brown's Bank of England reforms – that simply says "thank you", which the Chancellor has framed on his office wall.

Permanent and serious damage had however been done elsewhere. Brown blamed his Permanent Secretary, Burns, for the mess. He felt the crisis could have been avoided if he had announced the regulatory reform right at the start, as he had wanted to. And he also suspected that Burns had persuaded George to read too much into his agreement to consult the

Bank, perhaps raising a hope that Brown might be dissuaded from going ahead. The first Labour Chancellor in almost 20 years had lost confidence in the judgement of his most important official, whose formidable analytical skills would have been useful to him. The relationship between the two of them – one of the most important in all the government – never recovered.

***

Brown and Balls had one more battle to fight to create the kind of Bank they wanted. This was over the question of what the new inflation target should be. In 1992, the previous Tory government had set itself a target that the rate of increase in the retail price index should be in the range 1 per cent to 4 per cent and had amended that in June 1995 to a target of $2^1/_2$ per cent or less for beyond the end of the parliament – which was inherently ambiguous. There was an absence of clarity about whether the actual objective was for inflation to be $2^1/_2$ per cent or "less than" $2^1/_2$ per cent. Now, this may seem like a subtle distinction, but it carried significant implications for interest rates and the economy. A target of forcing inflation to any level below $2^1/_2$ per cent implied that interest rates should be consistently higher than if the aim was to hit $2^1/_2$ per cent on the nose. A senior Bank of England official describes the problem:

> We would try to explain that in practice the target means that you want to keep the inflation average pretty close to between 2 and $2^1/_2$. But we could never make that sound entirely plausible because it wasn't actually explicit and there was no way that you could persuade people that our interpretation of it was obviously the correct thing, since the words just didn't correspond to it. It didn't say '2.5 per cent' it said 'below 2.5'. So what did it mean?"

Clarke when he was Chancellor had faced regular sniping from economic commentators about this ambiguity. But in some ways, it was an interesting theoretical debate rather than one of great practical importance, since the Conservative government never actually hit the target on either interpretation (although, gallingly for Clarke, the underlying rate of retail price inflation did hit 2.5 per cent a fortnight after the Tories lost the 1997 election). Even so, setting the new goal was tricky for Brown and Balls. If they set it higher than it had been under the Tories, they would be accused of being soft on inflation. And if they set it lower, they would face accusations from their own colleagues that they were sacrificing growth on the altar of a zealot's crusade against inflation.

Their commitments in opposition on all this had been vague. In a speech to the annual conference of the Confederation of British Industry on November 11, 1996 Brown had said: "Labour in government will have a target for low and stable inflation. And let me tell you that we will not be satisfied with simply talking as tough as the Tories. For unlike the government, we plan to deliver on our inflation target. We will want our inflation performance to match that of our competitors in Europe." Brown was implying that the target would be $2^1/_2$ per cent, but he didn't actually say this.

What Balls really had in mind was to go for $2^1/_2$ per cent but to drop the "or less" aspiration. It would be a so-called point target. So the Bank would be "failing" not only if inflation was above $2^1/_2$ per cent but also if it was below $2^1/_2$ per cent. This was a sensible innovation, which would remove the suspicion that the Bank would have a basic instinct to keep interest rates too high. In fact, it's probably one of the more under-rated reforms pushed through by Brown and Balls.

Its worth was proved when the Bank cut interest rates steadily and over an extended period as the economy showed signs of weakness between February 2001 and mid 2003 (the Bank was cutting rates because of its obligation to ensure that inflation was not less than 2.5 per cent). And these cuts helped to sustain faster economic growth in the UK than in France and Germany, where interest rates may well have been too high because the European Central Bank has an inflation target of the "x per cent or less" variety (although the precise meaning of the ECB's target has been a matter of some dispute, reminiscent of the arguments in the UK during the 1990s). In a way, therefore, the introduction of the point target for the MPC was a sensible response to the traditional socialist fear that an independent central bank would be too deflationary and it obviated the need for an explicit growth target.

Even so, Balls feared that the purists in the Treasury and the Bank would complain that this move – from "$2^1/_2$ per cent or less" to just "$2^1/_2$ per cent" – meant that the new government was going soft on inflation. And because Brown and Balls did not wish to be accused of being any less committed than their Tory predecessors to the battle against price rises, they kept a veil drawn across the target in the run-up to the general election and when they announced plans to give control of interest rates to the Bank. But within the confines of the Treasury there was an anxious debate about Balls's plans for the target in those early weeks in government. Burns and Budd were concerned that the City would regard the new objective as too soft. And once again, Burns was worried about how Eddie George – who had staked his recent career on crushing inflation – would react. So Burns suggested that the target should be reduced to 2 per cent, saying this was what the Governor would have wanted (he was right, according to a Bank official).

In retrospect, all this agonising seems slightly surreal. At the time, it would have been an astonishing breakthrough in the battle against inflation if the new Monetary Policy Committee were to hit a $2^1/_2$ per cent target consistently: $2^1/_2$ per cent was even below the average achieved by the fearsome and respected German Bundesbank throughout its entire history, and was incomparably better than had been achieved in the UK since the Second World War. So in the end there was recognition that Balls's position – which had the useful support of Mervyn King, then the Bank's chief economist – was reasonable. Brown announced the point-target of $2^1/_2$ per cent in his speech to the City at the Mansion House on June 12, 1997. And there was a second important innovation. If inflation were to diverge in either direction by more than 1 percentage point from $2^1/_2$ per cent, the Governor would have to write an open letter to the Chancellor explaining why inflation was off course, what the Bank intended to do about it and when it would be back on course.

The package was viewed inside the Bank as a challenging set of rules. On the basis of precedent, it expected to be writing such explanatory letters to the Chancellor every couple of months or so (its current Chief Economist, Charlie Bean, wrote a paper before joining the bank estimating that – on the basic of precedent – such letters would need to be written between 40 and 50 per cent of the time). In fact, the Monetary Policy Committee has not written a single such note. In other words, inflation has been more or less bang on target every month since 1997 – a unique phenomenon in the annals of modern British economic history. The Monetary Policy Committee has been a greater success than either Brown or Balls could possibly have expected – and although part of that success probably stems from global trends towards lower inflation or even deflation in a whole range of manufactured goods, it would be churlish to deny the efficacy of the MPC.

From the moment it was established, markets concluded that it was an effective way of combating inflation. This can be seen in two ways: the gap between the respective interest rates on British and German government bonds dropped immediately and continued to fall, reflecting the belief that the inflation rate in the UK would no longer be significantly higher than that in Germany. Also, economists quickly reduced their inflation forecasts to around the 2.5 per cent target rate. However, it took slightly longer for the general public to be convinced that the monster of endemic price rises had been vanquished. But a relatively buoyant trend to average earnings may reflect the absence of recession for well over a decade, a run of steady growth that's also without precedent in the modern era – and in part reflects the price stability engendered by the MPC (the Treasury claims the UK is experiencing the longest period of unbroken growth for more than 200 years, although the data to back up the claim is not wholly robust and there is also an argument that the underlying growth rate of the economy at 2.5 to 2.75 per cent is not quite high enough compared with the US and – especially – Asian economies).

Are there no clouds on the horizon? Well, a change to a new measure of inflation, the Consumer Price Index, at the end of 2003 – as part of preparations for possible future membership of the euro – made the MPC's task a little more tricky for a few months. The reason was that inflation seemed to be tamed, almost slain, on the basis of the CPI numbers, but there were lots of other signs that inflation might be bubbling up again – especially the rampant price rises in the housing market – which provided a solid reason to raise interest rates. The disjunction between what the MPC did, which was to raise rates, and minimal inflation as measured by the CPI also sowed some confusion outside the Bank. The MPC's effectiveness could well have been damaged, since its success had hitherto stemmed in part from the fact that most businesses and many consumers could understand why it was raising or lowering rates and could make a reasonable stab at what it might do in the future (and plan their economic behaviour accordingly).

Meanwhile, if there's a further flaw it's that the process of making appointments to the MPC is neither open to applications or subject to transparent rules. Unlike other public appointments, the selection of MPC members has not been "Nolanised" – that is, the choice is not made on the basis of advertisement followed by the adjudication of an independent panel. Members have been hand-picked by Brown, Balls and O'Donnell (who has been more influential than is widely appreciated). The respectable argument for their grip on the appointments process is not that it enables them to wield day-to-day influence over MPC members. The process was originally conceived to allow the selection of more unconventional and imaginative characters to the MPC than the play-safe Nolan route might have allowed for (early members who made an important contribution included a former member of the US Central Intelligence Agency and a Dutchman with an American passport). But now that the MPC has acquired a distinct identity and a high reputation, Brown and Balls should cut the cord – or at some point risk seeing the MPC's reputation for independence marred.

However, that's a quibble. The creation of the MPC is probably – still

– their finest achievement. It wasn't an idea out of nowhere. In a sense it was the culmination of reforms begun after the 1992 ERM debacle, which introduced inflation-targeting, the publication of the Bank's inflation report, and the publication of minutes of interest-rate discussions. But even if the transfer of control over interest rates can be seen as the end-point of a continuum – which is the argument made by Lord Burns – there was certainly no guarantee that it would happen. If the Tories had won the 1997 election, they would not have given independence to the Bank. Both John Major, as Prime Minister, and Kenneth Clarke, as Chancellor, were opponents of handing over control of interest rates. When Gordon Brown rang up most of his living predecessors as Chancellor – James Callaghan, Denis Healey, Nigel Lawson, Norman Lamont and Kenneth Clarke – to tell them about the bold reform on the morning of May 6, 1997, only Clarke told him definitively that it was a mistake (Healey was not enthusiastic about it, but has since been gener-ous in his praise of Brown). And for several years after 1997, the Tories continued to oppose the empowering of the Bank, even though it was demonstrably an unqualified success (astonishingly, they only embraced it in February 2000, after Michael Portillo became Shadow Chancellor). But these days, there is a broad consensus that the Bank of England's Monetary Policy Committee is a lynchpin of the British economic sys-tem. It's almost unthinkable that its power to set interest rates could ever be removed. So Brown and Balls were not overdoing the fanfare and the-atre on that spring morning eight years ago: they were making history.

CHAPTER FIVE

How Brown won the confidence of the financial markets
so that he could be a real socialist

When the final judgement is made of Gordon Brown as a politician and Chancellor, his approach to public expenditure will weigh heavily. And if control of the purse strings were the only factor, it would not be an easy judgement. There have been distinct phases in his approach to spending – and they cannot be explained easily by reference to simple ideology. On the face of it, the charge of inconsistency sticks.

In the early years of government, he put a tight corset on public spending growth. Faced with pressure from his cabinet colleagues for significantly increased resources, he said no to a quite remarkable extent. Labour's landslide victory and the sheer enormity of its parliamentary majority meant that he could ignore the wishes of many Labour MPs to be tougher in his expenditure controls than they wanted and than a government with a more fragile grip on power could have been. But then, in the run-up to the 2001 general election and in the early years after Labour's second win, the corset was loosened and finally removed altogether. He made long-term commitments to grow health spending and – to a slightly lesser extent – education expenditure at annual percentage rates of increase that were almost without precedent.

And there was an associated change, which in a way was even more remarkable. While he was Shadow Chancellor and when he was new to office, his rhetoric was all about the need to eliminate waste, to be "wise spenders" (not "big spenders"). This looked like the true Brown, the proper expression of his Scottish Presbyterian antecedents. But by the time spending had started to gush, he had achieved little in the way of structural reform of the public services, notably in health and education, to ensure that significant sums would not be frittered away on the creation of superfluous jobs or white elephant projects. Some of the spending, if not unwise, seemed potentially superfluous.

Possibly this failure was not his fault, since "modernisation" of public services was not touched on in the Granita agreement: it fell between the cracks of what was Brown's territory and what was Blair's. It is, however, relevant and striking that when Brown felt that his vision of effective and socially just public services was threatened by policies emanating from 10 Downing Street, he fought hard – and increasingly in the public arena – to see them off: in this category are the battles over Foundation Hospitals, a more independent breed of hospital, and over university tuition fees. Brown was happy to engage in the debate on education and health when it suited him (See Chapter Nine).

Anyway, belatedly, there's been a third phase, known as Gershonisation, after a former businessman, Sir Peter Gershon, who has been working with the Treasury since late 1998 on improving the efficiency of the Whitehall machine. From 2005 to 2007, there will be a modest deceleration in the rate of spending increase (except in Health), accompanied by an ambitious programme to reduce civil service costs and improve public service efficiency, with the aim of making every pound of new money go further.

What does all this meandering mean? Well in part it shows that Brown's decisions on public spending have been pragmatic, they have been means to an end. The original prudence was "for a purpose", as he still says to almost anyone who spends more than five minutes with him. But what was that purpose for? Well, winning a second term of office – so long as the power once seized was not squandered – was not a bad result. The hair-shirtism was crucial to acquiring economic credibility, to restoring the strength of the public finances and averting the kind of economic crises that undermined all previous Labour governments (no cap-in-hand emergency trip to the International Monetary Fund for Gordon Brown, no humiliating re-run of Denis Healey's request for financial succour from the IMF of 1976, just lectures from him to other finance ministers on how they should manage their respective economies with prudence). And the dividend was another landslide in 2001, whose scale was magnified by the promise to voters of magnificent public-spending rises to come.

It was an outcome Brown was trying to engineer from the moment of victory in 1997. One of his closest advisers said to me, in the summer of 1998 when Brown had announced only modest budget increments for the public services in his first Comprehensive Spending Review, that the subsequent general election had been won that very second in the act of self-denial.

But among Labour sympathisers and within the Party's ranks, even at the highest level, the question of whether Brown was excessively cautious still rages. To have taken the reins in 1997 after so many years in the wilderness and then to have stuck with spending plans inherited from the Tories – thus depriving vital public services of succour – is viewed as a terrible betrayal, even by moderate ministers and economists of the soft-left (the *Observer* columnist, William Keegan, is probably the standard-bearer for those who believe Brown's prudence was overdone – see his book *The Prudence of Mr Gordon Brown*, 2003 – and a professional economist of the stature of Gavyn Davies also has his doubts about whether Brown needed to be quite so frugal). And what's worse, or so they say, the betrayal was unnecessary, since the City would have been more tolerant of a little more expenditure than Brown believed.

The price of not spending was bigger than simply the facilities and services foregone, according to the critics. Civil servants lost the habit of spending, so that when they were finally given the funds, they did not know what to do with them. But if that's true, and it probably was, it doesn't mean that Brown's belt-tightening was wrong on balance. The shock for voters and the financial community of seeing a Labour Chancellor show such budgetary discipline – greater than the Tories whom Labour replaced – eventually endowed him with a greater freedom to spend and take financial risks than any modern Chancellor of any political affiliation.

Here is the real point, or the purpose, of all that early restraint. It was to allow Brown, over time, to spend more than if he had splurged initially and then had been forced to tighten his belt, which had been the fate of his Labour predecessors at 11 Downing Street. When Labour came to power in 1997, public spending was £315.6bn, or 40.8 per cent of GDP. After Brown's famous squeeze, the ratio actually fell to 37.4 per cent in 1999/2000, which was its lowest level since 1960, according to official statistics (the lowest it became under Margaret Thatcher was 39.4 per cent in 1988/9). But after the last Comprehensive Spending Review of 2004, spending is now set to reach £580bn, or 42.3 per cent of GDP by 2008. To put it another way, the government was spending £865m per day in 1997 and now expects to spend £1.6bn every single day by 2008. However, the steady creep of the state should not be exaggerated: under the Tory governments of 1979 to 1997, public spending as a share of the economy was usually in the range 42 per cent to 48 per cent, consistently higher than what has happened under Brown.

But, although the statistics show that the Tories were not particularly adept at curbing public spending, it was their desire to do so: they wanted to limit the size of the state, because they were convinced that the efficiency of the economy as a whole reduces as the share of overall spending taken by the public sector increases. So the view of the right, since the collapse of the Butskellite consensus with the advent of Margaret Thatcher as Prime Minister in 1979, has been that public spending is a necessary evil. This was manifested under Thatcher and then John Major, first with the privatisations of the 1980s and early 1990s and then with new tighter budgeting rules to limit growth in public expenditure. On this view, the whole purpose of government is to re-engineer the state, to transfer as much as possible of the provision of public services to the private sector (one of the theological debates that gripped the Tory Party in the 1990s and is still current on its wilder fringes is over what precise percentage of the economy should be taken by the public sector, based on the apparent belief that there is a holy ratio whose attainment – by cuts and more cuts – would precipitate our economic redemption).

Brown, in stark contrast, believes that public spending, on health and education in particular, is a good thing – which is not a statement of the obvious, because for several years even Blair was convinced that his Chancellor actually hated spending. For Brown, investing in education and health is socialism in practice, redistribution of a particularly effective kind. So part of Brown's importance as a Chancellor – his place in history, to use the cliché – lies in his rejection (not immediately, but by stealth and then in a great splurge) of a Tory viewpoint that had almost become a law of nature, that the point of being Chancellor is to gradually reduce the share of the economy that goes to public expenditure. The measure of his success in this respect is that promoting a slash-and-burn approach to spending on public services would now be regarded as the height of folly – political suicide, in fact – by the Tory frontbench.

Apart from a political mission to make public spending respectable again, there has been a great personal benefit to Brown from exercising total control over the public spending tap, allowing only a dribble in 1997 and 1998 and then gradually opening the valve. It's shown who's really in charge. To begin with, Brown's sway over all his ministerial colleagues was reinforced by his determination to rebuff their requests for more funds, which have, however, been fewer and further between than he expected. Few Chancellors have ever been quite so insistent that the right to disburse was his alone, not the Prime Minister's. When, finally, he was in a mood to spend, he left no one in any doubt about whom should be praised for his magnificent generosity: not Blair the Irrelevant, or Brown the Prudent (who had gone on a long vacation), but Brown the Binger.

***

The years of feast seemed extremely remote in 1992, after John Major staged one of the great all-time comebacks in a general election campaign to beat a resurgent Labour Party. Brown's analysis was that Labour had lost in part because it was viewed as profligate and lacked economic credibility. So the imperative for him, as Shadow Chancellor, was to establish that credibility by curbing its enthusiasm to spend.

As Shadow Chancellor from 1992, his first public expenditure initiative was simple and blunt: he made it clear that there would be no spending, or – more precisely – that Labour in opposition would make no promises unless it could demonstrate precisely how it would fund those promises. The previous approach of saying that any particular Labour project would only take place "as resources allow" had failed spectacularly, Brown felt, because the Tories in 1992 were still able to add up all the items on the Shadow Cabinet's list of possible future commitments and allege that a Labour government would spend many billions more than them. The Conservatives had thus created the fear that taxes would be going up under Labour by £1,000 per year on average for every family (the reality was that Labour was actually planning to hit only those on above-average earnings: the "average" family would probably have been better off under Labour).

So it wasn't the spending aspirations *per se* which damaged Labour, but the implications for taxation, as a minister recalls:

> We had a lid on spending commitments and then John (Smith) developed the idea that if you could raise X in tax you could spend Y on pensions and child benefit. The truth is that nobody remembered what we promised to spend it on, but they remembered what we had promised to tax it on.

When in February 1992, in preparation for the general election, the Tories launched their "double whammy" campaign – alleging that taxes and inflation would go up under a Labour government – there was no easy way for Labour to prove it wrong, as the opinion polls showed.

As it happens, the previous Christmas, Brown had advised Smith and Kinnock – then party leader – to drop the shadow budget and develop a campaign blaming the Tories for the recession then gripping Britain and highlighting Labour's plans to create employment. As the general election approached, Brown – as Shadow Trade and Industry Secretary – focused his own rhetoric in this way, but Labour as a whole continued on its Kamikaze flight. Brown was permitted to do press conferences on the economy, so long as they were not major ones.

After the electoral defeat, when Smith took over as leader on July 19, 1992, Brown – as the new Shadow Chancellor – was given a relatively free rein. And he then took a leaf out of Margaret Thatcher's book as leader of the Tories in opposition in the mid-1970s: members of the shadow cabinet were instructed to keep their mouths shut, promise nothing at all, give not even a hint that they might want to build a few more hospitals or schools. Looking back on it in 1997, this is how he described what he had done:

In 1993, I said the new Labour Party would never construct economic policy by drawing up a wish-list of spending, seeing how much of it could be financed by taxation and meeting any gap by borrowing. There would be no return to the days of careless demand management, masquerading as Keynesianism. [speech to Labour activists on January 20, 1997, given at the QEII Centre in Westminster]

The logic was inescapable to him. Unfortunately, much of the Labour Party did not share it. So 1992 and 1993 are Brown's years of personal sacrifice and struggle, an almost religious trial of his inner strength. He seemed determined to find out how unpopular he could make himself within the Labour Party, by brutally ditching its historic commitments to massive increases in public spending and then abandoning its determination to oppose privatisation. Brown appeared to see a positive correlation between the amount that he was hated by his colleagues and the success of his mission. "The problem with Gordon is that there are no half measures when he thinks he's right and you're wrong," says a cabinet colleague. "He's determined to kill you. And even though, with the passage of years, you begin to see that indeed he was right, you never forget the way he humiliated you."

These days Brown shudders very slightly when talking of the way he was forced to alienate colleagues after the 1992 general election, when he ditched the economic programme put together by John Smith in the late 1980s, the Shadow Budget. But he doesn't seem to have any regrets. Although there was a huge personal cost to him, in that Blair's popularity soared as his waned, he does not manifest a doubt that it was the right thing to do. Shadow ministers may have been irked to be shackled by a blunt Shadow Chancellor who was a great deal younger than most of them, but having been prevented from creating an expensive agenda of prescriptions for the UK's ills, they devoted their skills to undermining the Tory government. And on the plausible theory that governments almost always lose elections (and that oppositions rarely win them), this was probably no bad thing in the short term. The almost total block on policy creation helped to refashion New Labour into the most fearsome "oppositionist" opposition of the 20th century. There was, however, a long-term price for this stress on negative campaigning rather than the development of positive initiatives: Blair, Brown and their colleagues would be in government for many years before they started to define themselves for what they are and what they wanted to achieve, rather than as "not as bad as the other lot" (see Chapter Nine).

From the outset, only one piece of new spending was allowed by Brown – and typically it was one of his own pet projects, the New Deal to help the young unemployed and the long-term unemployed find work and acquire relevant skills, which was permitted because it would be funded by the windfall tax on the privatised utilities (see pages 260-5). If the Tories queried the cost of the New Deal, Brown could reply that it would financed by an impost on the gas, water and electricity companies – and he was confident that this would not be an unpopular tax, since the reputations of these utilities was at an all-time low.

***

One of Brown's earliest and most symbolically important punch-ups was against the Tribune group, the leftish group which represented 100 Labour MPs, in the latter half of 1993. Its flamboyant secretary, Peter Hain, together with Roger Berry, had in July of that year called for a £10bn to £15bn "reflationary package" to kickstart growth and reduce unemployment after the downturn of the early 1990s. In a pamphlet entitled "Labour and the Economy", Hain also advocated a new top rate of income tax for those earning £50,000 or more each year. And then, in September 1993, Hain published a further pamphlet, "What's Left", which was a fairly explicit attack on Brown and Blair for being seduced by allegedly unprogressive social democratic thinking (the bodysnatchers of New Labour eventually captured Hain, who has been an enthusiastic senior member of Blair's government for many years). All this was Hain's rallying cry for the large dispossessed wing of the Party that still hankered after a relatively crude, Keynesian tax-and-spend policy. However the proposals were derided in the media by "senior Labour sources" as "kiddy economics". Brown still recalls the incident with annoyance, because it might have undermined his mission to reinvent Labour as a credible manager of the economy: Hain's call for increased borrowing, when the public finances were in a mess, reinforced a perception of Labour as spendthrift. As for Hain, when asked about this bruising encounter with Brown, he still winces.

At precisely the same time, Brown was evolving a more muscular, market-oriented policy for economic recovery, which was summarised in his own pamphlet, "How we can conquer unemployment" (which was in fact largely written by Ed Balls and John Eatwell, a Cambridge economist who advised Labour at the time). Its title pays homage to Lloyd George's famous 1929 paper, "We can conquer unemployment" – though, in fact, Hain could have claimed to be honouring Lloyd George's Keynesianism rather more than Brown (by a wonderful irony, the Treasury has uncovered an original copy of Lloyd George's work, adorned with a scribble by an anonymous official who complained of its "extravagance, inflation, bankruptcy"). The pamphlet says:

> Unemployment today is not simply the by-product of cyclical fluctuations in the economy which can be tackled by the old medicine of boosting demand... The UK economy in its current state cannot operate at full employment and go on borrowing and borrowing... We will stick to strict low inflation targets... The threat posed by Britain's looming budget deficit must not be ignored.

The thesis was praised by Gavyn Davies, who was that rare thing a decade ago, an influential City figure who supported Labour (at the time, he was a partner in charge of the international economics team at the leading US investment bank, Goldman Sachs). Davies wrote a column about it which began with extracts and then asked his readers to guess the author – with the implication that the pamphlet must have been written by a right-wing politician.

It was probably inevitable that Brown should feel increasingly isolated from most of his colleagues, including his leader, John Smith. He felt particularly exposed because his remaking of Labour's economic policy became wrapped into a wider power struggle within the Party over the role of the trade unions, which was expressed that autumn in the One Member One Vote (OMOV) fracas at Labour's annual conference in Brighton. Smith and Brown agreed that the role of trade unions in selecting MPs, the Party leader and making policy should be reduced, but Smith was more open to compromise than his maddeningly bright and tenacious young colleague. Smith was prepared to trade with the unions to obtain their votes in a conference plebiscite on the issue – which sowed mistrust between him and Brown. The Shadow Chancellor also feared that whatever credibility he was painfully winning for his revised economic approach was being undermined by Smith's use of traditional Labour rhetoric about the need to use "all the levers of macro-economic policy" to secure full employment and his willingness to scrap Tory legislation delimiting the power of unions. "There was a bit of a crisis among the modernisers," says a friend of Brown. "The '93 conference was not a good conference. We got OMOV through, but with John Smith appearing to turn back the clock on economic reforms we thought were crucial."

***

The death of John Smith in 1994 has subsequently led to a thriving "what if he had lived" industry. And the question is most resonant in respect of Labour's approach to government spending. Smith's Chief of Staff and old friend, Murray Elder – who was a school contemporary of Gordon Brown – is persuaded that Smith would not have adopted Tory public spending budgets for his first two years in office, which is what Brown eventually did. "When it came to Gordon's economic policy, especially curbing public spending in the first few years of a Labour government, I think it would have been far harder to convince John Smith of the need for that than Tony (Blair)" Elder says. All that's to jump the gun, but it is striking that there was a hiatus in Brown's "modernisation" of public spending policy until the spring of 1995, a year after Smith had died.

Much of the groundwork for the next great leap was once again laid by Ed Balls. His paper, "The Macroeconomic Framework" – which was presented to Blair and his close allies at a meeting held in March 1995 at the country home of Chris Powell, the advertising executive (see page 124) – was the first hint that Brown and Balls were trying to devise rules on how much a Labour government could borrow to provide comfort to the financial markets that it would not be profligate and imprudent. They looked at the Treasury's undistinguished record of economic management and at the early performance of the US President, Bill Clinton, and concluded that the absence of such rules was a form of freedom that was not worth having. "The problem which Clinton had in 1992 to 1993 is that he didn't have a framework at all, which made him too vulnerable to pressure from markets," recalls Balls. "What we wanted was a framework that simultaneously forced us to be tough on the budget while building up credibility to invest." A central conviction of Brown and Balls was that once bankers and currency traders had acquired confidence in their borrowing rules, they would not panic when a Labour government started showing its true colours by directing resources to the public sector. "Constrained discretion" on their ability to borrow and spend would – paradoxically – allow them to spend more over the long term than no constraints at all.

Brown began to set out his framework for borrowing in a speech on May 17, 1995 to Labour's Finance and Industry group, a motley collection of Labour-supporting business people, bankers and party activists. The relevant passage, setting out his "fiscal" rules, was this one:

Two rules for borrowing will guide our approach in government. First Labour will be committed to meeting the golden rule of borrowing: over the economic cycle, government will only borrow to finance public investment and not to fund public consumption.

Secondly, alongside this golden rule commitment, we will keep the ratio of government debt to GDP stable on average over the economic cycle and at a prudent and sensible level.

The first fiscal rule, the golden one, meant that it was allowable for the government to borrow for the building of schools, hospitals or for other capital projects that would increase the stock of national assets. But over the years of an economic cycle, any borrowing on the so-called current account – for example to pay the wages of public servants, or to make social security payments, or to service the interest on the national debt – had to be offset by government revenues. Importantly, this rule did not prohibit borrowing for current spending – as opposed to investment – in any one year. As for the second rule, the so-called "sustainable investment rule", Brown refined it in government to mean that the ratio of net public debt to GDP should be no greater than 40 per cent, which was consistent with the Maastricht criteria for joining the euro.

Now, in some ways these innovations were as important in establishing Brown's economic credibility as the giving of independence to the Bank of England. They limited the ability of a Labour Chancellor to borrow excessively in a way that had never happened before – so investors were able to have much more confidence in him than his antecedents. That said, there's been plenty of carping subsequently that the rules aren't as tough as they look – which is right. Brown is able to borrow enormous sums for investment. He can even borrow for current spending over an extended period, so long as he is able to demonstrate that – at another point in the many years of the same economic cycle (and defining the cycle is not a pure objective science) – there's a corresponding surplus.

As events have turned out, it's been beneficial that Brown retained this constrained discretion to spend and borrow. British economic growth from 2001 onwards has probably been stronger than in many other countries in part because public expenditure has risen in a counter-cyclical way, offsetting a worldwide economic downturn (or, more properly, Brown wasn't forced by tight rules to cut back on expenditure increases that had been planned for some years). Meanwhile, members of the euro zone have probably suffered lower growth because their ability to spend during a downturn has been limited by a less flexible set of fiscal rules which they were forced to follow under their Growth and Stability Pact.

On the other hand, it is arguable – and the Tories do argue this – that there is too much fuzziness around the edges of the fiscal rules. For instance, Brown acquired a fair amount of latitude to shift borrowing off the government's balance sheet through the so-called Private Finance Initiative (PFI) and through Public Private Partnerships (PPP). These were a Tory invention, warmly embraced by Brown, on the basis that they transferred some of the financial risks of building a school, prison or hospital – for example – to a private sector contractor, and therefore put pressure on the contractor to complete the said project on time and to cost (which almost never happens in conventional public sector construction projects). And if the risk of these projects were transferred, the borrowing associated with them (the finance acquired by the contractor to pay for the work) could be taken off the public sector's balance sheet. However, there is controversy about the extent to which the risk really has been taken away from the public sector, about whether the government in fact retains residual liability for the debt associated with the relevant projects – and if the government retains some risk, perhaps it should declare more of the associated debt as part of the public sector debt than it does at the moment.

Critics of Brown's fiscal rules also say that he has too much ability to move the goalposts, to ensure that he never faces the humiliation of breaking them. In particular, the Treasury has considerable control over the definition of the economic cycle, which leaves it open to the charge that it will manipulate the length of the cycle to ensure that the golden rule is always met. In this context, it is amusing that the important 1995 speech by Brown also contained a commitment that a "panel of independent forecasters" would be asked to comment regularly on the "sustainability of the public finances" in the light of the new fiscal rules. As it turned out, such tough independent external scrutiny of whether the rules are being met – in the spirit and the letter – did not become a characteristic of the system as eventually implemented.

However, the fact that the debate today is about whether the rules are rigorous enough shows that they are a success – because this is a world away from the fiscal crises that characterised all previous Labour governments. If opposition politicians and City economists whinge about whether Brown and Balls are taking risks with their own commandments, that's irksome for the duo. But it's an almost theological argument which is relatively harmless to the government. Far worse would have been an escalation of public borrowing of the sort that destroyed the reputation of the Labour government in the mid 1970s.

***

By coincidence, May 1995 was also the last time that Blair made any significant contribution to the shaping of economic policy. On May 22, in the Mais Lecture at London's City University, he cautioned Labour supporters not to expect significant rises in the level of public spending after victory in a general election. He said that "the boundaries for changes" in taxation and spending were "much reduced", adding that "both are dependent on the performance of the economy, not on *a priori* assumptions about the desirability of particular levels of either". In an interview with me, which I conducted at his Islington home a couple of days before, he explained the background to the new economic conservatism: "The determining context of economic policy is the new global market. That imposes huge limitations of a practical nature – quite apart from reasons of principle – on macroeconomic policies."

Blair's subsequent remoteness from economic policymaking, either as Party leader or Prime Minister, is almost without precedent. In the 1980s, by contrast, Nigel Lawson as Chancellor felt almost constantly undermined by the interventions of Thatcher and her influential adviser, Sir Alan Walters. And although Blair agreed to this delegation of powers when Brown allowed him a clear run for the Labour leadership, the entente would probably never have held if Brown had ever made any serious errors, if there had ever been a full blown economic crisis. But Brown has retained his autonomy to a large extent because there have been no crises and few failures, no mess for Blair and 10 Downing Street to clean up. "Historically Prime Ministers had to be involved in broader day to day economic management because the economy kept going wrong," says an official. "The truth about Tony Blair is he hasn't had to be at all. He did the Mais Lecture in 1995. But that's about it."

Brown also strengthened his grip on the economic controls by securing a promise from Blair – while still in opposition – that he would chair the relevant cabinet committees, especially the one that oversees public spending (now called PSX, though it was called PX in the late 1990s, and EDX under the Tories).

Anyway, the message developed by Brown in the latter part of 1995 and the following year was that Labour spending would be smart not huge. The best expression of this was in a lecture he gave at the Manchester Business School on April 29, 1996, entitled "The Treasury's Mission under Labour". He said:

> We do not believe in a policy of simply spending more and taxing more... Our aim will be to save money before we spend money. And that is my advice to my Shadow Cabinet colleagues. I want our government to be remembered as wise spenders not as big spenders and that is how we will proceed.

Brown's most important speech on public expenditure was the one he gave on January 20, 1997 at the QEII centre in Victoria, which is largely remembered for giving the historic commitment not to raise income tax rates (see page s 257-9). What Brown said about public spending was just as significant, probably more so. The preamble was all about the need for greater efficiency in government, less waste and clearer priorities. And there was confirmation that Labour had renounced its traditional opposition to privatisation or the use of the private sector to deliver public services (an argument which he did not re-examine till the beginning of 2003 – see page 302):

> Our first principle then is that pursuing the public interest does not mean government must act on its own using public spending in every area. The public interest can also be pursued either through government setting standards for the private sector or by the public sector working with the private sector to meet shared objectives.

Much more shocking, at that moment, was Brown's announcement that Labour would stick with the public expenditure limits – the so-called control totals – laid down by the Conservative government of John Major (as Prime Minister) and Ken Clarke (the Chancellor).

The crucial parameters for the scope of action by all Labour ministers for pretty much the entire first parliament were set in this speech, which was drafted by Ed Miliband. But – and this is characteristic of Brown's big initiatives – there had been no shadow cabinet debate about it at all. Brown and Balls had planned the coup for months. But – with the exception of Blair – no Labour frontbencher was told about it, until the eve of the announcement. The full extent of Brown's consultation with his colleagues was that he telephoned some of them the night before the speech, having faxed the bare bones of it to Blair at home.

It was intrepid stuff: maintaining reasonable control of public spending was one thing; pledging to spend no more than the Tories was quite another. Even a very untraditional Labour supporter like Gavyn Davies regarded it as excessive hair-shirtism and told Balls as much shortly after the speech had been given. Davies's view was that President Clinton's accumulation of a vast budget surplus was persuading international investors that left-of-centre governments could be trusted, that they would give a new Labour government more latitude to spend than Brown and Balls feared.

So what was the counter-argument of Brown and Balls? Well, their fear of a financially unfettered future was a reaction to the sins of their forefathers, as a colleague of Brown explains:

Our reading of history is that Labour governments went wrong by losing credibility on the economy and public spending in the first two years. Roy Jenkins was always for us the model of what we didn't want to be doing. We never wanted to be a great Jenkins-style Chancellor, because he was a great Chancellor for doing everything that Labour didn't want to be doing in the second half of a parliament. In the past you tended to have a Labour Chancellor who did not establish credibility early enough, did not take the tough decisions. So you would have a crisis and they would be replaced: Dalton went in 1947, Callaghan went in 1967. And the new Chancellors, Cripps, Jenkins, would then make their reputations by having to slow the economy, cut public spending and raise taxes in the run up to a general election. The *Financial Times* then writes editorials saying what great Chancellors they were for doing the right thing in the end. But the Labour Party thinks, 'that's all very well but we just lost the election'.

Brown's and Balls's conviction was that there was no sensible half-way position in practice between imposing an apparently unbreakable straitjacket and appalling profligacy. They were persuaded that if they gave any hint that departmental budgets could be expanded, there would have been a torrent of demands for additional resources within days of the election – which would have been a dreadful distraction from the priority of preparing his first budget, whose centrepiece would be a windfall tax on the privatised utilities to fund his cherished New Deal employment-creation programme. A colleague of Brown explains: "We were worried there would be pressure in the first few weeks of government, because ministers would want to get on and spend." And it would be hard to resist, because they would be supported by their senior civil servants. "We thought there would be the normal full frontal assault," says a Treasury official. "We were right. All across Whitehall the spending officials briefed their cabinet ministers to ask for more money." Bizarrely, most of the ministers behaved with self-control and didn't take their civil servants' advice.

***

The creative interaction of Brown and Balls is particularly evident in the detail of this public spending policy. Brown had in 1996 come up with the important innovation of a Comprehensive Spending Review, which would be a fundamental assessment of the whole of spending that would take place every two years and would set departmental budgets for three years. The point of it was to allow public services to plan with more confidence than was possible under the traditional system of annual spending reviews, which had a bad habit of chopping or augmenting budgets with little warning. And it would also allow the Treasury to allocate resources between departments in a more strategic way.

But this initiative on its own would not prevent recently appointed Labour ministers from screaming for lots more dosh for their pet projects just as soon as the election was over. And it was with this fear at the back of his mind, that Balls held a meeting at the Treasury in December 1996 – with Burns, Paul Gray (who was in charge of the budget), Robert Culpin (responsible for public spending) and John Gieve (Culpin's deputy). During the course of this, the idea for the two-year expenditure freeze began to take shape for Balls. At this meeting, Balls also became excited when he learned that there was a substantial reserve of £7.5bn to cover public spending emergencies, because this provided him with a device for softening the inevitable complaints that the Treasury under Brown would not be doing enough for schools and hospitals. In his first budget, Brown could pre-allocate £1bn from the reserve to Health and a further £1bn to Education, without flouting the symbolically important public spending limits.

Even so, few of Brown's colleagues and almost no one in the Treasury believed he would actually stick to the spending targets. "We all thought it was a clever wheeze," says a senior Treasury official. "The Conservatives had almost never stayed within budget, so we could see no reason why Brown could or should." And the Labour frontbench was convinced Brown would lighten up and allow them some extra money, once the dream was realised and they were actually in office. Even Ken Clarke, Brown's predecessor as Chancellor, told me after the election he probably wouldn't have stuck to the budgets.

However, Brown possesses a Thatcher-like resolve to deliver on his promises. And once he's set on a course, it's almost impossible to knock him off. This unwavering quality doesn't always rebound to his credit. He caused himself absurd difficulties in the autumn of 1997, not long after the election, when as Chancellor he pressed ahead with plans to cut benefit payments to single parents that had been proposed by the Tories. His bloody-mindedness, in the face of passionate opposition from his own backbenchers, was caused quite simply by his calculation that if he softened his stance on this, no one would believe he was serious about staying within the overall public spending limits. Any sign of weakness from him would encourage other ministers to demand a loosening of the public spending corset, or so he feared.

During the furore, he was unrepentant about this dogmatic pursuit of fiscal rectitude. But his colleagues now acknowledge that the fight over what was called the lone parent premium was probably unnecessary (Brown's recalcitrance won him the distinction of prompting the first resignation of a minister from this government, that of Malcolm Chisolm, an obscure and decent minister in the Scottish office). A friend of Brown says: "The lone parent benefit row in the first few months was 'very bad politics'. We thought it was important for our credibility to stick to our spending plans. But we under-estimated the conviction in the Party that any Labour government will betray the Party. The loan parent cut proved this to them, because our action was 'against Labour people'."

Despite the squealing from the backbenches and Labour supporters all over the country, Brown kept to the spending squeeze. In fact, thanks largely to a reduction in payments of interest on the national debt and a fall in social security payments, public spending during the first years in government was actually less than the budgets set by Brown that were – supposedly – impossibly tight. There is also a Whitehall legend that not even Health and Education spent their allotted funds from 1997 to 1999, while an examination of Treasury figures shows that they actually over-spent marginally in this early period. However, there was an under-spend by both departments from 1999 to 2002, after their budgets were increased significantly, which may prove that the lean years had indeed deprived them of the mechanisms and the will to buy and invest.

Meanwhile, one of Brown's hopes, that ministers would respond to the lack of new money by shifting resources from low priority areas to high priority ones, was largely disappointed. Some reallocation went on in social security, with the transformation of benefits into tax credits (see page 275) and other reforms. But in these early years, there was a notable absence of creative reorganisation of budgets in most departments.

On the other hand, Brown's prudent approach to spending was generating reserves of goodwill in financial markets and he famously never lost an opportunity to laud his own prudence (the sport of the press gallery was to take bets on the number of times he would use the "P" word in a budget speech). This theme was sustained in the first ever Comprehensive Spending Review, in the summer of 1998, when he resisted the temptation to splurge.

For the three years beginning in April 1999, Brown allowed growth in current spending of just 2.25 per cent a year in real terms, which was in line with the Treasury's estimate of the trend rate of growth in the economy. What's amusing in retrospect – now that Brown is under attack for spending too much – is that his attempts to prove that this was an exceedingly generous settlement, by a slightly devious accounting technique, led to ferocious criticism of him for pretending to be more generous than he was.

He announced, for example, that Education spending would be rising by £19bn and Health spending by £21bn. But those numbers were the aggregated totals of each year's increment over three years. They sounded a lot, but they told you nothing at all about the proportional annual increases in resources for schools or hospitals, which is what gives the best indication of whether there are going to be more books or teachers or nurses.

As it happens, expenditure on Education and Health was beginning to accelerate – and was rising faster than spending on all the other departments. But on this occasion, this positive economic reality was obscured by the hype. These days the Treasury excuses itself for doing this by saying that it was simply sharing with the world its internal methodology. But as someone who was a political editor at the time, I know that Brown and Balls were endeavouring to have their cake and eat it: they wanted to be generous in the eyes of the Labour Party and mean in the eyes of the City. Amazingly, they more or less got away with it.

Their mindset at the time – which was to keep spending ministers on a short leash – was manifested by their attempt to increase the efficiency of spending by establishing "Publish Service Agreements" with all departments. These were supposed to be lists of practical targets for the improvement of public services and were scheduled to be announced in the Comprehensive Spending Review on July 14. But implementing this innovation in such a short time was far too ambitious. So in the end, the deadline was shifted to the autumn. And what emerged was something of a dog's breakfast. There were a staggering 700 targets, which was far too many for them to be monitored effectively. Since then, the process of setting targets in this way has been refined and improved – though it's moot whether the right balance between setting goals and decentralising the delivery of public services has yet been achieved (see page 305).

The point of all this prudence and the parsimony from 1997 to 2000 was to prepare the ground for a massive expansion of the role of the state by demonstrating to the markets that Brown, as Chancellor, could be tough when he needed to be. And, in particular, it was to facilitate generosity in the run-up to the 2001 election. Balls and Brown were desperate to do a "Jenkins-in-reverse". Rather than cutting at the end of a term in office, as Roy Jenkins had done as Chancellor in 1969, they wanted to splurge, to buy votes.

But would the City and international investors turn against them, once the trend to spending moved upwards? Under Brown's new system of comprehensive spending reviews, expenditure plans are set for three years, but reviews are every two. So the crucial one was to be in 2000, a year before the date when Labour would ask the electorate for a second term in office. It was the moment of truth for the Chancellor and Balls. Would the prudence have its promised purpose? Would they at last be able to show their Labour colours and not be punished by markets?

Financial markets are most interested in the aggregated expenditure figure, rather than how it is divided between departments. So the budget of 2000, on March 21, 2000, was the big credibility test of Brown's and Ball's fiscal rules, because it set out the overall totals for current and investment spending – which would be divided between the departments when the spending review was completed that summer. If Brown could announce a significant increase in overall expenditure without spooking investors, then perhaps Labour really had shed its reputation of being an untrustworthy steward of the economy.

Balls was probably more obsessed with this credibility question than even Brown. He sees the 2000 budget as the most important of his time at the Treasury (Brown sees the 2002 budget as more important, because the huge rise in health spending that it announced – funded by a special one per cent National Insurance levy – was the justification for all the pain he suffered in the early 1990s when being attacked by his colleagues for allegedly abandoning socialism in pursuit of financial respectability (see page 274).

Anyway, Brown pushed up the growth rate of current spending to $2^1/_2$ per cent a year in real terms, while more than doubling net capital investment. Most strikingly, there was to be 6.1 per cent average annual real terms growth (that's adjusting for inflation) in NHS spending for four years – which the Treasury claimed was the longest period of sustained high growth in the 50-year history of the NHS.

One consequence was a significant shift from net redemption of debt to net borrowing. Would commentators and economists see it as an inflationary package? Would there be pressure on the Bank of England to raise interest rates? Would the Bank in fact raise interest rates? The answers to these resonant questions – the tests of Brown's credibility – hinged to a certain extent on whether an analysis of the budget was a short-term one or a longer-term one. The Treasury was projecting higher repayments of debt in 2000-1 and 2001-2 than it had originally forecast in its Pre-Budget Report the previous November. So it was hard to argue that Brown was being incautious on that basis. But between 2002 and 2004, public borrowing was projected to rise quite sharply, by an amount equivalent to a significant proportion of GDP (0.7 per cent, according to estimates at the time).

It was fortunate for Brown that the Bank and the City tend to focus their forecasts on the shorter term. The Bank of England tends to take account only of the economic outlook for two years when setting interest rates. And that was apparently its modus operandi on this occasion. There was no immediate rise in interest rates (in fact, interest rates were set to decline for another three and a bit years, till being raised in November 2003). As for the City in general, it didn't seem unduly fussed. If anything, sterling remained stronger than Brown might have liked. Brown went into the general election promising a public spending bonanza and anyone who cried foul – such as the occasional Tory MP – was widely regarded as slightly unhinged.

Part of the reason Brown has been given the benefit of the doubt in financial markets for so long is that he oversaw a spectacular reduction in the national debt and in the government's interest rate bill. Debt as a proportion of GDP fell from 43.7 per cent in 1996-7 to 30.2 per cent in 2001-2 (it has risen a couple of percentage points since then), through tight control of spending, planned and unplanned increases in tax revenues, and one or two amazing windfalls. In 2000-1, Brown repaid £37bn of the national debt, which was a huge amount by any standards. And as a result of this reduction in debt and a fall in interest rates, Brown was able to claim in his 2002 budget that interest payments on the national debt in 2002-3 as a proportion of national income were less than for any government since 1914.

The biggest one-off contribution to the reduction of debt was the £22.5bn proceeds from an auction in early 2000 of licences to provide so-called third generation (3G) services over mobile phones. The Treasury's timing for the sale was spot-on, because at the time there was euphoria in the City about the value of internet businesses (it was soon replaced by depression). So Brown ended up selling these licences, to Vodafone, BT and others, for a massive multiple of what they were really worth (at the time, Sir Chris Gent, then chief executive of Vodafone, acknowledged to me that he was probably paying too much for his company's licence, but said that his shareholders would not understand if he pulled out of the auction).

***

172

Funnily enough, Brown and Balls did not feel wholly comfortable about being in surplus to this extent – about being quite so successful as financial conservatives (strikingly, even the Tories said they wouldn't have used the mobile phone proceeds to pay down the national debt but would have endowed universities with the billions as part of a policy to give them greater financial independence). The last thing Brown and Balls wanted was to have the success or failure of their economic stewardship judged by whether they were repaying debt, because that would limit their ability to carry out a progressive spending programme. And they were also worried about the electoral implications of creating the impression that somehow the foundations of the economy were now so strong as to be unbreakable, even by a change of government.

In that respect, they took an important lesson from what they perceived as the complacency of the Democrats in the US after the Clinton administration started to generate huge budget surpluses in the mid-1990s. Brown and Blair and the New Labour vanguard took a particularly close interest in the policies and plans of President Clinton, because – in the most general sense – his politics were similar to theirs. And they were alarmed to hear Sydney Blumenthal, Clinton's adviser, claiming that all the Left's problems were over now that Clinton had eliminated the government deficit. "Blumenthal was doing this whole rap around London in the late 1990s about the politics of the surplus," recalls a friend of Brown. "America had got a surplus so this now resolved all dilemmas. You didn't have to worry about the competence and credibility of left-wing governments any more. Politics was now just a debate about how you use the fruits of economic growth." Brown rejected Blumenthal's analysis, partly because it meant that the left's newly won economic credibility could not be exploited properly. One of the Chancellor's colleagues explains:

Our view of Blumenthal's thesis was that it would be disastrous, because if you simply move into a debate about distributing revenues generated by a successful economy, then you give credibility to Bush's call for tax cuts. And, more importantly, you give away at a stroke your biggest card – which is that the economy was weak before you came on the scene and that it was you who came along and struggled for stability and competence.

Our view was that we had to preach eternal vigilance. The struggle must go on, because you can't take the surplus for granted. So if you look at our 2001 election campaign, the first two-thirds of the election campaign were on the economy, stability, not putting it at risk, attacking the Tories for lacking economic competence.

It was crucial for Brown that in the 2001 general election and the one after that there was not such an enormous surplus that the political debate would all be about whether to hand it back in tax cuts. The mountain of cash had to be spent: Labour's priorities of education and – above all health – had to be properly funded.

***

The big spree came in 2002, with a dramatic step-up in the funding made available for the health service. Because this was so closely bound in with arguments about personal taxation and National Insurance, it is discussed in detail in chapter eight (pages 265-74). But what's slightly odd is that the Brown of this period is uncharacteristically gung-ho. Tax revenues were sliding at the time, mostly because of the delayed effects of the stock-market slump at the turn of the millennium, which led to reduced receipts from capital gains tax and stamp duty on securities transactions. There was (and still is) a risk that he would break his golden rule (that he must not borrow to fund current spending over the course of the cycle) with his decision to increase current spending from 2004 to 2006 by 3.3 per cent per annum including health, well above the economy's intrinsic growth rate (though any breach would probably come in the next cycle, not the current one). He also imposed a little more strain on the government's balance sheet with an increase in net public sector investment from

174

a target of 1.8 per cent of GDP in 2003-4 to 2 per cent just two years later.

As I've said, it's probably the case that the pace of actual and planned spending was partly responsible for the notable fact that the UK continued to avoid recession, while much of the euro zone was enduring a sharp economic slowdown (although, as Keith Marsden has pointed out in a paper for the Tory-leaning Centre for Policy Studies, comparisons with the performance of much of the rest of the world are less flattering for the UK). Business confidence was low, after the pricking of the internet bubble on the stock market in 2000 and the 9/11 atrocity in 2001. That said, Balls and Brown insist that their main spending decisions were primarily motivated by a political commitment to improve public services, not by old-fashioned Keynesian demand management.

However, Balls is a great proponent of the "automatic stabilisers", which are characteristics of the tax and spending regime that serve to smooth out bumps and dips in the economic cycle: when the economy is growing fast, government tax receipts tend to rise and assorted payments to the unemployed tend to fall; when the economy slows, the reverse usually happens. So government borrowing automatically falls in a boom and rises during a slowdown, all other things being equal. There is a built-in dampener to demand when the economy is growing and a stimulus in a downturn.

Now, part of the reason Balls regards his and Brown's fiscal rules as a success is that they allow full effect to these automatic stabilisers – which is less true of the euro zone's Growth and Stability Pact, since that imposes constraints on borrowing independent of the economic cycle. However Balls would not sign up for the kind of active demand management that characterised the Labour governments of the 1960s and 1970s. Probably the most he would claim is that he and Brown have challenged the orthodoxy of the world's most powerful economic institutions – notably the International Monetary Fund and the European Central Bank (which is still in thrall to the monetarist ideology of the German Bundesbank, though its new president, Jean-Claude Trichet, is showing some sign of wanting to shed these shackles) – by demonstrating that it's possible for a government to be prudent while not spending every waking moment at every stage of every economic cycle endeavouring to reduce public debt. He thinks that they have proved that a Chancellor or finance minister who wants to boost public spending is not necessarily someone rushing headlong to bankrupt his or her economy.

On the other hand, a resonant concern for the avowed penny-pinching son of Scots Presbyterians, Brown, is whether the sheer size of recent spending settlements is precipitating grotesque waste. This is a critique which he has acknowledged in his actions to have some force. In June 2003 he asked Sir Peter Gershon – an émigré from the private sector, the dismantled GEC, who was put in charge of government procurement (how it buys all its goods and services) in 2000 – to review whether substantial efficiency improvements could be made throughout Whitehall.

Gershon's initial report shocked cabinet ministers, when he presented it to them in December 2003, because it indicated that tens of thousands of jobs across the public sector were surplus to requirements. There was then an anxious few weeks for the Treasury, as it endeavoured to assess whether Gershon's proposals were practical and deliverable – and whether there would be a revolt by the spending ministers most affected.

Help came in an unanticipated way from an unexpected source. In February 2004, Oliver Letwin, the Shadow Chancellor, announced that the Tories would significantly limit the growth in public spending if they won the next election. This made it easier for Brown to persuade colleagues that the Labour government had to be seen to be cutting out waste and then reinvesting the proceeds in so-called front-line services. The political climate for what the Treasury has taken to calling Gershonisation suddenly became a whole lot easier.

Letwin could, in fact, have really put Brown on the spot. He had in his possession a leaked copy of Gershon's unpublished recommendations (or so Letwin told me). So what he should probably have done was to press Brown day after day about whether the government was going to implement the painful cuts recommended by the efficiency guru, while saying nothing about his own plans (if the tables had been turned, with

Letwin as Chancellor and Brown as the Shadow, those would have been Brown's tactics). The drip-drip of judiciously timed disclosures of extracts from the report – especially those that implied chronic over-manning in Whitehall – would have been a severe embarrassment to the Chancellor. In the annals of missed political opportunities, this was a big one.

Anyway, Brown returned to the familiar territory of his earlier years in government with a relatively cautious budget on March 17, 2004. Growth in current spending would be $2^1/_2$ per cent a year between 2006 and 2008, which pushed it back into line with the Treasury's view of the underlying growth rate in the economy – although there was another sharp rise in investment spending to 2.25 per cent of GDP. Health and Education benefited once again from particularly generous settlements, ostensibly underwritten by Gershon's efficiency savings, which – proba-bly thanks to Letwin – were accepted by the Cabinet. Brown announced a staggering 54,000 job cuts in the Department of Work and Pensions, the Inland Revenue and Customs alone. Customs and the Inland Revenue were to merge, in a radical reorganisation of the way the government conducts business. And in the Comprehensive Spending Review of July 12, 2004, Brown announced that the Gershon process would lead to total job reductions across the public sector of 104,000 by 2008, which would allegedly save more than £20bn a year.

The human cost of all this was worthwhile, according to Brown, to free up funds for schools and hospitals. This was the cut-to-spend budg-et. In a way, therefore, although it may not have been his favourite budg-et, it is the one that most neatly sums up Brown's political persona. He's neither a mean-spirited person nor a mean-spirited politician, but – and perhaps this is the legacy of his father – he never seems really happy unless there has been toil and sacrifice on the path to economic redemp-tion.

CHAPTER SIX

"Clear and unambiguous" – how Brown took control of
the historic decision on whether to join the euro

Except for the decision to go to war against Iraq, Tony Blair has faced no more momentous choice as Prime Minister than whether to sign up for European monetary union, whether to join the euro. And for a long while he created the impression – and believed, though not as consistently or wholeheartedly as is widely believed – that his place in history would be as the deliverer of the UK into the European single currency, in order to restore the UK to its rightful place as a leader in Europe. But there was an obstacle (apart from British public opinion, which has been largely hostile to the idea of giving up the pound). As it turned out, it was not his decision to make. For Gordon Brown, as Chancellor, has kept almost total control over the process of whether to join. He and Ed Balls have manifested a mastery over the machinery of government that left the Prime Minister with little discretion over what perhaps should have been a test of his judgement and his judgement alone (or, more properly, the judgement of the Cabinet under his lead).

There is a temptation to see this marginalisation of Blair as proof that Brown has been the real Prime Minister. And there is some truth in that interpretation. But it would be an over-simplification, because it would imply that Brown has over-ruled Blair or bullied him into a particular course of action. But Brown wasn't in this case simply exercising what he saw as his proper powers under the Granita agreement – it would have been stretching even that unprecedented deal for Brown to argue that it gave him complete, independent control over a question so vital to the UK's future. What Brown and Balls in fact did was subtler: they secured Blair's agreement that the evaluation of whether to join should be based purely on an economic assessment.

Balls, as a professional economist, knew it would be hard to find a credible professional economist who could prove that the economic case for joining was unanswerable. To be clear, there are plenty of credible economists in favour of monetary union, but their arguments tend to be influenced by political considerations; demonstrating beyond a reasonable doubt that the economic benefits outweigh the costs is trickier.

And just to make doubly sure that politics would not taint the evaluation, Brown and Balls persuaded Blair that the assessment should be led by career civil servants in the Treasury. The officials delivered precisely the negative opinion that Brown and Balls wanted – but (and this is worth noting) without direct subversion by Brown and Balls of their impartiality and independence. In fact, career civil servants have told me – in all seriousness – that this process was a reassertion of the power of Whitehall after years of being undermined by Blair's government (which is rather stretching the point, in my view).

Brown and Balls staked everything on the way that they had framed the economic issues that needed to be evaluated and the innate mistrust of our friends in Europe that has been a characteristic of the Treasury for decades (when Edward Heath as Prime Minister was negotiating British entry into the European Economic Community – the precursor of the European Union – in the early 1970s, he simply ignored the Treasury's view that the costs, especially those associated with the Common Agricultural policy, outweighed the potential economic benefits; Heath would not have dreamed of giving the Treasury a veto). Balls's role in the construction of this process cannot be understated.

Now, there is no modern precedent for a Prime Minister being neutered to this extent by his or her Chancellor on an issue of such import. The most relevant analogy is with Margaret Thatcher, who hated the idea of joining the European Exchange Rate mechanism and resented the pressure she faced from her Chancellor, Nigel Lawson, to do so. Lawson eventually saw his ambition realised in 1990 – but accession to the ERM came almost exactly a year after he resigned over differences with her on exchange rate policy. By contrast, in 2003, it was Blair who signalled that he was chomping at the bit to take the United Kingdom into the European single currency – and who, for a couple of days at least, was hopping mad that his Chancellor had made it impossible for him to do so. He and his Downing Street team made a last-ditch attempt to exert some influence on what kind of statement would be delivered that spring about the UK's future intentions towards the single currency. But any success they had was in changing the style of presentation, not the substance of what was announced.

As it happens, I think Brown and Balls are correct that the economic price of joining the euro is probably too great at present – which is not the same as saying there will never be a good time to sign up. Brown believes that the trend to economic reform within the European Union – however slow that trend may be – means that the UK could well become a member one day, though putting a date on this is difficult. And it's striking that whenever he talks in private about the euro, he always sounds far more positive about the long term prospects for joining than his public image would suggest would be his view (he is, for example, remarkably sanguine that the European Central Bank will in time become a more open and less deflationary institution, such that a British government would have more confidence in its interest rate decisions).

***

When it comes to their views on the euro, Brown is the inverted image of Blair: far less hostile to monetary union than is widely believed. In fact, Brown has consistently been pro-European throughout his political life, though not to the extent that it has defined his politics, in the way that it did for the late Roy Jenkins (that rarity, a relatively untarnished former

Labour Chancellor and founder of the Social Democratic Party) or for Ken Clarke (Brown's predecessor as Chancellor) or even for Peter Mandelson (the most pro-European of Blair's close confidants). But when he was on the brink of his parliamentary career in 1983, he does not appear to have taken any kind of a stand against Labour's absurd and unrealistic call for withdrawal from what was then called the European Economic Community (and became the European Union). Indeed, Brown has no memory of doing so.

More than 20 years ago, Labour's extreme anti-European stance was an element in the notorious "longest suicide note in history", a Party manifesto – "New Hope for Britain" – which also called for draconian industrial intervention and unilateral nuclear disarmament. At the time, Brown was the candidate to become the MP for Dunfermline East. His message to his constituents for that election makes no reference to Europe, which probably shows that he wasn't encouraging anti-European hysteria. By contrast, Blair's 1983 address to the voters of Sedgefield was rather more in the spirit of the mad manifesto: "We'll negotiate withdrawal from the EEC, which has drained our natural resources and destroyed jobs," it says. The manifesto *in toto* was proof to Brown that Labour was not fit to govern. And his justification for keeping quiet on Europe at the time was that there was absolutely no chance of Britain making a unilateral declaration of independence from the EEC because there was no possibility of Labour beating a Tory Party led by Margaret Thatcher (who was basking in the glory of her Falklands triumph).

Through the 1980s, Labour abandoned its implacable hostility to the EEC and eventually picked up the pro-European banner, while the Tories began their slow but inexorable conversion to euro-scepticism. This remarkable change was to a large extent triggered by the policies of a French socialist, Jacques Delors, who in the 1980s was President of the EEC. Delors' vision of a "social Europe" of minimum employment standards and investment in under-privileged regions was a direct challenge to the Thatcherite *laissez faire* agenda. Margaret Thatcher was moving the terms of British political debate further to the right with every day that passed, but Neil Kinnock – Labour's new leader who was on a crusade to make the Party more representative of mainstream public opinion – could at least take comfort that in Brussels there was a friendly voice and potential ally.

For a brief moment in the late 1980s, the respective leadership teams of the Conservatives and Labour were united in their unwise support for Europe's precursor to fully fledged monetary union, the European Exchange Rate mechanism. In the Conservative Party, the economic and political disasters that were precipitated by British membership of the ERM simply accelerated the trend towards anti-Europeanism. The effects on Labour were subtler. It would not drop its new pro-Europeanism, but it became increasingly conscious of the eurosceptic tendencies of influential newspapers and therefore became more cautious in its European policies. As for the impact on Brown, who had been a supporter of the ERM, the debacle was probably the most important moment in his European education. He became much more hardnosed in his views of Europe's economic adventures, especially any further experiments with merging currencies.

The European Exchange Rate Mechanism was an arrangement between European currencies, which obliged them to trade within a predetermined price range. If, for example, the franc threatened to fall below its minimum value against the German mark, the Banque de France was obliged to raise interest rates or sell marks in order to push the price of the French currency up again. And, like any member of the ERM, the UK would be forced to set interest rates in a way that would lead to the convergence of our inflation rate with the German one, or risk seeing sterling's value against the deutsche mark fall below what was allowed. So the spurious attraction of the ERM for the UK was that, as a member, we too would be compelled to adopt the internationally renowned, anti-inflationary discipline of the German Bundesbank.

However, joining the ERM also represented a significant erosion of the autonomy of a British government when managing the economy, since British interest rates would in effect be set by the Bundesbank rather than the Chancellor of the Exchequer. It was, to use an inflammatory phrase, an erosion of national sovereignty. Why did it appeal to Brown as Labour's trade and industry spokesman from 1989 to 1992 – and also, more importantly, to his leader, Neil Kinnock (as well as almost every mainstream British politician of the time)? Well, his argument for joining was based on a seductive analysis of the Party's historic weakness (the analysis was correct, although the prescription turned out to be spurious). He hoped that the ERM would insulate a future Labour government from the sterling crises that had plagued its predecessors (the irresistible pressure on the Wilson government of the 1960s to devalue was probably the most relevant lesson).

Meanwhile, the Treasury, under Lawson and his successor as Chancellor, John Major, was pressing for ERM membership for slightly different reasons: the Treasury's anti-inflationary strategy – based largely on controlling various definitions of the money supply – had failed miserably in the late 1980s. The ERM would be the new bulwark against runaway price rises.

When on October 5, 1990, the Treasury got its way, Labour foolishly signalled its approval. But the UK had joined the ERM at the worst possible moment and at the worst possible exchange rate (it was a salutary lesson to Brown and Balls that so many brilliant economists, politicians, officials and commentators only spotted this after the event: they swore never again to allow a "belief in Europe" cloud their economic judgement). The British economy was moving from boom to bust and it would become desperately urgent for interest rates to be cut. But the pressure on interest rates in Germany was all in an upward direction, to curb the inflationary impact of the reunification of East and West Germany. In those circumstances, if interest rates were cut in the UK the value of sterling would collapse, probably to a level below the minimum permitted by the ERM. Interest rates in Britain therefore had to remain painfully high.

Here was the fatal weakness in Brown's case for joining the ERM in the first place. Far from providing a deterrent to the currency speculators, as Brown had been arguing, the ERM actually encouraged speculators to sell sterling, because it was blindingly obvious that the British government could not resist the economic imperative to cut interest rates forever. Currency traders simply did not believe the government when it insisted it would never allow sterling to fall through its ERM floor.

What Brown learned, the hard way, was that a monetary system like the ERM is only a sound defence against the destructive activities of speculators if it is credible. And the problem with the ERM is that it wasn't credible, or at least British membership wasn't credible: our economy was too weak to bear the recessionary pressure of the interest rates that were forced on us by it. Selling the pound became a one-way bet, a sure thing. And if Labour had won the 1992 general election (until the very last moment, it looked as though it would do just this), a Labour Chancellor would once again have faced the kind of sterling crisis that Brown had believed the ERM would prevent. In a humiliating repeat of its interludes in office of the 1920s, the 1940s, the 1960s and 1970s, Labour would have found itself fighting a losing battle to defend an overvalued exchange rate. Yet again it would have been forced to capitulate: sterling would have been devalued and Labour's opponents would have painted it as the Party of the easy option, of soft money, of economic incompetence.

On this occasion, Kinnock, as Prime Minister, might have sensibly negotiated a lower, more sustainable ERM rate within hours of taking office – which would have been a lesser embarrassment than toughing it out for months before capitulating. Some of his advisers say that was the plan. But if there was a secret plot to devalue, Brown was told nothing about it – which is odd. And the Shadow Chancellor of the time, John Smith, confided to Brown that he had been into the Treasury a few days before the 1992 general election and discussed raising interest rates by a breathtaking two percentage points, precisely so that sterling would not collapse. Smith told Brown that a Labour government would endeavour to stay within the ERM at the exchange rate that it had inherited – which shows that if Labour was unlucky not to win the election, Smith and

Brown were extremely fortunate that it lost.

The notion of Brown as the living embodiment of monetary stability and prudence would have been laughable if he had been a pro-ERM minister in a Kinnock-led government on September 16, 1992, Black Wednesday, the day when sterling was forced out of the ERM. What's harder to judge is how badly Brown's reputation suffered as an opposition politician, as a result of having got it wrong on the ERM. Characteristically, he is in no doubt that his position – in the context of Labour's history – was the right one. His consistent refusal to call for a devaluation of the pound won him respect in the City for his monetary machismo, for defending sterling as staunchly as the Tories, or – at least – that is what he believes. He acknowledges there was a modest price, in that he upset many Labour MPs, who thought the ERM was crippling the economy. But alienating his colleagues became par for the course for Brown from 1992 onwards: it was almost a duty.

Even after the 1992 general election defeat, when Smith had become Labour leader and Brown was Shadow Chancellor, Brown did not waver in his support for the ERM. This is what he said in a speech on September 7, 1992 (at an event called "Europe and the world after 1992"), just nine days before sterling's forced exit from the ERM:

I want to suggest that the logic of events is not to abandon the ERM but to work to the principle of greater integration within Europe side by side with greater coordination beyond Europe, that would diminish speculative pressures, reduce the transaction costs that penalise industry, commerce and the mobility of citizens and make for the stability necessary for growth and prosperity.

It's striking that he rooted his support for the ERM firmly in the context of his wholehearted enthusiasm for the European Community (its guise after "EEC"). In 1992, he was a paid-up member of a pro-Europe lobby that was happy to see powers transferred from national parliaments to Brussels. Not any more. Brown no longer embraces the goal of "greater integration within Europe". It's the other sentiment, that of "greater coordination beyond Europe" that he has developed over the past decade. These days he argues that Europe as a whole needs to be more integrated with the global economy, while its national members must keep a certain distance from each other.

***

If the ERM debacle did not turn Brown into an opponent of European monetary union, it shaped forever his views about the practicalities of embarking on a great economic adventure of that kind. The fear of joining the euro at the wrong rate and the wrong time overwhelmed his innate pro-Europeanism when he became Chancellor. But the task of translating this anxiety into a coherent policy was to fall from late 1992 onwards to Ed Balls.

In December 1992, Balls – who was then an opinionated, 25-year-old leader writer on the *FT* – published a Fabian Society discussion paper, "Euro-Monetarism: why Britain was ensnared and how it should escape". Brown likes to tease Balls that he never actually read the paper – although Balls sent it to him in draft in the autumn of 1992 and they discussed it. This was the start of the courtship which eventually led to the young economist going to work for the Shadow Chancellor in January 1994.

What's remarkable about this document is the extent to which it foreshadows both Brown's eventual approach to the euro and the transfer of control over interest rates to the Bank of England. Balls was analysing the 1992 Maastricht Treaty, which committed EU members to merge their currencies towards the end of the decade. His paper says: "Monetary union, in the manner and timetable envisaged in the treaty is an economically and politically misconceived project." It warns that the "timetable is rigid and overly ambitious while the treaty's inflation and fiscal convergence criteria are likely to impose slow growth and high unemployment". And it says that EMU (or Economic and Monetary Union) "would not deliver the stability, growth and full employment that Britain and Europe need".

Much of Balls's analysis was prophetic: the euro zone suffers from low growth and high unemployment (though Balls wrongly predicted that Germany would continue to be the economic powerhouse of Europe and that it would be other states that suffered). However, Brown himself would never and has never said anything as hostile to monetary union as Balls's early thesis. And even Balls tempered his opposition to the European single currency in the mid-1990s, in tune with the largely pro-euro sentiment of the Labour Party. One example was the influential paper he presented to Brown and Blair in the spring of 1995, called "The Macroeconomic Framework", which argued that creating an independent central bank, with control over interest rates, would be seen as a step on the way to joining the euro — and that was a good thing. It says:

> The status of the Bank of England and the making of monetary policy is important from a European perspective, given that the Maastricht Treaty requires moves towards independence. Howard Davies [then director general of the business lobby group, the Confederation of British Industry] has said that our attitude to the Bank of England will be the most important test of whether Labour is seriously committed to European integration. Obviously this will not be a prime reason for change – at least publicly and before the next election – but it is a consideration worth bearing in mind. Indeed as the European debate moves on to consider the possibility of monetary union in 1999 or beyond, the willingness of a Labour government to act in accordance with the Maastricht Treaty will be viewed with increasing importance both domestically and within Europe.

In the end, the blueprint for Bank of England reform adopted by Brown in 1997 was not consisted with the Maastricht Treaty (see Chapter Four). In fact the arrangements he put in place for setting interest rates turned out to be an alternative to joining the euro. But back in the mid-

1990s, Brown's priority was to keep his options open on the single currency, while his rhetoric was largely that of the ardent EU fan. Here's the euro-enthusiast Brown in a 1994 speech (taken from a Labour archive of his speeches, though the precise time and date of delivery has been lost and its heading is the unpromising "Europe: Investment, Global Economy and Long Term Success"):

> For us, the key question is how we can, through greater co-operation, achieve the degree of integration and convergence necessary, not just of inflation rates but growth and unemployment too. And in doing so, (we would) ensure that monetary union can not only begin but be sustained... Britain cannot afford for ever a government attitude which sees us hovering half in and half out for ever. The case must be made for full participation in Europe's future.

If this implied that Brown was keen to participate in European Monetary Union, that he was pro-single currency, that was certainly what I believed at the time. And as political editor of the *FT* from the beginning of 1995, I was seeing a great deal of both Brown and Balls. Neither of them explicitly said to me that they had a cunning plan to take the UK into the euro. But I didn't press them hard on this, mostly because it seemed irrelevant. It was highly uncertain that the euro would ever be launched: John Major and his cabinet, for example, were not persuaded that monetary union would become a reality until quite close to the 1997 general election.

These days, however, Brown and Balls insist they were always "realists" about the economic risks of monetary union, that they would never have advocated membership if there was the danger of damage to the British economy. And in 1996 – in the two most important European speeches he made while Shadow Chancellor – Brown began to construct the economic arguments that would eventually serve to keep the UK outside the euro zone. They were given in Bonn and Paris in May 1996 and are similar in tone and content. This is what Brown said in Bonn:

For currency union to work with Britain as a member, there is a minimum level of economic integration which must first be achieved, and minimum levels of accountability and transparency in European policy making. Without such convergence, currencies would be locked together without regard to differing economic circumstances, and, for the weaker economies, that could mean substantial rises in unemployment.

Unlike Blair at the time – whose focus was almost exclusively the domestic agenda – Brown was taking steps to deepen his knowledge of the EU's agenda and cultivating relationships with finance ministers. I witnessed this at first hand, when I was the sole journalist who accompanied him on the 1996 trip to Paris (whose logistics had been arranged by Balls in a preparatory visit, a month earlier). The Gaullist Finance Minister, Jean Arthuis, treated Brown as though he were already Chancellor – which was in part due to the French government's frustration with the eurosceptic drift of John Major's government. At a stylish dinner Arthuis hosted in a sumptuous, tapestry-walled private room of the 18th century Restaurant Laperouse – which was also attended by his opposite number from the Socialist Party, the flamboyant Dominique Strauss-Kahn – Arthuis implied that he had more in common with a pro-European Labour Party than with his putative right-wing soul mates in the Conservative Party. Brown's message to Arthuis was that he could not commit to joining the euro, because that would be electoral suicide in a UK dominated by a euro-sceptic press and where all the opinion polls indicated public hostility to the single currency. But the Shadow Chancellor said that he wanted to be in a position to sign up at the earliest practical opportunity (which was less disingenuous than it seems now).

While Brown was schmoozing EU ministers, Balls was getting to grips with the minutiae of European policymaking, with the help of Sir Nigel Wicks, a second Permanent Secretary at the Treasury (in effect number two in the department) who was also the influential Chairman of the EU's secretive and powerful monetary committee. Wicks is the

British civil servant who took European politicians' dreams of merging their currencies and turned them into a reality through the diligence of the technical preparations overseen by his committee (the irony that it was a methodical, British official who built the euro zone is stupendous). He is a stickler for form, who would never have talked to an opposition special adviser such as Balls in his capacity as a senior Treasury official. However, there was apparently a clause in the mandarin's secret code of conduct that meant he felt able to guide Balls when wearing his EU hat.

The establishment of a relationship with Wicks at this point was useful to Balls – and it became invaluable during early squalls in government. Balls also capitalised on Brown's friendship with the Irish Finance Minister of the mid-1990s, Rory Quinn, especially when Ireland occupied the EU presidency in the second half of 1996. The young Labour official would go to Brussels in advance of meetings of European Finance Ministers – gathered in a committee called Ecofin – and would be handed most of the relevant briefing documents by the Irish delegation. It meant he had an inside track on most of the important euro policy issues in the run up to the general election.

At this juncture, Tony Blair was much more interested in how the European issue was playing in the UK than in the detail of euro policy-making. Although Labour was well ahead in the opinion polls, Blair was worried that its pro-Europeanism was a potential weakness – especially when it came to winning the backing of British newspapers, most of which were sceptical about the European Union in general and were also opposed to the euro. The newspapers that Blair most wanted on his side, Rupert Murdoch's *Sun* and the *Daily Mail*, were rabidly anti-euro.

It was all the tougher for Labour to remain even lukewarm believers in monetary union when the Tory Party under John Major was moving in a much more eurosceptic direction (particularly in its use of language, if not the substance of policy). Major was not a fan of monetary union, but he was also not a headbanging sceptic. He took the principled position that it would be wrong to rule out membership for the lifetime of up to five years of the subsequent parliament – which is what a majority of his backbenchers wanted him to do. It was theoretically possible, Major felt, that staying outside the single currency area would wreak significant damage on the British economy.

However, he could not be totally deaf to the clamour from his own MPs. So in March 1996, Major announced that there would be a referendum, in the unlikely event that a Tory government were ever to recommend entry into the euro. This caused a dilemma for Brown. He wanted at all costs to keep open the option of joining the euro, but would that be achieved by making a copycat pledge to hold a plebiscite? Or would conceding a referendum deliver a morale-boosting victory to the eurosceptics in the Labour Party and the media, which they would then attempt to convert into outright opposition to the single currency?

Brown finally decided to make a referendum pledge, partly because he calculated that he would not otherwise be able to hold the line against ruling out euro membership for at least the term of a parliament (it's striking that this should have mattered so much to him at the time, given subsequent events). And characteristically he was determined that he, not Blair, should make the announcement. So, on November 17, 1996, he said in an interview in the *Independent on Sunday* that the electorate would be polled on the single currency if the Cabinet ever decided to join.

Brown's evaluation of the prevailing mood on Europe was very similar to that of his opposite number across the floor of the Commons, Ken Clarke, the Tory Chancellor. For this robust leader of the beleaguered pro-European tendency in the Conservative Party, Major's pledge to hold a euro plebiscite was almost intolerable. After Labour followed Major's example, Clarke feared that he might no longer be able to resist a further lurch towards outright hostility to monetary union in official Conservative Party policy. If Labour moved any further in an anti-euro direction, his own ability to persuade Major to give no more ground to the eurosceptics would be lost. So he asked his political aide, Anthony Teasdale, to do some sleuthing and – eventually – to send a secret message across party lines, to ascertain where Labour's policy on the euro would end up (see below, pages 196-7). The sporadic cross-party dialogue may have helped to dissuade Blair from adopting a more anti-euro policy: it would be useful to Labour to sustain Clarke as a divisive force at the heart of the Tory Party.

However, Blair was saying in private briefings at the time that he had profound doubts about whether it would ever be right to join the euro. He said this to me as late as the beginning of 1997. In other words, in 1996 and 1997 it was Brown who wanted the flexibility to join the euro, while Blair was much more hostile to monetary union – which looks like the precise inverse of where they were to stand in 2003. But Brown's position may have changed slightly less than is apparent. He's always been determined to retain the option of going in to the euro zone, even if he's never been committed to a firm date for entry. By contrast, some time in the autumn of 1997, Blair started to become much keener on joining the single currency – although this did not become particularly visible until 1999. Meanwhile, the position of Ed Balls on the euro has been fairly consistent, largely because he's always put great weight on the economic costs of joining prematurely. Either enthusiastically (Brown) or reluctantly (Blair), his more senior colleagues have ultimately adopted Balls's approach and recommendations.

Balls played his trump in the power game over euro membership in February 1997, when he and Brown were trying to come up with a more sophisticated policy that would enable them to answer the question, "Are you in favour of monetary union?" with something more than generalisations and platitudes that satisfied almost no one, least of all a eurosceptic media. Their solution – which for reasons best known to them they decided to announce while on a trip to the US to see the Treasury Secretary, Robert Rubin – was to establish five "British economic tests", to be applied as the criteria for making the decision on whether to sign up for monetary union. I was the first journalist to write about the tests (which I did in the February 20 edition of the *FT*), having been briefed by Balls in a phone-call to my office in the press gallery of the House of Commons, while he was looking over New York's East River. But I did not have the faintest idea that they were going to be so important in shaping the UK's future relationship with the European Union (I remember thinking that it was rather a dull story).

At the time the five tests (which were refined a little in the autumn) were:

- Whether European countries were at different stages of the economic cycle
- Whether members would have the economic flexibility to cope with shocks
- The impact on employment
- The impact on investment
- The impact on the City

Among political journalists, the received wisdom is that Balls made these up in the back of a New York taxi cab. When that's put to him, he becomes a little huffy – for the obvious reason that it would not be dignified for the UK's political and economic future to have been decided in such a carefree (and possibly careless) way. And to be fair to Brown and Balls, the tests are consistent with the general thrust of Brown's Bonn and Paris speeches of 1996. But for all that, he and Brown did put the finishing touches to them while being driven in a taxi. This was in keeping with the frenetic pace of their lives at the time and with their slightly manic attempts to stay one step ahead of their political opponents.

Inevitably, they had accidents. On this occasion, Charlie Whelan – Brown's political adviser on media matters who had remarkable licence to interpret and pursue his employer's objectives – put out a statement the following day on the newswires reporting that Brown had outlined the important five new tests to Robert Rubin, the US Treasury Secretary, in a private meeting. But Whelan had somehow calculated the time difference between New York and London incorrectly, so the story was running a full hour before the meeting had happened – which Rubin's deputy, Larry Summers, pointed out to Balls with some relish (there was history here: Balls had been Summers's know-all student at Harvard).

In the end, the five tests were what kept the UK out of the euro. But when they were first announced, Brown tried to temper the impression that he was putting a big block in the way of joining the currency. He insisted that he was retaining Labour's determination to join the euro "in the next parliament and in the first wave" if "the economic conditions are right". And he also manifested another sign of his pro euro instincts on the same US trip.

He had agreed with Blair that he would say in a BBC interview that there were "formidable obstacles" to joining the euro. This was a gambit to stoke up the Tory civil war over the single currency (the Foreign Secretary, Malcolm Rifkind, had just said that the Tories were "on balance... hostile" to monetary union, a view that was immediately denounced by Clarke). Anyway, the BBC's chief political correspondent, John Sergeant, had flown to the US for an interview with Brown, having been promised that the Shadow Chancellor would use the "formidable obstacle" words. Sergeant would have a scoop – that Labour had become significantly more hostile to monetary union – for the following morning's *Today* Programme. But Brown steadfastly refused to use the phrase.

After 45 minutes of recording Brown, with Balls trying to gee-up Brown and calm down Sergeant, the bluff BBC correspondent switched the recorder off and gave up. Why couldn't Brown bring himself to say it? Well his commitment to the pro-European cause was sufficiently deep for him to balk at the intense pressure from Blair and his aides to kowtow to the eurosceptic press. And when the formula "formidable obstacles" was finally deployed less than two months later, it was not used by Brown but by his keenest political rival, Robin Cook, the Shadow Foreign Secretary.

It may seem odd now, but the most dangerous division within the Shadow Cabinet in 1997 was between Brown and Cook, not between Brown and Blair. Cook's priorities at the time appeared to be first to exert an influence on the euro debate (Brown always tried to shut him out) and second – by a whisker – to get one over on Brown. His reputation was as passionately hostile to the euro, which was a deliberate contrast with

Brown's putatively pro-euro stance (within a couple of years, Cook would be seen as fervently pro-euro, as Brown became perceived as more cautious). So it was piquant that Cook should have said, in an interview on London Weekend Television with Jonathan Dimbleby, that there were "formidable obstacles" in the way of joining the euro at the 1999 launch date. Even more significantly, Cook added that it was "very difficult to see a government that has taken the decision that Britain wasn't [joining] in 1999 coming to the decision that it would be ready by the year after, or the year after that" – so "the probability is that it is looking towards the subsequent parliament".

This was explosive stuff. The campaign for the May 1 general election had started. And Labour, in the shape of Cook, was apparently ruling out joining the euro for the entire term of a new government – which was a eurosceptic trump that not even the Tories had tried to play. Brown was livid and stamped on it. He glossed Cook's statement as a prediction that Europe as a whole would not be ready for the euro at the scheduled date in 1999: nothing about Labour's basic attitude to the project should be read into his colleague's words, Brown said. But, for Blair, it was helpful that his Shadow Chancellor and Shadow Foreign Secretary were facing in different directions on Europe: they made it easier for him to appear ambivalent.

Extraordinary as it may seem, Blair feared up till the last moment that Labour could lose the 1997 general election and that a word out of place on Europe – especially a pro European one – could be its undoing. This was brought home to me in January 1997, when I interviewed him about the European Union. Here was a short hiatus in a media campaign conducted by him in patriotic rhetoric that bordered on chauvinism: he wanted to use the medium of the *FT* to send out a positive message on Europe to other EU governments (it was a characteristic example of him saying one thing to EU heads of state and another to the British electorate – a skill he would hone when Prime Minister). However, just before the *FT* went to press, Blair rang me to express concern and regret that he had said something that implied he was relaxed about a possible extension of majority voting in EU decision-making. He feared that the subtlety of his constitutional argument would be lost on the eurosceptics of the press and Tory Party, who would paint him as surrendering the great British veto that prevented Brussels imposing its will on us. Could I please reassure him that the story would be handled sensitively? I was astonished. The notion that some woolly remarks about the minutiae of EU voting arrangements could seriously damage Labour did not compute. But it is what he believed, in part because he was desperate for the public backing of the euro-hating *Sun* newspaper – and Labour did not receive the *Sun's* endorsement until March 18.

As the general election loomed nearer, Blair became increasingly desperate to minimise the impact of the Conservatives' charge that "Labour is selling out to Europe" (one notorious Tory poster had Blair sitting on the knee of Germany's then Chancellor, Helmut Kohl, looking like a ventriloquist's dummy). His use of nationalistic symbolism verged on the absurd. Blair – reinforcing the bonds with Murdoch – put his name to an article in the *Sun* on April 22 in which he wrote, "On the day we remember the legend that St George slayed a dragon to protect England, some will argue that there is another dragon to be slayed: Europe." Perhaps the most surreal moment was when Blair's closest ally and adviser, Peter Mandelson – the *ne plus ultra* of Europhiles – led out a British bulldog at a press conference. To describe this as disingenuous doesn't really do it justice.

Meanwhile, within the government, Ken Clarke, the Chancellor, disliked the way that his party, the Conservatives, seemed to be in a game of leapfrog with Labour over which of them could be the most hostile to monetary union and Europe. He wanted to know whether Labour would cease its eurosceptic jumps: if it didn't, there was no way that he would be able to prevent John Major from adopting a more explicit policy of opposition to the euro. Anthony Teasdale, his advisor, therefore asked for clarification of where Labour was heading on all this from Roger Liddle, a political consultant for whom Teasdale had done some work in the early 1990s. Liddle – who is a close friend of Peter Mandelson (and who worked for Blair on European policy in the Downing Street Policy Unit from 1997 to 2004) – took soundings and then called Teasdale. He told Teasdale: "Do you remember that thing you were asking me (whether Labour would rule out joining the euro for the duration of the next parliament)? Well it's not going to happen."

Fortunately for Clarke, Blair had calculated that in an unbridled contest with the Tories on which of them could be the most beastly about the supposedly meddling Europeans, the Tories would win. There was even a terrifying risk for Blair that, if Major became wholeheartedly anti-euro, Labour might lose some of its precious media support. So it was in Blair's interest to give hope to Ken Clarke and the other Tory Europhiles that there was a fight worth fighting on Europe. Also the electorates' perception of a Conservative Party in the grips of a civil war between the pro-Europeans and the anti-Europeans was hugely valuable to Labour. Blair's eurosceptical drift went so far, but no further.

However, there were lasting consequences from Labour's opportunistic waving of the union flag. Having voiced his doubts about European integration, Blair had limited his ability to argue the pro-European case with credibility for some years. The *Sun* newspaper had bought his patriotic line and would not give it up lightly. For the following couple of years, the tabloid that wields the most clout in 10 Downing Street – along with much of the media – persisted in perpetuating the conceit that Blair was the staunch defender of British sovereignty, especially when it came to whether the UK should join the single currency, whereas Brown was painted as a misguided Europhile. This gap between perception and reality became more confusing in November, when Blair and Brown – as members of a new government that needed to make a real decision on whether to join the euro – seemed to lose their European bearings altogether.

***

On May 1, just before the magnitude of Labour's landslide was confirmed, the Treasury was gearing up for the arrival of a Chancellor who was viewed – by senior officials – as in favour of joining the European single currency. Lord Burns (then Sir Terry Burns), the Permanent Secretary, believed that a decision to go for the euro could be taken quickly by the new administration, so he commissioned a paper from a bright, young official, Tom Scholar, on how the Bank of England would have to be reformed in preparation for monetary union (see page 130). However, in those early months after the election, Brown refused to disclose his hand on the euro, in public or to his new Treasury colleagues. "We assumed he was in favour of the euro, that he was pro-European, because that's the expectation we had before he arrived," says a former senior official. "And although he did nothing to persuade us we were wrong, he said nothing that confirmed this view either."

The experience of government would in fact quickly influence Brown's positive views about the European Union. When he attended the regular meetings of Ecofin, the committee of European finance ministers, he felt more isolated than he had expected. A desire on the part of his fellow ministers to harmonise and integrate European taxes – which was anathema to him – turned out not to be the hysterical fabrication of the British eurosceptic lobby. He was surrounded by European politicians who were less questioning than he was about whether it was sensible to transfer more powers from national members of the EU to the EU's own decision-making bodies. The alleged plot of the French and Germans to create a "European superstate" or a United States of Europe was not quite the myth he had thought it was.

He became the lonely advocate, or so he thought, of a hardnosed economic agenda of encouraging the completion of Europe's single market, of promoting competition between companies throughout the EU, of preventing an escalation of the costs of doing business in Europe. But he revelled in being one against the rest: it was almost a conscious act of homage to Mrs Thatcher, with whom he has more in common than he would probably choose to admit (such as – on the positive side – tremendous tenacity and an ability to think strategically; and, less attractively, a

198

mistrust of those who are not "one of us"). His obstructionist tactics seemed to pay off when – after years of arguing and lobbying – he finally blocked a European savings (or withholding) tax, in 2000.

Brown became persuaded that he would rather beat his fellow ministers than join them. He never became explicitly hostile to the EU. But his credo became one of nationalistic support for Europe – a pragmatic view that the EU was a good thing only insofar as it delivered practical benefits of peace and prosperity to Britain.

Meanwhile, Blair's experience as Prime Minister of conducting business in Europe was moving him in precisely the opposition direction. He was frustrated that his words did not resonate with his fellow government heads on the Council of Ministers as much as he would have liked. It became plain that unless and until the UK signed up for the euro – as unambiguous proof that Blair was breaking definitively with the half-in and half-out approach to Europe of John Major and Margaret Thatcher – they would not wholly trust him. Blair's publicly stated desire to transform the UK into one of the EU's most influential members – an agenda-setter, not the agenda-spoiler that it became under the Tories – explains why he gradually became a keener advocate of monetary union.

But even with the UK outside the euro zone, Blair's pragmatism and charm significantly improved relations with the rest of the EU (until the chill that was brought on by the build-up to his decision to follow the US into battle in Iraq during 2002 and 2003, when France and Germany were urging restraint). In private conversations with EU heads of governments and senior Brussels officials, he consistently sent out as positive a message as he could about Britain's attitude to the euro. As early as a month or so after the election, Blair told the then President of the European Commission, Jacques Santer, that "although Britain would be unable to join (the euro) in 1999, he hoped any delay would be short" (according to Blair's Economic Adviser at the time, Derek Scott: *Off Whitehall*, 2004). However, during his debut, there was a startling sign that he slightly over-rated his own persuasive powers.

In the early summer of 1997, Blair gathered his most senior advisers and colleagues – Jonathan Powell, his Chief of Staff, and Lord (Robin) Butler, the Cabinet Secretary and head of the home civil service, plus Brown, Wicks and Balls – to talk over whether it was remotely sensible to join the euro right from the start at the January 1999 launch-date. There would be a cost to Britain's reputation in the EU if it refused to participate. But the new Prime Minister reassured his team that the decision might be less pressing than they thought. He would ring up his friend, Chancellor Kohl of Germany, and ask him to delay the project till Britain was ready. Wicks, in *haut*-mandarin mode, congratulated Blair on a "great strategy, Prime Minister", with an almost indiscernible trace of irony: there was no chance of the EU postponing the start of monetary union.

Brown, by this time, had made only one serious public foray into the territory of setting euro policy. In a speech on July 17 at the Royal Institute of Foreign Affairs in London, he announced that he would set up an advisory group of business leaders to advise on practical issues arising from monetary union (which eventually became a more broadly based group of business, City and trade union grandees, whose role was to devise a National Changeover Plan for swapping pounds into euros, in preparation for the moment – whenever it might come – that the UK joined the euro zone). Brown also said that "today the government is throwing open the EMU debate" – which is quite funny in retrospect, because eight years on the government is still incredibly uptight about what any minister says on the merits and drawbacks of Economic and Monetary Union (EMU). So the speech was more significant for what happened during its preparation. Blair had been kept in the dark about its contents until close to the date it was delivered and he felt Brown had encouraged the media to interpret it as unduly positive towards the single currency. Mutual distrust between the Treasury and 10 Downing Street on this vital issue was already deeply ingrained.

Brown's relative failure, during the first months in office, to map out a more detailed euro policy for his Treasury officials was incongruous for a politician obsessed with removing as much dangerous uncertainty as possible from his political life. But he was still feeling his way, still agonising about what the right position was, while fully engaged on matters that seemed more pressing (like preparing his first budget which was due on July 1). At the same time, Treasury officials tried to inter-act with him in the way that they had with previous Chancellors: they sent papers to him urging that he write to the Prime Minister with an outline euro strategy. He never did, largely because he wasn't willing to commit anything to paper, least of all for distribution to 10 Downing Street, until he was absolutely sure, down to the minutest detail, that he had a robust policy – which Balls, in consultation with Wicks, was at a very early stage of preparing.

In the meantime, there were risks in allowing a policy vacuum – as became clear within days of the election, when a story with a Brussels dateline appeared on the newswires early one morning saying that the government was considering rejoining the European Exchange Rate Mechanism as a precursor to monetary union. Investors thought it was true which is odd since Brown was by this stage sending out unambiguous signals that he had become implacably opposed to re-entering the ERM (he never believed that it was in practice necessary to sign up for the ERM as a first stage towards monetary union, even though that was a condition of the Maastricht Treaty). Sterling sunk like a stone, because traders assumed that if the pound did rejoin the ERM, it would have to be at a lower exchange rate than the prevailing one. At 10am on that day, Balls learned about the currency volatility and rushed to see the Treasury's director of communications, Jill Rutter, to find out what was going on. Rutter said she had assumed – wrongly – that Balls had planted the story, so she was talking to Wicks about what the Treasury's "official" statement would be. Balls was furious. After talking to Wicks and Balls, Rutter eventually put out a denial that re-entry to the ERM was on the cards. However, the incident helped to sour relations between her and Brown's clique of advisers – which is a shame, because she is a brainy and dedicated public servant.

The cock-up was a precursor of a genuine crisis in the autumn that stemmed largely from this same absence of a clear policy. Balls, however, tried to move the debate along in a meeting before Parliament's summer recess with Gordon Brown and Geoffrey Robinson, who was then Brown's closest ministerial colleague as Paymaster General. In his autobiography, *The Unconventional Minister*, Robinson describes the conversation, which mostly consists of Balls explaining why joining in the first term would be too dangerous. Balls stressed the risk that the British economy was neither strong enough or flexible enough to withstand any serious shocks as a member of the euro zone. Robinson agreed with him. But Robinson says Brown was non-committal. He says:

> Gordon listened for the most part. He could see the obvious political attractions of being in the EMU; but it was clear, too, that he saw the real dangers of premature entry. The discussion of EMU rather petered out.

And that summer, Brown told one of his oldest friends that he hoped to take the UK into the euro shortly after the 1999 launch. Even so, Balls was persuaded that Brown was heading towards ruling out membership for at least a few years.

In the first week of September, Balls went to see Wicks, who concurred with Brown's young and influential consiglieri that it would be wrong to join at the launch date in 1999. But the problem remained of how to keep the option open of going in later, without making the government vulnerable to constant speculation about when it might happen. This was a keen concern of the Treasury, which had acute and painful memories of the "noise" generated in the run-up to ERM entry in 1990, as journalists and MPs constantly speculated about whether the so-called Madrid conditions for signing up had been met and whether the UK would join within days or weeks or months. All that media and political chatter made it much harder for Thatcher and Major to weigh up the pros and cons of joining in a cool and rational way, which in part explains why the UK ultimately joined at the wrong time and the wrong exchange rate.

The best way to stifle speculation and obtain sufficient stability, Balls and Wicks concluded, was to make it clear that membership was unlikely for the lifetime of the parliament (or till after the general election, which would be in 2001). All they needed now was the assent of the Chancellor and the Prime Minister. In the meantime, they were neurotic that there might be a leak of their preference, which would shake financial markets and prompt a furious backlash from the europhiles. To prevent this, they told their conclusions to no one and instructed Treasury officials to draft a paper which would discuss seven different euro scenarios – from joining in the first wave to ruling it out for the foreseeable future. The officials were asked to write the relevant five paragraphs for each of these different scenarios, with the intention that one of the euro vignettes would be included in a future statement by the Chancellor to the House of Commons.

Balls and Wicks knew which of these scenarios they wanted Brown to pick. Brown himself was aware of the direction in which they were heading (and, by the way, this was a classic example of the way he works, which is never to make a final decision until there has been a detailed evaluation of all possible options). However, the Prime Minister did not have the faintest idea what the Treasury was up to.

Now this is where I became an accidental protagonist, rather than simply a chronicler. On September 26, 1997, I wrote a story for the *Financial Times* under the headline "Cabinet shifts towards EMU". It began: "The government is on the point of adopting a much more positive approach to European economic and monetary union, with a statement shortly that sterling is likely to join at an early opportunity after the 1999 launch." I'd written this primarily on the basis of conversations with officials and ministers close to Blair and in the Foreign Office. They had become much less hesitant than they had been only a few months before about how they wanted to sign up for the euro within only a few short years of 1999. This was significant – or so it seemed to me – since the main opposition to joining the euro in the run-up to the general election had come from Cook and Blair. However, although I talked to my contacts in the Treasury, one of them misunderstood what I was planning to write. For reasons that I don't understand, he thought I was on the verge of writing a story that the government was to rule out euro membership, which was too strong a version of what was under consideration – so he pushed me too far in the "options open" direction. Also, like most observers of the political scene, I remained persuaded that Brown was in favour of going for monetary union sooner rather than later. In retrospect, what my story should have said was "Government in disarray over euro policy" – which is what became crystal clear within just a few days. But the immediate consequences of my article were remarkable. The FTSE100 share index jumped 160.8 points, which was a record at the time, the price of gilt-edged stock soared and sterling shed 4.1 pfennigs (having at one stage during the day been 6 pfennigs lower). My head swelled to a disgusting size when on September 29, Gavyn Davies – who was then the chief international economist at the investment bank, Goldman Sachs, and was a close friend of Blair and Brown – wrote in the *Independent* newspaper: "Robert Peston, the *Financial Times* journalist whose work nowadays has more impact on the markets than the budget speech itself, set the cat among the pigeons on Friday…" Meanwhile the response of Gordon Brown's influential political spokesman, Charlie Whelan, was to describe the article as "bollocks" – which was his trademark "non-denial denial" (Whelan had at some point disclosed to political journalists that "bollocks" was a term of art for rubbishing stories that weren't, in fact, untrue). In the subsequent few weeks, assorted cabinet members congratulated me on the scoop – which goes to show how far out of the loop most of the Cabinet was.

From this moment of market mayhem, well over a month was to elapse before a definitive euro policy was nailed down. And there would be more and worse embarrassments for the government along the way. The first gaffe was on a visit to Italy by the Chancellor in early October, when he was accompanied by Balls, Whelan, Robinson and a gang of journalists (including myself). I can't remember what the ostensible reason for the trip was, but have a vague memory that Brown had organised a chat with the Italian Finance Minister. The real reason for the trip was that England was scheduled to play Italy in a crucial qualifying match for the World Cup finals and Robinson – whose skills as a provider of hospitality are world class – had persuaded the Football Association to find 11 tickets for us. The problem arose the following morning, when Brown, Whelan and Balls endeavoured to provide a "genuine story" to those reporters who feared that their employers might question whether watching a famous England success (a nil-nil draw that guaranteed a place in the World Cup finals) was what they were being employed to do. So the Chancellor's team briefed details of the UK's so-called "convergence programme", or statistics which showed that Britain would comfortably meet the economic and financial criteria for participating in monetary union set down in the Maastricht Treaty.

In retrospect, Balls and Whelan were naïve (to an almost incredible extent), since they believed the data on trends to public sector debt and budget deficits would be written up as evidence of the UK's strong public finances. In the feverish atmosphere of the time, journalists instead interpreted their swanking that there were no formal obstacles to joining the euro as evidence that a decision to join had to be only days away. The *Daily Mail* used the briefing as the hook for an article that was very similar to the one I had written the previous month – though the *Mail*'s tone was more sensational. The media was doing the thing that was anathema to New Labour, with its obsessive need for control: it was running with an agenda not of the government's choosing.

The reaction of 10 Downing Street was fast and furious. Alastair Campbell, who was then the Prime Minister's Press Secretary, telephoned Balls in a rage demanding to know why he and Brown were "bouncing the government into the euro". Balls had flown to Luxembourg for an Ecofin meeting and had retreated to his hotel room with flu. His defence to Campbell was that he and Brown could not be held accountable for "mad" journalists. Now, at the time, Campbell's "favourite" journalist – as he took pride in saying at Downing Street briefings – was the late Anthony Bevins, political editor of the *Independent*. It is reasonable to assume that an article by Bevins on the front page of the *Independent* the following day stemmed from a conversation with Campbell. It said:

> The Treasury is trying to bounce Tony Blair into a decision which could lead to the early death of the pound. Sources close to the Chancellor of the Exchequer are actively briefing selected reporters that Mr Blair is poised to announce early membership of the single currency, as soon as possible after the first-wave launch in 1999....
>
> There are signs that the Chancellor, Gordon Brown, could be over-reaching himself, by trying to bounce the Prime Minister, the country and sterling into a single currency. Mr Brown, who is said to regard himself as the government's managing director – with Mr Blair as non-executive chairman – could be under-estimating the Prime Minister's determination not to repeat past mistakes, particularly the disastrous decision to join the European Exchange Rate mechanism in 1990.

This was the first manifestation of a serious conflict between Downing Street and Treasury, between the respective gangs of Blair and Brown. And the dispute appeared to be over the most important policy issue of all. But there was a mind-boggling solecism at the heart of Bevins's article: for in reality, Brown was not actively trying to bounce Blair into joining the euro and Blair was becoming much keener on the euro (as became clear within days). In fact, at this particular moment, their views on the euro were probably not that far apart. So, in a pattern that would be repeated again and again over the subsequent years, the fight (which was real) between Brown and Blair was probably precipitated more by mutual mistrust and jockeying for position than by principle.

Even so, Brown was worried. Having witnessed the disagreement between Lawson and Thatcher in the late 1980s over whether to join the ERM, he feared that when there is a conspicuous rift between Chancellor and Prime Minister, both end up losing, although the Chancellor is usually the first casualty. Perhaps Brown would be the exception to that rule. But he wasn't going to test the theory so early in the life of the parliament. So the dispute had to be ended and fast. Unfortunately, the method chosen for settling the row precipitated a worse crisis.

Brown had by now made up his mind to rule out membership of the single currency at the launch date of 1999 and for the lifetime of the parliament. In the preceding weeks, it had become clear that the risks of political and economic instability from keeping the option open were simply too great. If the decision against joining were not taken, the whole of his first term as Chancellor would be marred by speculation about when the government would sign up for monetary union, which could create all sorts of tension between senior ministers – or so he feared. This was a momentous conclusion for a country whose political and media classes were (and are) obsessed by Europe. And such was its constitutional importance that it had to be announced to parliament before the wider world was told. But parliament was in recess. Also Balls had already made an agreement with Jonathan Powell – the Prime Minister's Chief of Staff – that the Chancellor would make his statement to parliament on November 12 (though characteristically, Balls did not tell Powell what that statement might say). The idea was that Blair would be the warm-up act on the big day, giving a pro-European speech in the morning to the annual meeting of the CBI, the lobby group for big companies' executives (who, at the time, were largely enamoured of Blair and he of them), before Brown dropped his bombshell at the House of Commons in the afternoon.

When Bevins's story appeared on Tuesday October 14, there was still around a month to go, which was too long for Brown, who feared there could be any number of further accidents and skirmishes with Downing Street. So he, Balls, Whelan and Alastair Campbell decided to employ a tactic that had been very effective in opposition – but would turn out to be controversial (to put it mildly) in government. They decided to leak the government's euro intentions to a friendly journalist on a friendly newspaper.

Blair had been kept almost totally ignorant of the Treasury's euro plans until this point, but a Chancellor could not rule out joining the single currency for some years without informing his Prime Minister. Brown went to see him and – as is par for the course for these two – no one else was with them to take notes and ensure they really were on the same wavelength (this habitual informality is a break with the longstanding custom and practice of the British system of government, that there should be thorough noting of meetings between a Prime Minister and his Chancellor).

The Chancellor came away persuaded that Blair had given his consent to ruling out the euro for the duration of the parliament and also for the device of floating the decision in the press. However, subsequent events were to prove that Blair did not regard their conversation as quite so definitive (such confusion seems to be a characteristic of their relationship: my impression is that Brown is not always as blunt and explicit in discussions of tricky issues as he might be, and Blair dislikes pressing him). Still, Blair had taken in enough to brief Campbell in a fairly unspecific way about what Brown was proposing to do.

Separately, Whelan and Balls were discussing which newspaper should be given the scoop. Balls recommended Philip Webster, political editor of the *Times*, who is an unusual member of the parliamentary lobby – the collective term for British political reporters – in that he's trusted by MPs of all parties (he goes to football with the Brownites and plays golf with Tory whips and Downing Street press officers). Equally important in the context of a New Labour government, he's liked by officials from both the Blairite faction and Brown's cohort and was regarded by both as an exceptionally safe pair of hands.

Although Balls was at home in Islington, still suffering from flu and writing a speech that would become the definitive account of the government's monetary reforms (a lecture to the Scottish Economic Society given on October 22, 1997 – see page 133), he informed Campbell that Webster had been selected. The choreography, which was to be overseen by Balls, was that Webster was to be offered an interview with Brown. The Chancellor would not say the words, "We are ruling out membership of the single currency for the lifetime of the parliament". But he would make some comments – on how the Tories had made a terrible mistake in the way they had kept open the option of joining the ERM eight years earlier – from which Webster would be steered by Balls to form the appropriate conclusion.

The operation had to be handled with immense care. Brown had already offended the sensibilities of the Speaker of the House of Commons once before, in May, when he announced independence for the Bank of England in a press release, before making a statement to MPs. Miss Boothroyd would not be amused if the Chancellor repeated the grotesque breach of parliamentary form. So a balance had to be struck between getting the message out through the *Times* while not actually making the historic declaration. As it happens, this was probably an impossible task, but it was made more difficult by a chronic lack of co-ordination between Brown's political team, the official Treasury press office and Downing Street (time and again this government would be embarrassed by a lack of trust between Brown's people and Blair's people, although the gulf between Brown's political team and the rest of the Treasury was closed within a year).

Anyway, Balls telephoned Webster on the morning of Friday, October 17, to map out in general terms what was proposed. At midday Balls rang again to say that the great interview was proving difficult to arrange, because Brown was out and about in his Scottish constituency and could not be pinned down. It may seem slightly strange that an event described as an interview was missing the most vital ingredient, viz the interviewee, but this was an almost routine occurrence at the time, when New Labour's post-modern approach to media relations was in the ascendant.

In the fuzzy world of Campbell, Whelan and Mandelson, the connection between newspaper stories and real events often became severed. Speeches were routinely briefed and written about in newspapers a day or two before they were actually made, if they were ever delivered at all. What was important was what the newspapers reported that the Prime Minister or Chancellor were going to say (and the interpretation put on these putative statements by their media advisers), not what was eventually said. Frequently, the speech as eventually delivered would be substantially different from the speech as described in advance to journalists and then written up by them, but no one seemed to notice or even care. The important thing therefore on this occasion was that Webster should report what Brown wanted to say, whether he actually said it or not.

Brown faxed to Balls a draft of the quotes he was proposing to provide to the *Times*. Balls then spoke to the Chancellor, they agreed some amendments and the approved text was faxed to Webster. Thus the "interview" primarily consisted of Webster reading a page of A4 presented to him by Balls, who then explained what it all meant. The idea was still that Webster would speak to Brown at 4pm, to put some "background" gloss on the printed words. I'm unclear whether this actually happened – and, to be blunt, it's an irrelevance. If they spoke, it's inconceivable that Brown would have departed from the words on his crib sheet, because the stakes were too high. So in that sense, Webster was just as well off reading them.

Now, in spite of this attempt to control the process minutely, Balls was feeling slightly anxious. The reason is that in his midday chat with Webster, before he had sent off the fax, the *Times* journalist had appeared to have greater knowledge of what Brown was planning to "say" than he should have done. Balls had said to Webster that the Treasury and Number 10 were co-operating on this stratagem, in response to which Webster replied that he had already "had the call": Campbell had spoken to Webster, which meant that Balls could no longer have complete confidence that he was in total control of the flow of information.

What Balls and Brown wanted from the *Times* was a story about a journey rather than an arrival: they wanted it to say that the Chancellor was "moving towards deciding" that it was unlikely sterling would join the euro during the parliament, because anything more definitive would have breached the rule that such announcements have to be made in the Commons. However it was tricky to capture such nuanced conditionality in the headline of a front-page splash. And it's not what was eventually printed. When the early editions of the *Times* came off the presses that evening, the headline on the front page was "Brown rules out single currency for lifetime of this parliament" – which didn't leave much room for doubt.

Subsequently, Balls, Brown and Whelan have claimed that it was only the headline that was unfortunate, that the body of the article as written by Webster contained a more subtle message. But there's an element of wishful thinking here. The story said:

> Gordon Brown is on the verge of ruling out British membership of a European single currency before the next general election.
>
> The Chancellor will, as expected, announce over the next few weeks that Britain will not join the first wave of monetary union on January 1, 1999. But at the same time he will act to protect the economy from damaging speculation about the Government's long-term intentions by making plain that Britain will not join in the present parliament.

The thrust was clear. And at around 6.45pm, Whelan started to tip off journalists on other newspapers – including me – that this big decision had been taken and would be in the *Times* (there was a bit of a furore subsequently when MPs learned that Whelan was briefing this portentous statement of government policy on his mobile phone, from the saloon bar of the Red Lion pub in Whitehall). "I'm tipping you off that we're ruling it out," he said in his nasal cockney bark, the origin of which is a mystery to me, since Whelan is a public schoolboy. Hats off: if you are going to trample on venerable parliamentary etiquette, it's as well to do so in style.

But events would soon become farcical, because Balls and Whelan had forgotten to tell their own press office in the Treasury what was going on. When the BBC's *Newsnight* programme rang up Peter Kirwan, the Treasury's director of communications, Kirwan insisted that no decision had been taken on whether or not to join the euro – which was what Evan

Davies, who was then *Newsnight's* economics editor, broadcast that night. But the climax of the comedy was a telephone call by the Prime Minister himself to Whelan in the Red Lion. Blair was unable to get hold of Brown or Balls, but eventually tracked down the Chancellor's spin doctor. The Prime Minister asked, in apparent innocence, "What is this story?" Whelan said in his characteristically gruff way: "The euro's been ruled out for this parliament". Blair seemed to be dumbfounded. "It's got to be stopped," he ordered Whelan. The phlegmatic Brown aide replied that the story was now everywhere and nothing could be done about it.

Why should Blair – who had been lauded only months before by the *Sun* for wishing to slay the European dragon – wish to keep open the option of joining the euro? The most plausible explanation is that he was beginning to assess the political cost to the UK of semi-detachment from the rest of Europe which would follow a definitive "we're staying out" statement. Also there had been that message sent before the election to Ken Clarke, to the effect that a Labour government would not retreat down a eurosceptic cul de sac. It was still not in Labour's interest for pro-euro Tories to cease their battle against the Conservatives' eurosceptic majority.

The other government member furious about these euro developments was Blair's closest ally, Peter Mandelson, who at the time was the minister without portfolio in the Cabinet Office, a post that more or less allowed him to engage with any aspect of government policy. "Mandelson was on the phone spitting," says a senior Treasury official. Although he petted the British bulldog during the general election campaign, Mandelson thought of himself as the keeper of the European flame and was even more angry with Brown than normal.

Mandelson was determined to make Brown repudiate the *Times* story – which became clear in a conference call he took part in on the day after it was published (a Sunday) involving Brown, Balls, Blair and Campbell, and also from subsequent coverage in the *New Statesman* magazine. Mandelson and Campbell – who have not always seen eye to eye – sensed an opportunity to embarrass Brown and build up their hero, Blair. Mandelson alleged that Brown had undermined the confidence of the City, by releasing a price-sensitive statement in such a slapdash way. And Campbell wanted Brown to apologise to the House of Commons for failing to tell MPs about the historic decision before divulging it to the press (which was ironic, to put it mildly, given that many MPs have complained that Blair's presidential style – promoted by Campbell – has undermined parliamentary democracy). "Campbell was obsessed with whether we were going to issue an apology for the way it came out," says one of Brown's colleagues. "He went on and on about it. He was obsessed by it. He thought we should say sorry for the way the story came out."

There was now no possibility that Brown could wait till mid November to make the formal announcement to the House. It had to be made as early as possible after MPs returned from the recess. So Wicks set to work feverishly refining the preliminary work already carried out within the Treasury. Balls and he had a week to come up with a robust policy that would withstand the detailed scrutiny and criticism it was bound to receive over the coming years.

Mandelson's hope that he could engineer a complete volte face, to allow the prospect of euro membership shortly after 1999, vanished fast, largely because Blair – who had still not completed his metamorphosis into a euro enthusiast – was not going to challenge the main thrust of Brown's policy. But there was an opportunity for Mandelson to influence the nuances of the wording of Brown's eventual parliamentary statement. For Mandelson and the ardent pro-Europeans, it was a matter of life and death that Brown should not categorically rule out *any* prospect of participating in monetary union before the next election, subject to *no* exceptions, which is precisely what Brown was planning to do at the time of the Webster article (that was the formula Brown had chosen from the seven options presented to him by the Treasury). Blair backed Mandelson, to placate his pro-European friends at the top of big companies (the business lobby, the CBI, was, at the time, largely united in support of the euro: these days large companies are no longer the champions of monetary union that they once were) and also so that Clarke, Heseltine and their pro-euro chums should not be deprived of their *casus belli* in the struggle for the soul of the Conservative Party.

So when Brown finally made his statement to the Commons on Monday October 27, he left open the very faintest possibility of joining the euro sooner rather than later. He said:

> It is not in this country's interest to join in the first wave of Emu starting on 1st January 1999, and barring some fundamental and unforeseen change in economic circumstances, making a decision, this parliament, to join is not realistic.

However Mandelson's victory was of little substance: Brown and Balls had won the war. They had established the core of the policy without reference to anyone else (except Wicks). And what they had also engineered was that they would continue to have sway over *when* and *whether* the UK should join the single currency.

The coup that shut out Blair and Mandelson from any further serious influence on this issue was a bald declaration that the constitutional and political implications of joining the euro were of subsidiary importance. Brown put it to MPs like this:

> There are those who argue that there should be a constitutional bar to British participation in a single currency, regardless of the economic benefits it could bring to the people of this country.
>
> In other words, they would rule out a single currency in principle, even if it were in the best economic interests of the country.
>
> That is an understandable objection and one argued from principle. But in our view it is wrong. If a single currency would be good for British jobs, business and future prosperity, it is right, in principle, to join.

As an economic decision, the Treasury – rather than any other part of the government, including 10 Downing Street – was best equipped to determine whether the UK should join the euro zone. And to put a quintuple lock on the Treasury's euro hegemony, Brown said there was no possibility of signing up until his department had concluded that the five economic tests had been met, which had been reworked into these ones:

- Whether there can be sustainable convergence between Britain and the economies of a single currency
- Whether there is sufficient flexibility to cope with economic change
- The effect on investment
- The impact on our financial services industry
- Whether it is good for employment

Blair himself hated the expression "the five tests" and rarely used it. He preferred to talk about the "economic conditions", which sounded rather less rigorous and showed his regret at the scale of the transfer of power he had made to the Treasury. For him, the problem of the concept of "the five tests" was that it implied that the government's economic department, the Treasury, genuinely could assess in a wholly impartial and objective way whether the moment would ever be right to join the euro.

This conceit that a judgement about the euro is a matter of dry, logical economics has always been seen by Brown and Balls as vital to their authority: they would never, even for a second, countenance renouncing it. But if there was even the tiniest residual opportunity for Blair to exert his sway over an eventual euro decision when it was made years into the future, the Prime Minister gave it away with a remarkable insertion he made into Brown's Commons statement. He urged his Chancellor to state that the economic benefits of joining the euro had to be "clear and unambiguous" before the UK could think about signing up. At the time, the phrase was employed as a piece of political expediency, to reassure Blairs' friends in the eurosceptic tabloids that the hurdle to joining the euro remained high. But Blair rues the phrase today. It meant that over the subsequent years, as the Prime Minister became more sympathetic to the idea of being inside the euro zone, the Treasury could – with loyalty – remind him that this was out of the question, based on his own logic: a political era would come and go before the economic benefits would be demonstrably "clear and unambiguous".

CHAPTER SEVEN

"The man in the white coat" – how Brown kept
the UK out of the euro

For all the drama leading up to the Chancellor's euro statement of October 1997, it had the intended effect of insulating the government from the buffeting of the assorted euro lobby groups, inside and outside parliament, prior to the subsequent election. Between 1997 and 2003 – when the Treasury finally presented its assessment of whether the five tests had been met – there were occasional ministerial disagreements over the euro policy and periodic attacks on the government from both the proponents and opponents of monetary union. But there was only one full-scale crisis, a stand-off between 10 Downing Street and the Treasury in the spring of 2003, as the very final touches were being put to the Treasury's assessment of the five tests (which has never before been made public). On Wednesday April 2, 2003, Blair asked for Brown's resignation in a fit of frustration at his inability to influence the decision on whether the UK should join the euro and Brown duly offered it to him – though when tempers had cooled, they returned to their roles as though nothing had happened, much in the way that dysfunctional partners in a marriage would do.

That near-disastrous collision was the exception. Brown and Balls had designed their policy in part to create an equilibrium between the opposing euro factions. So when the government's pro-euro friends in business complained that being outside the euro-zone meant that the British economy was losing valuable investment from abroad and the British government was punching below its weight in world affairs, Blair and Brown could say that a process had been started that would eventually lead to the UK signing up for the euro. They would highlight Labour's "historic" decision to state publicly that it was in favour of monetary union as a matter of principle. There was simply a practical issue – of timing entry to minimise the risk of economic damage – that was left to be settled. And as a sign of their supposed intent, they created a magisterial standing committee, consisting of the Trade and Industry Secretary, the president of the CBI, the General Secretary of the Trades Union Congress, and the Governor of the Bank of England, to review the practicalities of joining and to prepare a National Changeover Plan that would list the practical steps needed for the introduction of a new currency.

Such a gloss on the policy would be deeply alarming to an anti-euro newspaper such as the *Sun*, whose support for Labour was cherished by Blair. So to prevent that influential tabloid turning on Blair and Brown for an allegedly grotesque sell-out of Britain's right to rule its own economic affairs, the Prime Minister and Chancellor would point to the mountainous economic hurdles that had to be surmounted before the government would even think about asking the British people to vote in a referendum on whether to join (Brown has courted the tabloids as assiduously as Blair and he's had less success in wooing the *Sun* but rather more with the *Daily Mail*, which for some years has been a vicious critic of the Prime Minister: Paul Dacre, the euro-loathing editor-in-chief of the *Mail* told me in 2001 that Brown is one of the "few great men of our age", before hurriedly adding the qualification that Brown is wrong a great deal of the time).

There is another way of viewing this political stability which is less flattering to Brown and Balls. The sceptics and the euro enthusiasts were as one in their lack of respect for the five tests, which were widely described as economic nonsense, to be manipulated by Brown either to keep the UK out of the euro or to take us in (depending on the point of view of the particular critic). However, on this occasion, Brown didn't in the least mind being denigrated. The Chancellor preferred being attacked by everybody rather than being worshipped by one lobby and vilified by the other: it left him in control of the agenda.

That said, the strategy of facing both ways probably confused the electorate. Voters became progressively more opposed to monetary union, in part because the only intelligible voice heard by them was that of the starkly eurosceptic printed media. What must also have bemused the general public was a total rewrite by newspapers of how they presented the respective euro views of the Prime Minister and the Chancellor. Some time towards the end of the 1990s, Blair started to be characterised as the government's passionate pro-European and a true patriot no longer, while Brown was viewed as a eurosceptic.

There was a small element of truth to this image swap, although – as I've described – Blair was never as hostile to monetary union as he implied around the time of the 1997 general election and Brown was never quite as pro-euro as his image. The difficulty in elucidating their real views is that their stance on important policy issues like this is inextricably bound up with the power struggle between them. When Blair would periodically make pro-euro statements that Brown plainly hated, this was as much an attempt to prove that he still had a voice as with his ideological convictions. And it's hard to blame him for manifesting exasperation with Brown periodically. After all, he is the Prime Minister, and Brown had comprehensively shut him out of the euro assessment.

There were sporadic attempts by pro-euro ministers, such as Mandelson and Charles Clarke – who is now Home Secretary – to challenge Brown's control of the decision on when and whether to join (the Treasury always believed that they were ciphers for a frustrated Prime Minister). But their interventions only ever generated noise: they never changed anything of substance.

Even an event billed as Blair taking a strong lead – the announcement to the Commons by the Prime Minister on February 23, 1999 of details of the National Changeover Plan – was in fact a confirmation of Brown's power. Blair was presenting the results of a year-long study, initiated by

Brown's statement of October 1997, into the practical preparations that business and the government would have to make if a decision was ever taken to join the single currency. It concluded, for example, that it would take between 24 and 30 months for euro notes and coins to be introduced into the UK following a referendum vote in favour of joining.

This evaluation may now seem of largely academic interest, but at the time Blair's speech was seen as the Prime Minister putting himself at the head of a campaign to take the UK into the euro – and Downing Street officials encouraged this interpretation. The resonant description came from Paddy Ashdown, a passionate believer in monetary union who was then leader of the Liberal Democrats. Ashdown claimed that Blair had "crossed the Rubicon" and could no longer retreat back to his cautious approach to the single currency. Equally excited and welcoming of Blair's conversion to the cause were the senior pro-Euro Tories, Ken Clarke, Michael Heseltine and Sir Edward Heath.

They were right that Blair was happier than hitherto to be seen as in their camp. However, they grasped only part of the significance of his Commons statement. It was an important public endorsement of Gordon Brown's euro strategy. And the words Blair used confirmed that the Treasury owned the decision-making process. This is what Blair said right at the opening of his statement:

Madam Speaker, in his statement of October 1997, the Chancellor made clear the government's view that membership of a successful euro would bring benefits to Britain in terms of jobs, investment and trade. He said that in principle the government was in favour of Britain joining a successful single currency. And he set out the conditions necessary to satisfy our national economic interest. So our intention is clear. Britain should join a successful single currency, provided the economic conditions are met. It is conditional. It is not inevitable. Both intention and conditions are genuine...

There is much focus, entirely natural, on the politics of the euro project. It is, of course, an intensely political act. But just as the euro cannot be conceived of, except politically; it cannot be made to work, except economically. It is, after all, an economic union. We have, as a government, resolved the political issues, in favour of the principle of joining, should the economic tests be met. But they must be met. The manner in which we joined the ERM is a standing monument to the danger of joining a monetary arrangement on purely political grounds.

Blair was confirming to the Commons that the decision was an exclusively economic one, which reinforced the implication that the Treasury would make it. He even used the "tests" word, with which he was always uncomfortable. Brown and Balls were delighted.

They had urged the Prime Minister to make the statement for the very reason that it would be almost impossible for him ever to wrest back control over euro policy once he had made this public declaration. And perhaps because Blair recognised this, he was initially reluctant to do so (also, it was slightly humiliating that Brown had made the first and more important statement on the euro in the autumn of 1997 and he had to make do with giving this second, supporting one). However Brown had briefly worried that he had made a terrible mistake. When it came to drafting the Commons statement, there was to-ing and fro-ing between 10 Downing Street and the Treasury because Blair was minded, under pressure from Mandelson, to weaken the economic tests of membership and emphasise the political benefits.

At the time, Mandelson was heavily engaged in creating Britain in Europe, the pro-European lobby group which was supposed to transmogrify at some indeterminate point into the campaign-organiser for a yes-vote in a euro referendum. Mandelson was conscious that influential Tories, who were being urged to join Britain in Europe, such as Michael Heseltine, wanted Blair to put much more stress on the political dividends of euro membership. In the end, however, Blair spoke a lot of pro-Euro rhetoric but did not change the fundamental policy – that the euro decision was all about economics – one iota.

Even so, Blair was now, in the view of the tabloid newspapers, a euro fanatic. This wasn't quite right, as became clear when Britain in Europe was eventually launched at a surreal press conference-cum-rally at London's Imax cinema on October 14, 1999. When I asked Blair whether his desire to be "a fully committed member of the EU" meant the UK must eventually participate in the euro, he stumbled for a few seconds and professed not to understand the question, before trotting out a version of the Brownite formula that the economic tests had to be met.

***

The next euro event of any significance would be the outcome of the Treasury's assessment of the five tests. But the Chancellor had never said when this would be announced or even when the work would be carried out. The original 1997 statement by Brown had simply said:

> In order to give ourselves a genuine choice in the future, it is essential that the government and business prepare intensively during this parliament, so that Britain will be in a position to join a single currency, should we wish to, early in the next parliament.

This implied that the tests should be applied "early in the next parliament". But when exactly was that? On February 7, 2001, responding to a question from William Hague, then leader of the Conservatives, Blair gave an answer. He said:

> Early in the next parliament is exactly what it says. Early in the next parliament would of course be within two years.

On the assumption that the coming election would be in May or June of 2001, the Treasury's assessment of the tests would have to be announced by May or June 2003.

Brown had not been expecting this announcement and was mildly annoyed. But it did not cause him any great difficulties, since the

Treasury was already gearing up for what would be the most ambitious evaluation project it had ever undertaken, to be co-ordinated by David Ramsden, the head of the Treasury's economic and monetary union team. His explicit mandate was that the work had to be rigorous, authoritative and objective. The *sotto voce* and (probably) more important condition to be satisfied was that the conclusions had to please Brown and Balls – which was made trickier by their scrupulous refusal ever to instruct him what the conclusions should be.

By the time the general election took place on June 7, 2001, Ramsden was steeped in statistics, analyses and forecasts. At the time, the economics pointed to a further delay on British entry, but that's not what the Prime Minister seemed to believe. A front page story in the *Independent* newspaper said that Blair favoured "a referendum in the autumn of 2002" and that he was about to "kick-start a national debate on Britain's future in Europe as early as September [at the TUC's annual conference] in an attempt to swing public opinion behind joining the single currency". The author was the *Indie*'s political editor, Andrew Grice, whose articles on such issues always cause a frisson in the Treasury, because for years he has been regarded as having a close relationship with Peter Mandelson, Blair's most influential friend.

To be clear, Grice has never – to my knowledge – talked about his association with Mandelson or with any of his contacts. However it's one of the givens of the parliamentary press gallery and among MPs that a sensitive piece under his byline about the Prime Minister would have come from Mandelson. That perception is probably what matters, rather than whether Mandelson really is the source of his scoops. So Grice's piece was – predictably – interpreted by the Brown caucus as a manoeuvre by Mandelson, Brown's great foe. And one of the great laws of British politics in recent years is that any action by Mandelson causes an equal and opposite reaction by Brown.

Within just a few days of Grice's article, there was an aggressive riposte from the Brown camp: Balls and – amazingly – the Governor of the Bank of England, Eddie George, both made speeches on June 12 warning of the economic risks of joining the euro too soon. In fact, Grice was right about Blair's plan. However, it didn't work out that way. Events in New York on September 11 created a more pressing problem for the Prime Minister and an ambitious push to persuade the public of the euro's merits would have to be put on hold.

That said, there was also evidence at the time of continued prevarication by Blair on this most contentious of issues (so the notion that it was Al-Qaeda's attack on the World Trade Centre that kept the UK out of the euro, as some ministers believe, does not fit with the facts). For example, Blair and Campbell reacted very unexpectedly when they read an early draft of the Chancellor's speech for the annual Bankers and Merchants dinner at the Mansion House, to be held on June 20. Brown and Balls wanted to use this City platform to further dampen the rampant speculation – fuelled by Grice's story – that there would soon be a government decision to go for the euro. So they dreamed up a new phrase to describe their hard-edged approach to monetary union: "pro-euro realism".

This phrase was supposed to mean that the government was in favour of joining as a matter of principle but would make a tough-minded assessment of when the time was ripe. If Balls and Brown had a worry about this new gloss, it was that the media would interpret it as a significant nudge in the direction of euroscepticism. So they tried to redress the balance by peppering the early version of the address with lots of warm phrases about the EU. "The Europe bit was quite strong," concedes a Treasury official. They also took the rare step of sending the text to Blair on the eve of the event – which was something they did only when they regarded an initiative as particularly important.

Blair's reaction was precisely the opposite of what Brown and Balls had expected. They had expected to be berated for being too negative about monetary union. But in a meeting with them on the very day of the speech, Blair said he was worried that it was too pro euro and he then invited Campbell into the room. Campbell – who by then was Downing Street's Director of Communications – said: "If you make this speech, we're going for it. It will be seen that you're firing the starting gun [for joining the euro]." Blair added: "I'm really worried about it. We're not in a position to do this now."

Brown and Balls were bemused. They retreated to the Treasury and cut out many of the pro-European elements – which were only window-dressing in any case. The predictable consequence was that most commentators viewed the speech, when it was finally delivered, as massively reducing the likelihood of the UK participating in the euro-zone, at least for the subsequent few years. Newspapers wrote that the eurosceptic Brown had made his most cautious statement ever on the euro and had once again reined in the ambitions of the euro-loving Blair – which was not precisely what had happened.

But why did Blair behave as he did? As his Economic Adviser of the time, Derek Scott, has noted in his memoirs (*Off Whitehall*, 2004), in the autumn of 2001 his message to other EU states was that "early entry was still being pursued as an objective". So why did he push Brown to make a more eurosceptic pronouncement? Again, his actions probably stemmed from their rivalry. A speech he was then planning for the TUC in September was supposed to hype up the positive aspects of monetary union. Blair wanted all the credit for making a dramatic out-of-the-blue repudiation of the Chancellor's euro caution and seizing the euro reins: Brown would be demoted to the more proper subsidiary role.

However, because of the New York atrocity on 9/11, Blair said nothing of the kind and Brown's dominance remained unchallenged. The speech that had enduring effect was Brown's Mansion House one, which also served a second purpose for Brown and Balls: it helped them answer the incessant questioning from MPs and journalists about when the assessment of the five tests would be completed.

Speculation about this had been rife ever since Blair had announced that the deadline was two years from polling day. But, predictably, Brown wanted his own way of talking about the timing and not just for reasons of pride and vanity. Leaving nothing to chance (as usual), he wanted to put yet another barrier around the euro-evaluation process, so that it was even more insulated from any influence that Blair or his

Downing Street colleagues might wish to exercise.

Brown has for many years used his speeches – the word as spoken in public – to set out his intentions in such a definitive way that it becomes very hard for his opponents to push him on a different course. He raises the stakes, even on issues that seem fairly trivial, so that if the Prime Minister (for example) were to want to do anything different from what Brown has said, he would probably have to dump his Chancellor in the process. And quite often the important sections of his speeches in this context are not the flashy stuff for media consumption, but phrases that seem tedious and dry – such as a statement by Brown at the Mansion House that the Treasury was doing a series of background studies on the euro and that this "technical and preliminary" work, as he dubbed it, would eventually be published. He added that the formal assessment of whether to join the euro could not start until this preliminary work was completed. Here is the relevant section of the speech:

> Before any such assessment is started, we must, of course, continue to do the necessary preliminary work for our analysis – technical work that is necessary to allow us to undertake the assessment within two years as we promised.

When the Prime Minister read and approved this statement, he probably thought it was insignificant. But its effect was to further undermine him, which he learned with growing frustration as the months of the new parliament passed by and he endeavoured to obtain a steer from Brown about how the Treasury's assessment was likely to come out. Each time he would ask his Chancellor for the result of the five tests, Brown would say: "Look, we haven't completed the technical and preliminary work." And then Brown would add, with the considerable gravitas of which he is capable: "I refuse to allow it ever to be said that this was not done in the best way, in an objective way, in the national interest. We must go through the process properly. I'm not going to pre-empt the outcome. And I'm not going to get into the discussion."

Blair's attempts to cut through the wall of silence by using Whitehall's mandarin net were equally futile. He would ask his Principal Private Secretary, Jeremy Heywood (who is now a banker at Morgan Stanley), and his adviser on EU affairs, Sir Stephen Wall, to meet with Balls and Gus O'Donnell, the Treasury's Permanent Secretary, to discuss relevant "process issues". But in these meetings, as in the Brown-Blair ones, Balls would reply to the only question that mattered – "Are we going to join?" – with the blocking mantra: "We've got to do the technical and preliminary work."

Prime Ministers are not often thwarted by the construction of administrative barriers around territory they regard as properly their own. Is it, for example, remotely conceivable that Margaret Thatcher would have permitted her Chancellors – Nigel Lawson and John Major – to cut her out of the decision on whether to join the European Exchange Rate Mechanism. Lawson famously kept her in the dark about his 1987 initiative to keep the value of sterling relatively constant in relation to the deutschmark (which she was furious about, when she found out). But even Lawson, at the very pinnacle of his reputation in the mid 1980s, would not have conceived that he could have shut her out of a decision as momentous as the one on the euro.

***

At Labour's annual conference on October 2, 2001 Blair issued his call to arms for a campaign in favour of monetary union:

> If they (the five tests) are met, we should join. And if met in this parliament, we should have the courage of our argument to ask the British people for their consent in this parliament.

But it was a conditional rallying cry. He could only go over the top and ask the electorate to back the euro in a referendum if the Treasury concluded that the economic conditions for joining were favourable. And he became increasingly frustrated, as became clear in a stream of newspaper articles, at being shut out of the Treasury's evaluation process.

In private, he was putting enormous pressure on Brown to nobble Ramsden and fix the outcome of the five tests in favour of joining. And he endeavoured to exploit what he perceived as Brown's greatest personal weakness, his unsated desire to be Prime Minister. So on December 11 2001, Blair's most trusted aide, Anji Hunter, told a Treasury official that Blair would quit and make way for Brown, so long as the Chancellor "delivers on the euro" (and see page 330). And the message was repeated by Blair at a private dinner in Downing Street on December 18. Given his ambition to be premier, Brown's response was strikingly robust whenever Blair endeavoured to trade his premiership for the single currency. He would always say: "History will never forgive us for having that conversation: I'm not going to do it."

But Blair resolutely refused to believe that it was a matter of principle for Brown that the assessment be carried out by Ramsden free from political pressure. "He thought that the whole of the five tests and the work of Ramsden was just a smokescreen," says a colleague of Brown. "And when Brown refused to tell him what the outcome of the assessment would be, he would get very upset. Because he thought he was being lied to. He could not conceive that we had not prejudged the outcome. He always thought the whole thing was a charade and it was going to end in a bargain."

Based on this analysis, he adopted assorted tactics to strike that bargain. Thus he asked cabinet colleagues to intercede on his behalf, to tell Brown that he would quit before the subsequent general election if only the Treasury would facilitate his desire to take the UK into the euro. A minister who carried this message for Blair was Alistair Darling, one of Brown's oldest and most loyal political friends, who – unusually – always contrived to remain on good terms with the Prime Minister. Another was John Prescott, the Deputy Prime Minister, who has long played a role of helping Blair find his place in political history, in the apparent hope that this would facilitate a handover to Brown that would wreak the least damage on the unity of the Labour Party. Meanwhile Clare Short – then the International Development Secretary and a supporter of Brown – was asked by Blair, when they were away together on a tour of Africa in February 2002, to relay that he had no desire to serve a third term in office, and his departure would be speeded if only Brown would "work more closely with him so that he could make progress on the euro" (*An Honourable Deception*, 2004). Short put this offer to Brown over lunch the following week. And in September of the same year, she again put the deal to Brown on behalf of Blair. Both times Brown turned it down. And on the first occasion, Short records him as saying that "he would not contemplate recommending that we join the euro in order to advance his own position rather than advance the economic interest of the country." Which seems admirable and wonderfully disinterested, when in fact it was totally consistent with his personal interest: Brown calculated there was no point being Prime Minister of a country gripped by economic crisis, but that was more than likely to be his dire fate if the price of his succeeding Blair was that he allowed the UK to join the euro at precisely the wrong time.

Anyway, by the summer of 2002, it was clear to me, having spoken to ministers and officials in the Treasury, that there was no possibility of the assessment coming down in favour of immediate membership of the euro. There were many reasons for this, all of them captured by the five tests. Although the economies of the UK and of the euro-zone had converged to a certain extent – with differences between rates of inflation having lessened – one of the more structural disparities had become, if anything, even more of a problem than in 1997. This was that disproportionate numbers of Britons own their own houses and have bought them with variable rate mortgages (in the euro zone, there are relatively more people renting than in the UK and relatively more people with fixed-rate homeloans). This means that the net spending power of British consumers is far more closely linked to changes in interest rates than for consumers in the euro zone. Every rise or fall in interest rates feeds through to UK mortgage rates, which in turn increases or decreases the amount of cash homeowners have to spend on other things and has a separate impact on their spending patterns by influencing their expectations about whether house prices are likely to rise or fall (or whether they are about to become wealthier or poorer). Now the Bank of England can adjust interest rates in the UK with a weather eye on the condition of the domestic housing market. But it is impossible for the European Central Bank to be as sensitive to conditions in Britain: it must set interest rates on the basis of average inflationary conditions throughout the euro zone and can pay little heed to specific conditions in just one of the constituent economies.

Over the past few years, this structural disparity between housing markets here and on the continent has become more of an obstacle to euro membership because house prices in the UK have been rising at alarmingly rapid rates (of more than 20 per cent per annum, according to the leading surveys). Arguably, one of the principle challenges faced by the Bank of England and the Treasury (which, at the time of writing, is just possibly being achieved) was to help cool this market, without precipitating a slump. But going into the euro and imposing the euro zone's lower interest rates on the UK – and thus cutting mortgage costs – would only have served to pump up the housing bubble.

A further hurdle to joining was that general economic conditions in the euro zone – or at least in the core economy of Germany – were significantly less buoyant than in the UK. So the low interest rates that were needed to kickstart euro zone growth were less relevant to the UK.

Meanwhile, the British method of constraining the build-up of government debt and of managing interest rates both seemed superior to the euro zone's arrangements. Or to put it another way, Brown's economic reforms had been too successful: throwing them away for the euro zone's seemingly less robust arrangements did not seem wise. Strikingly, however, Brown seems less protective of his domestic economic architecture than many of his colleagues and he sees signs of the euro zone adopting reforms that may one day satisfy his concerns.

But in 2002 and 2003, the Treasury's detestation of the EU's Stability and Growth Pact was visceral. The pact had the laudable aim of preventing any intrinsically profligate member countries from bankrupting the euro zone as a whole by limiting the amount that any one of them could borrow in any given year. It was, however, drafted too crudely for Brown's tastes, in that it put too little pressure on countries to reduce their total indebtedness, as opposed to the amount of new borrowing they took out in any given year (even though the Maastricht Treaty that created the euro said that members' national debt should be no more than 60 per cent of GDP). The point is that a country with massive debt as a percentage of the size of its economy – such as Italy, with debt equal to 106 per cent of GDP at the end of 2003 – is probably more of a potential threat to the long-term stability of the euro zone than a country breaching the annual limit that borrowing should be no more than 3 per cent of GDP.

Brown and Balls are also believers that it's economically healthy to borrow a bit more in an economic downturn and to repay debt in boom times – which is the approach they captured in their own fiscal rules (see page 161). But the growth and stability pact's rules do not distinguish between different phases in the economic cycle. These rules say annual borrowing should be minimised whatever the prevailing climate – so in an economic downturn, a euro zone government would be under pressure to cut spending and borrowing, which would have the effect of reinforcing the downturn. To express all this in more nationalistic terms, Brown, Balls and the Treasury could claim with some justice that the growth and stability pact was inferior to their own fiscal rules, which had provided a framework for Brown to redeem vast amounts of the British national debt in the late 1990s when the economy was growing strongly, while allowing a sensible rise in public spending during the economic slowdown of 2002 and 2003 (see page 175). And the proof of the pudding was that growth in the UK has in recent years been at a higher average rate and has been less volatile than growth in the euro zone. Anyway, the pact is now in disarray, having been breached by France and Germany (which, as one of those glorious ironies, was the country which originally designed it, because it was so worried that its longstanding fiscal rectitude would be compromised by other fast-and-loose countries).

As for the setting of interest rates to curb inflation, the design of the Bank of England's Monetary Policy Committee was viewed by Balls and the Treasury as superior to that of the European Central Bank in a fundamental respect. They disliked what they perceived as the ECB's deflationary tendencies: it aims for inflation of less than 2 per cent, which means that it is predisposed to keep interest rates a little higher than may be sensible, since overshooting 2 per cent is a breach of the rules, but it's never wrong for inflation to be below 2 per cent. And if interest rates are always marginally on the high side, growth will always be marginally less than it could and should be. By contrast, the Bank of England's MPC aims for a "point" target (of inflation at $2^1/_2$ per cent on the old measure called RPIX and 2 per cent on the new CPI target). What this means is that if inflation is below the target, the MPC is obliged to cut interest rates, to actually increase the inflation rate – so, in theory, there is no bias in favour of higher interest rates.

For these reasons (and others) it was clear inside the Treasury and to most dispassionate observers that the time was not right for the UK to join the euro. There was no great mystery or secret about any of this. But Blair seemed to be in denial, since he continued to licence ministers such as Peter Hain (who was then Minister for Europe) and the staunchly pro euro Charles Clarke to make public statements implying that membership of the single currency in the short term was a plausible and attractive idea. Blair was unwilling to let go of his dream that the UK could and should be the driving force of the EU, which was impossible while outside the euro zone.

***

The imperative for Brown was for the assessment to be so rigorous, detailed and comprehensive that it would be impossible for Blair or anyone else to undermine its conclusions. In terms of its sheer scale and sophistication, it was to be like no other document ever produced by the Treasury. Huge resources were devoted to the project: 25 Treasury officials worked on it full time; over 100 officials, academics and experts played a role. And the cost was almost £5m. The project left little space in the Treasury for other significant policy initiatives. But it would be worth it, if all uncertainty and argument about monetary union could be silenced by its sheer enormity.

However, it wouldn't silence the assorted lobbies if Brown and Balls were vulnerable to the charge that they had distorted the assessment by imposing their own views and prejudices. So, although Balls had to be intimately involved in its preparation, he was always obsessively careful to be seen as a facilitator, rather than an author. Ownership of the assessment belonged to Gus O'Donnell, the Permanent Secretary, John Cunliffe, the Managing Director of Macroeconomic Policy and International Finance, and Ramsden – or more, properly, to the Treasury as an ostensibly apolitical institution. As its form began to take shape, these senior officials met either in Ed Balls's office (with its view over St James's Park) or in 11 Downing Street. They would review Ramsden's slide presentations of between 200 and 250 charts, in an iterative process, during which the chaff was gradually sifted away.

During the summer of 2002, the core of the assessment took shape, in the form of five "issues papers" on the five tests – which would ultimately turn into the main chapters of the final review. The time for Blair to have any kind of an influence was fast running out. So just a few weeks later, in the autumn, Jeremy Heywood – Blair's Principal Private Secretary – made a brave, belated attempt to influence the presentation and timing of the assessment on behalf of the Prime Minister. "It was the Principal Private Secretary's job to get the Prime Minister what he wanted," says an official.

Heywood had read the runes and recognised that it was highly unlikely that the Treasury would conclude it was the right moment to join. And he intimated to Treasury officials that he agreed with this verdict. But he thought the conclusion could be presented as "not quite yet, we don't quite meet the tests". And the point of this "almost there" evaluation – especially if it was announced early enough – was that it would allow the possibility of holding a referendum later in the parliament. However his initiative fizzled out after he had futile meetings with Balls and with his old friend Gus O'Donnell, the Permanent Secretary. On the largely political question of whether the assessment could and should be portrayed as pointing towards the possibility of signing up for the euro before the election, even if the five tests had been flunked for now, Brown was giving no guidance to his Treasury colleagues. And without the Chancellor's leadership on this hugely important issue, there was nothing Balls or O'Donnell could offer Heywood.

So the Treasury stuck to its own timetable. And by Christmas 2002, the 18 background studies commissioned by the Treasury were completed. Shortly before, on December 4, Balls made a final, futile attempt to persuade the Prime Minister and his pro-Euro allies in Downing Street that it would be foolhardy to fix or distort the outcome of Ramsden's assessment. That day he gave a lecture at St Peter's College, Oxford, the Cairncross Lecture, which went into inordinate detail about the heavy price paid by previous governments that had taken important decisions affecting the currency for political reasons, rather than thinking through the economic consequences (he cited the 1925 decision to return to the pre-First World War system of global fixed exchange rates backed by gold reserves, the Gold Standard, the rejection of devaluation by the Attlee government in 1946, and the ERM debacle, *inter alia*). "Central to these past failures has been that politicians and policymakers paid insufficient attention to the economics in making key decisions and then paid a very heavy economic and political price," Balls said. He hoped he was talking directly to Blair.

Balls then took the 18 studies away with him to read over the holidays, having agreed with Heywood that they would be reviewed in five or six joint Treasury/Downing Street meetings in January, February and March. Their average length is 100 pages of A4 size and O'Donnell, Cunliffe and Balls were revising three of them a week. "It's hideous," was how Balls described the burden to me at the time. Then, in January, the delicate task of sharing the technical and preliminary work with

Downing Street began. Meetings were arranged and then almost always rescheduled, because the Prime Minister's understandable priority at the time was the build-up to war with Iraq.

The Treasury's team for these discussions – which routinely began with a presentation by Ramsden of around 45 slides – was Brown, Balls, O'Donnell and Cunliffe. On the Downing Street side were Blair, Heywood, Powell and Sir Stephen Wall (the Prime Minister's adviser on the EU). They lasted around 90 minutes each and were – in the words of one of those present – "incredibly technical". An official recalls: "TB called Ramsden 'the man in the white coat', because he went into the minutiae of complex economic analysis with lots of graphs and so on, while never looking at the big politics". Another one says: "Blair couldn't stand the presentations. Ramsden was schooled in this mad professor approach."

By now, Heywood had informed Blair that the Treasury would conclude that the five tests had not been met. But Blair – egged on and encouraged by his closest advisers, including Wall and Campbell – refused to accept this as a *fait accompli*. The notion that the Treasury was producing an impartial and objective assessment was anathema to him. He was convinced that Ramsden and his civil service colleagues would produce whatever result Brown ordained – and that it was up to the Chancellor to steer them in the right direction, a more pro-euro one. If the assessment was to be a "no", it had to be glossed as "one more push and we're in," so that a referendum on joining could be held before the general election.

Against that background, Blair wanted the euro decision to be announced in the budget, scheduled for Wednesday April 9. That would allow for a plebiscite to be held about 12 months later. Also the Chancellor was planning to incorporate into the budget a series of initiatives that could be presented as helping the UK to pass the five tests: he would announce that the Bank of England would adopt the euro zone's measure of inflation, called the Harmonised Index of Consumer Prices (later renamed as the Consumer Price Index), and he would also launch reviews of the housing and mortgage markets – all with the aim of accelerating the convergence of the British economy with the euro zone's. So although Brown was delighted to unveil the assessment in the budget, it was not his suggestion (which is why it was slightly odd that on April 8, just ahead of the budget, the *FT* ran a story saying that Brown had put strong pressure on Blair to announce the euro decision in the budget but that Blair had fought Brown off).

Just what would the assessment actually say? Brown was confident that Ramsden would come up with the right answer (in his terms), a "no" that would be far less ambiguous than Blair would like – and not because he had the slightest intention of ordaining it. In a way, it is odd that anyone should ever have thought that Brown and Balls would need to interfere (Wall and Roger Liddle – a pro-euro member of the Downing Street policy unit – in a state of high dudgeon, complained to other officials that they were certain Balls had fixed it). Having established the tests and with his acute knowledge of the Treasury's innate wariness of monetary union, Balls had no doubt that any rigorous assessment would lead unerringly to one conclusion.

However, Balls wasn't completely right. When in early March, Ramsden prepared his preliminary thoughts about the assessment and presesented them to Balls and O'Donnell, they went into mild shock: the paper was incomprehensible. Ramsden was sent away for another week to rewrite it in more accessible language, with help from any Treasury official, except Balls and O'Donnell.

After that, there was another week of the document being reviewed by Ramsden's peers. And, on the weekend of March 29, 11 days before the budget, Ramsden – on behalf of the Treasury – submitted the assessment to the Chancellor.

Brown was delighted with the vital sentence in the assessment, which had been written by Ramsden and modified by O'Donnell. It read that "a clear and unambiguous case for UK membership of EMU" had not been made and "a decision to join now would not be in the national economic interest." Thus Blair's insistence in 1997 that the case for joining had to be "clear and unambiguous" had come back to thwart him. And however furious he might be about this, the Chancellor could say – hand on heart – that at no time had he ever had a meeting or a discussion with anybody in the Treasury about the conclusions of the assessment. Balls too could swear that never at any time, either on or off the record, did he issue an order about what the conclusion should be.

It looked like a done deal, except in one respect. The Prime Minister had still not seen the assessment. But on Monday, March 31, Heywood – ignorant that the assessment was finished – spoke to Balls and urged that the Treasury wrap the process up. Balls, disingenuously, said that would be tricky, but he would do what he could and try to obtain the conclusions for the Prime Minister. Mark Bowman, the Chancellor's Principal Private Secretary, then informed Ramsden that he would have to produce a 50 page slide show for the Prime Minister, to be presented the following day (fortunately Ramsden had anticipated this would happen).

So on April Fools Day, the normal cast – of Brown, Blair, Balls, O'Donnell, Heywood, Powell and Wall – gathered for the momentous unveiling at Number 10. Ramsden was unequivocal that the five tests had been flunked. And although they should not have been surprised by what they heard, Blair and Wall were profoundly shocked. The Prime Minister said (according to one of those in the room with him): "This is all fine, but I don't accept it." Brown's response was simply that the conclusion was the conclusion and there was nothing he could do about it: it was not open to negotiation.

What Brown and Balls did next was certainly impetuous and probably impertinent: they arranged for a messenger to walk one copy of the assessment to the Prime Minister's office and another to the Cabinet Secretary, Sir Andrew Turnbull (who never attended the crucial Ramsden seminars). Brown and Balls were simply saying to the Prime Minister, "Here's the assessment, like it or lump it." A Treasury official says: "This was probably the most direct gesture we have made."

An hour passed. And then Heywood telephoned, to tell Bowman that he had consulted the Prime Minister and they had decided that they would not accept that they had received the formal assessment. And he added that Turnbull too was upset. As far as they were concerned, they had received an initial draft – and negotiations would now take place to get it right. The scene was set for a major confrontation. It would deteriorate into the worst dispute of the 20-year relationship between Blair and Brown.

The Prime Minister's officials requested another meeting, which would be held at 4.30pm, this time in Number 11 Downing Street. The Treasury line-up was Balls, O'Donnell and Cunliffe. And as they were walking across the yard in front of Downing Street, one of their colleagues rushed up with a copy of the assessment, having noted that Cunliffe had left his behind. But he was told to take it away, because Balls did not want to give any sign that the contents of the document were up for negotiation. Inevitably therefore the meeting – with Wall, Heywood and Powell – was very strained. "There was five minutes of very tense stand-off," recalls an official. Balls was typically blunt, insisting that the assessment was finished and submitted: all that was up for negotiation was the content of a parliamentary statement to be made by the Chancellor on the day it would be published; but the assessment itself was set in stone and could not be changed in any fundamental way. This meeting was short.

The impasse was such that there was no way through, unless Brown and Blair themselves could reach some kind of compromise. They met on Wednesday, April 2, 2003. But instead of an agreement, there was a head-on collision. Blair insisted on the right to amend the assessment, to allow for the possibility of holding a referendum a year later. He said to Brown: "If you are not going to give me what I want, then you should consider your position." Brown replied: "I'll do just that." And he stormed out.

Brown went back to the Treasury unsure whether he had been sacked or whether he had resigned. And he also knew that Blair would be simultaneously meeting with his advisers wondering the same thing. In retrospect, it's extraordinary that Blair should have risked losing his

Chancellor in this way. If Brown had gone at that juncture, Blair would have been finished too: the eurosceptic press would have bayed for the Prime Minister's head, if he had sacrificed Brown in the unpopular cause of taking the UK into the euro.

The Prime Minister and Chancellor were behaving like exasperated spouses. But they calmed down and the next day they had a make-up chat, without their respective consiglieri. They agreed that Heywood and Balls would endeavour to find a way of satisfying honour on both sides.

Heywood went to Balls's room in the Treasury at 9pm that night of April 3. Together they went through the whole assessment till half past midnight. There was plenty of redrafting, to make it less starkly negative. Heywood's contributions were balancing phrases such as "despite the risks and costs from delaying the benefits of joining". And they deleted an account of a narrow range of supposedly safe values for the pound's exchange rate against the euro at the time of entry. But Balls was satisfied that nothing of substance was altered: it was still the Treasury's paper and it still said that joining was not in the national economic interest.

At this stage the plan was still to announce the euro decision just six days later in the budget. The entire document had already been typeset and the printers were waiting for a direction to start producing copies. So when Heywood left at half past midnight, having settled all the outstanding points, Balls rang the Chancellor to check he was happy with the changes. Then, between 12.45am and 1.45am, Balls briefed Ramsden, who went straight to the printers to make the alterations. It was all done by 7am, at which point a new proof was delivered to 10 Downing Street.

Blair and his advisers pondered it for a couple of hours and then sent a message back that the assessment would not be in the budget after all. They said that the Iraqi conflict was approaching a positive climax, and it was crucial that the government should not be thought to be using the cover of the war to sneak out its euro decision. So the exhausted Treasury team knuckled down to completely rewriting all the budget documents, including the Chancellor's speech, so that they contained no reference to the euro assessment.

But although the budget had been robbed of its main event, it retained the initiatives designed to facilitate the convergence of the British economy with the euro zone's. To help bring more stability into the British housing market and eliminate the disjunction with that of continental Europe, studies were commissioned from leading experts – Kate Barker of the Monetary Policy Committee and Professor David Miles of Imperial College – on ways to increase both the supply of homes and of long-term, fixed-rate mortgages. Brown also signalled that the Bank of England would start using the euro zone's inflation measure when making its interest-rate decisions (the Monetary Policy Committee adopted the harmonised index of consumer prices in December 2003 which should minimise any confusion and uncertainty for British businesses and consumers if the Monetary Policy Committee is eventually replaced by the European Central Bank).

Another two months were to elapse before the euro verdict was finally announced on Monday, June 9. Throughout all those weeks, 2,500 boxes of 18 euro studies sat in a warehouse and the separate euro assessment – including Heywood's changes – sat fully typeset in the memory of the printers' computer, waiting for the button to be pressed. And during those weeks, there was (for the first time) genuine negotiation between Brown and Blair over precisely how the Chancellor would describe the conclusions of the still-unpublished assessment to MPs in his Commons statement (and once again it was the Chancellor making the historic statement, not the Prime Minister).

In some ways the to-ing and fro-ing was reminiscent of the dispute of 1997. Would the Commons statement rule out membership for the lifetime of the parliament – as Brown wanted – or would the Treasury be forced to reassess within a year whether the economics of joining had become tolerable? These were private discussions between the government's two biggest beasts, with no officials present, not even Heywood and Balls. Brown went to Chequers, the Prime Minister's country residence, to thrash out the final wording.

Blair and Brown also embarked on a cumbersome process of consulting the entire cabinet on the 18 studies and the assessment. Each senior minister received the studies in a single batch on May 17, followed by the *plat de resistance*, the assessment itself, a fortnight later. Their homework was a mere 1,982 pages of closely argued economic analysis. All of them were also given an opportunity, either on their own or in pairs, for tutorials with the Prime Minister and the Chancellor on the huge documents – which was presented as an exercise in the great British tradition of collective Cabinet responsibility. But it's striking that on the Prime Minister's original plan, of announcing the whole thing in the budget, senior ministers would have had next-to-no opportunity to have any kind of a say on this most crucial of decisions. Also, the ministers I have spoken to about it felt there was an element of going through the motions by Brown and Blair. Alan Milburn, who was then Health Secretary, had the meanest deal, being granted just $10^{1}/_{2}$ minutes to discuss all 2000 pages. Curiously, the two ministers most sceptical about going for the euro were both in the House of Lords: the late Lord Williams, then Leader of the Lords, and Baroness Amos, who succeeded Williams and was the Secretary of State for International Development at the time. The most important point is that the assessment was – in all material respects – done and dusted long before the Cabinet discussions.

By contrast, Brown had used his chairmanship of the influential Economic Affairs cabinet committee to brief 19 senior ministers about the material implications of the assessment prior to the budget. The Chancellor's behaviour in this case is redolent of a *de facto* Prime Minister. An official says:

On all the issues that matter in the assessment, the substantive economic issues, Gordon had a whole series of meetings of the EA Cabinet Committee in January, February and March. Ministers had been briefed on all the substantive stuff in relation to the euro: housing, planning, economic flexibility, the exchange rate. He gave presentations to the Cabinet

Committee himself on all these things. He never made a big fuss about it. It was the most extensive process of cabinet consultation we had ever done.

The last set of changes to the executive summary of the assessment were agreed in series of telephone calls on Friday May 30 between Blair and Brown on the one hand and then between Balls, Bowman and Heywood. Blair was in Chequers, and Brown was at home in Scotland. Meanwhile Heywood was in 10 Downing Street, Bowman was in the Treasury and Balls was in Yorkshire. Blair was concerned that that an impression should be created of the UK being significantly closer to passing the tests than it had been in 1997 (even though this was a largely false impression). And he came up with the slightly odd device of presenting two of the tests as having been passed in a conditional sense. Brown accepted the amendments, because they changed nothing that mattered to him.

When it came, on June 9, 2003, the verdict was clear enough for them. The first test was described in the assessment as: "Are business cycles and economic structures compatible so that we and others could live comfortably with euro interest rates on a permanent basis?" And the answer was no, largely because of "structural differences with the euro area, some of which are significant, such as in the housing market".

The second one was: "If problems emerge, is there sufficient flexibility to deal with them?" Again the answer was no, pending "progress on a range of economic reform policies to enhance flexibility and resilience to shocks, particularly in labour markets".

Those first two tests are the most important by far: they are the ones that capture whether there is a huge risk to British prosperity and economic stability from joining. Once they were flunked it was impossible to join. However, the third test, whether joining EMU would improve the climate for firms making long-term decisions to invest in Britain, was passed in the conditional sense that Blair and Heywood had insisted on. The final published version of the assessment says that the quantity and quality of investment would increase, once the UK economy had converged with the euro zone's in a sustainable way. Brown and Balls could live with this semi-positive result for the simple reason that there was not sustainable and durable convergence between the British and euro zone economies – however the weasel words were an affront to cold Treasury logic ("it was a nonsense" says one official).

The last test – would joining EMU promote higher growth, stability and a lasting increase in jobs – had the same conditionally positive answer: "We can be confident", the assessment says "that the growth, stability and employment test would be met once sustainable and durable convergence has been achieved."

So only one test was met in an unconditional way, which was the fourth one: would joining be beneficial for the City and financial services? The answer was positive, but that had also been the judgement in 1997.

All in all, it was a dire outcome for proponents of joining the euro as soon as possible. On the other hand – and thanks in part to the redrafting of Heywood – the summary manages to convey an impression of strong progress towards meeting the tests at some indeterminate point.

Blair also had one modest success: he secured the Treasury's agreement that there would be a review at the time of the 2004 budget of whether to carry out a second assessment of the five tests (note that this was a commitment to holding a review to decide whether to have an assessment, not a commitment to a further assessment). This obligation to consider revisiting the tests was irksome and potentially destabilising. It might have led to a round of bickering between the pro-euro and anti-euro factions in the government during the winter of 2003-4. In the event, with the euro-zone's economy still performing worse than the UK's, there was no possibility of re-opening the assessment. Anyway, the Prime Minister lacked the heart to push for it, since he was consumed by the fall-out from the Iraqi conflict, especially the David Kelly affair. So Brown, for a second time, postponed a decision on whether to participate in monetary union till after a general election.

Funnily enough I'm persuaded that Blair was not in the end unhappy about the outcome, in the sense that a referendum on the euro would have been utterly unwinnable in the subsequent years, when economic conditions in the euro zone were expected to be considerably less benign than in the UK. That said, he remains livid to this day at what he saw as a blatant affront to his stature and authority by Brown and – even more exasperating for the Prime Minister – also by Balls. His pro-euro colleagues, such as Mandelson, Liddle, Wall, Peter Hyman (one of Blair's most loyal and longstanding aides) and even Alastair Campbell were even more furious at the way they had been out-manoeuvred by Brown. Their hopes of being at the forefront of a big national battle to turn public opinion in favour of the single currency were dashed. A great and noble cause, the whole point of being in government, had been lost. And in the succeeding months, they all left the Prime Minister's side: Wall to a post as adviser to Cardinal Cormac Murphy O'Connor, head of the Roman Catholic church in England and Wales (and in an interview with the *Daily Telegraph* in September 2004, Wall accused Blair of "letting down" pro-Europeans); Mandelson to Brussels, as the EU's trade commissioner, with Liddle as his adviser; Hyman to become a classroom assistant at a central London comprehensive.

However, the man in the white coat, Ramsden, and the Treasury team were right: this was the wrong moment to participate in monetary union. So it is possible to view the process as a vindication and rehabilitation of the Whitehall machine and the mandarin class: for the only time since 1997, a momentous decision was taken in the old-fashioned way, of civil servants doing a serious piece of work which was subsequently adopted by ministers. Of course, that is an over-simplified view. Brown and Balls would never have entrusted the work to the Treasury, if they weren't sure in their bones that the Treasury would produce an outcome that would please them. But they did trust the Treasury and they did not subvert the evaluation process. And what's striking is the contrast between the way that the work of these Treasury officials reinforced the authority of the Chancellor, whereas when Blair looked to his officials on the

Joint Intelligence Committee to underpin his build-up to war against Iraq, the pivotal document it delivered – the September 2002 dossier on Iraq's alleged weapons of mass destruction – did not ultimately withstand sustained scrutiny.

And what does this epic of government policymaking tell us about Brown's underlying attitude to monetary union? Is he a "never" man, an ideological opponent of joining the euro? Or is the pragmatism that he claims for himself real? Having spoken to him about Europe several times over many years, I am persuaded he has a passionate commitment to the EU and to making a success of the UK's EU membership.

It's true that he infuriates the more ardent pro-European campaigners by constantly and very publicly putting the case for the European Union to concentrate more on liberalising its markets in goods and services and to abandon all pretensions to be a superstate with a centralised government in Brussels. What he wants to build is what he calls "Global Europe", a Europe efficient enough to trade successfully in a globalised economy, not a "Fortress Europe" trying to be self-sufficient and insulated from the rest of the world.

His critics in the Britain-in-Europe lobby group say that he undermines the pro-European case by constantly finding fault with the EU. His riposte is that the pro-European case is not credible if it pretends that everything in the Brussels garden is lovely, when most British voters can smell something slightly rotten wafting from that direction. Anyway, what I have always found striking is that when he talks about the obstacles to joining the euro, he discusses them in a practical way, highlighting how and when they might be removed. There is no hint of a principled objection to monetary union, quite the reverse (Balls too is not an ideological opponent of monetary union, though his practical reservations about the project are probably greater than his senior partner). However, as a pragmatist, Brown will go for the euro when he can see only a clear upside for the UK economy – and for the reputation of G Brown – from the abandonment of the pound. And here's a certainty: it will be his decision, not Blair's.

CHAPTER EIGHT
Progressive universalism – redistribution in the age of globalisation

I t was March 10, 1999. I was sitting on the backseat of Gordon Brown's official car, some kind of dark, utilitarian saloon, the antithesis of flashy. Brown – who was in front – was giving me a lift back to the House of Commons, after a lunch at the *FT* (where I was the political editor). He screwed his neck round, looked somewhere past my left shoulder and asked: "Why did you write that the budget would be 'seriously redistributive'?" This was an unexpected question, since this budget – like most Brown budgets – had disproportionately rewarded the working poor. I had foreshadowed this in an article published on the *FT's* front page on the morning of the budget of March 9. It said:

> Gordon Brown will today launch a Budget designed to shift resources significantly to the low paid and disadvantaged, while abolishing a series of so-called middle class tax breaks. The Chancellor's third Budget since the 1997 election is 'seriously redistributive', said a government member, but it would also endeavour to encourage enterprise and corporate productivity. It may be seen as a return to Labour's traditional values, following criticism from within the Party that Mr Brown has concentrated on fiscal prudence at the expense of redistribution.

At the heart of this budget was the abolition of the flat-rate Married

Couples Allowance, which had been payable through the income tax system to all married people, whether or not they had children, and no matter how large their income. It was being replaced by a Children's Tax Credit, which was directed specifically at people with children and whose defining feature was that it was means-tested. For families on slightly higher incomes, the new tax credit's value reduced by £1 of tax credit for every £15 earned until none was payable to any household where the main earner's income was £38,500 or more (this emphasis on the remuneration of the higher earner in a home was particularly significant). It was an emblematic Brown initiative: those on higher earnings wouldn't get it; and those who wanted it would have to work for it, by filling in a form that would prove their entitlement (which would, in Brown's view, increase their sense of identification with the bountiful state).

This budget measure also went some way to reversing what Brown views as one of the more regressive tax changes enacted by the previous Tory government, which was to tax spouses in a marriage as independent economic entities. Now it may seem odd that anyone on the left, like Brown, should have qualms about independent taxation, since surely it was a good thing (progressive even) – from a gender-equality perspective – that a wife should be taxed on the basis of her own earnings, rather than her husband's. However, there was a significant defect to independent taxation from a left-of-centre viewpoint: it meant that a multi-millionaire's spouse who had only small earnings would receive more generous tax treatment and family-linked benefits than households with two earners on relatively low incomes.

What on earth was Brown's problem with the *FT* story? "It was profoundly unhelpful" Brown expostulated. "I'd like to know why you wrote it. Who talked to you?" I was nonplussed. Here he was, at the height of his political reputation – when he was widely viewed as the most successful and influential Chancellor in a century – displaying a profound insecurity. Did he really think that voters would turn against Labour if they cottoned on that Brown was redirecting funds from the well-heeled to the impoverished? Was a penchant for redistribution his guilty little secret? Could he not be socialist and proud?

It's astonishing how anxious Brown and Blair have consistently been about the perception of what they are doing – or not doing – to close the gap between rich and poor. After all, in 1997 there was a seismic shift in the political landscape, when Labour had won the biggest landslide election victory of any party for a century. And the Tory Party was in a ragged condition, not a credible opposition in any sense. But they didn't seem to appreciate the strength of their grip on power. If they said anything that might, for example, allow their media critics to allege that they were "penalising success", well that would be curtains – or so they feared.

However, there is a crucial difference between Blair and Brown when it comes to their attitudes to taxation. Neither are taxers for the sake of taxing. That said, Brown believes in raising additional revenues through the tax system – from companies and individuals – as and when there is a demonstrable social benefit. By contrast, Blair regularly manifests a Tory-like wariness to any kind of tax increment. In a way, it's possible to accuse them both of dishonesty: Brown misleads when he implies that he hates raising taxes; and Blair is being disingenuous as a member of a party founded on the notion that the gap between rich and poor should be closed. Or to put it another way, Brownism is a rejection of Thatcherism while Blairism is the humanisation of Thatcherism.

The hackneyed point is that all the "prudence" of Brown's first years in office – when he gave control of interest rates to the Bank of England and kept a relatively tight rein on public spending – was "for a purpose" (as he has tediously repeated time and again over the years). And the purpose was not so different from that of previous Labour governments: it was to invest in public services and augment the income of the poor.

But his policy framework was unlike that of previous Labour Chancellors. He couldn't take for granted that his government had an explicit mandate to raise taxes (unlike its predecessors), because his rhetoric from 1992 to 1997 was always designed to give assurances that Labour was no longer a high-taxing party. So in the first few years he took advantage of a growing economy and a general sense of optimism to raise revenues from new imposts in ways that weren't widely noticed (eventually prompting the Tory charge that he was taxing by stealth) – although occasionally, as with the quadrupling of stamp duty on sales of residential property worth more than £500,000 and a trebling in the duty on homes worth more than £250,000 (which was carried out in two phases, in the budgets of 1998 and 2000), his taxing ambitions were hard to miss.

All the while, however, he trumpeted his record as a cautious manager of the economy, in order to build up the requisite public trust that would one day allow him to explicitly raise direct personal taxes to pay for the Party's spending priorities, especially health. And it worked. Brown's active taxer has prevailed over Blair's anti-taxer. Brown lost one important battle – over what kind of pledge to make on income tax rates in the run-up to the 1997 general election. But in other respects he has set the tax agenda.

***

Brown's current views on taxation (as with so many of his political convictions) were born in the frustration of losing the 1992 general election. Labour's defeat was attributable in large part to a successful Tory scare campaign focused on Labour's plans to introduce a new top rate of income tax and abolish the ceiling on National Insurance contributions (which is income tax by another name). As it happens, the majority of voters would probably have benefited from the implementation of what was called Labour's shadow budget, which promised increases to child benefit, pensions and income tax allowances – and was explicitly redistributive. But in the aspirational, anti-taxing mood of the time, too many voters believed that Labour was all about the politics of envy and taking from the rich.

The lethal damage to Labour's electoral hopes was not done by the votes of those who would have paid its new top rate of tax and extra

National Insurance contributions, because there were not enough of them. What probably cost Labour the election was the fears of millions of others on lower incomes, who felt that the Party would penalise them one day as their incomes rose. Brown's post-mortem analysis was that it was the Party's failure to persuade voters that it would keep tight control of public spending and public borrowing that fomented a widespread anxiety that taxes for all – not just higher earners – would inevitably rise under Labour.

Now, Brown did not believe then – and does not believe now – that the tax plans *per se* were the problem. In fact opinion polls throughout the election said that voters were prepared to pay more tax for better public services. But they did not believe that Labour would deliver those improved services. They were convinced the money raised through taxation would be wasted. And they were not going to vote for higher taxes to be poured down a black hole.

As a new Shadow Chancellor in 1992, Brown followed through his own logic by dumping the tax and spending plans of his predecessor. John Smith, who was now leader. His final act of atonement for his party's taxing past was a speech dated July 28, 1993, which was given to the Labour Finance and Industry Study Group, the apparatchiks rounded up for the unveiling of so many of his big initiatives (or at least the printed version of the speech, for distribution to journalists, specifies them as the audience). Actually, it's possible this speech was never really delivered, that it was one of those virtual events which exists only in the form of the photocopy presented to political correspondents – and whose point is simply to generate useful press coverage and headlines. At the time, I wasn't a political journalist and Brown's colleagues are slightly coy about what actually happened on the day. Anyway, Brown's words – spoken or just written – were significant.

The message he wanted conveyed was not that taxation was intrinsically a bad thing, but that "Labour was in April 1992 wrongly perceived as wanting to tax people for its own sake, because it was thought to be anti-wealth." He continued:

In the end what mattered was not so much the worry over Labour's actual plans but the willingness of many to believe the Tory lie that even those who, in truth, stood to gain from Labour were going to lose massively.

The task therefore for Labour since April 1992 has been relatively obvious – to show how it can advance economic opportunity, not hold it back, and to dispel the reputation about tax and spending… We do not tax or spend for the sake of it but for reasons – to increase opportunities for people. And where we spend, we do so efficiently and in a way that yields tangible opportunities for people. Put simply, we do not look for increased opportunities to tax; we will not tax unless we increase opportunities for people.

He's been pretty faithful to that ordinance since then. However, on one point, he was naïve. The speech says: "Once this position is put credibly, then a rational debate about tax and spending can take place." More than a decade on, Blair and Brown are still determined to silence any senior member of their team keen to argue the case in public for higher personal taxes. For example, when Peter Hain – in June 2003, in the full flush of having recently been promoted to be leader of the House of Commons – cackhandedly endeavoured to initiate a debate on whether a new top rate of tax should be introduced, he was slapped down in the most brutal way by Blair, who said: "I have not spent the last ten years ensuring the Labour Party is in a position of saying, 'We are not raising the top rate of tax' in order to do so now." Strikingly, the criticism of Hain from the Treasury was not about the principle of whether there should be a debate, but about the appropriate time and place for such a debate – an important nuance.

***

Brown would spend the next four years ensuring that Labour made almost no commitments that involved spending taxpayers' money. Every waking moment would be devoted to hammering home the message that it was the Tories under Major who were forcing the electorate to pay high taxes. So one of his more important symbolic gestures as Shadow Chancellor was to promise a cut in VAT on fuel from 8 per cent to 5 per cent, which was made at Labour's annual conference on October 2, 1995. The Tories had announced the VAT charge in March 1993 but had been prevented from increasing it further still to 17.5 per cent by a backbench rebellion. "This was our first and really only pre-election tax commitment, as well as the windfall tax on utilities," says an ally of Brown. "It was symbolically very important in that we were proposing a tax cut on fairness grounds."

However, the more important tax question was a long way from resolution: what should the Party say about income tax in the run-up to the election? Blair's instincts were made clear in the only important economic speech he gave as leader of the opposition, the Mais lecture, on May 22, 1995: "The objective of any government is to lower rather than increase the tax burden on ordinary families," he said. This implied that the basic rate of tax should not be increased.

But should Labour at least keep open the option of implementing a new top rate of tax? One of Blair's more influential advisers – Philip Gould, whose expertise was in analysing public opinion – told the Labour leader that would be highly dangerous. Gould makes this clear in his book, *The Unfinished Revolution* (1998): "I have never had any doubt: increasing the top rate put us at political risk," he writes. "Blair was always instinctively against raising the top rate, Brown more inclined to keep the option open. In meetings they would discuss it as a matter of principle: did increasing the top rate reveal your instincts as a tax-raising party, or did it not? Blair thought it did, Brown thought it did not."

This is consistent with what Blair said to me on a Boeing 747 on April 10, 1996 when I and other journalists accompanied him on a trip to New York, where he was expecting to receive the political endorsement of George Soros, the billionaire investor, international political activist and philanthropist. It was his first foreign trip with the political lobby in tow and he did not choose his words precisely enough. When he said to me that no top rate of tax would be imposed on anyone earning up to £40,000 per annum, I reported this as mildly interesting but an unsurprising staging post in Labour's journey to becoming a party opposed to high rates of personal taxation. However, after I retailed his words to my journalist colleagues on the flight – which I felt obliged to do by a convention of the Parliamentary lobby about sharing information on such foreign trips (political journalists are part of a *de facto* club with slightly fuzzy rules) – right wing newspapers spun the story in the opposite direction, as yet another Labour tax bombshell: they published headlines that Labour was considering imposing a new top rate of tax for those earning more than £40,000. Blair and his Press Secretary, Alastair Campbell, were apoplectic and blamed me for their own mess – which was bizarre. Whenever I saw Campbell over the coming fortnight, he would scream at me "Peston you cunt, are you still spinning for the Tories?" Meanwhile Blair, whom I found myself standing alongside in the urinal of an airport men's room, said in a jokey, self-effacing way that was typical of Blair at the time: "Alastair has said I mustn't talk to you." Anyway, the incident showed quite how explosive the income tax issue was. And it wouldn't be settled till January of the following year.

By the summer of 1996, the choice was between ruling out a new top rate of tax and keeping open the possibility of a new 50 per cent charge on earnings above £100,000 per annum. Blair, backed by Mandelson and Gould, was clear that any hint of a new top rate should be stamped on. Mandelson was fearful that, given Labour's history as a party that likes to tax, voters would see the imposition of a new higher band as a clue to the Party's "real" desire to hold back those who wanted to better themselves. And he feared that the Tories would campaign on the allegation that the £100,000 levy was just the start, that Labour would progressively reduce the threshold at which the 50 per cent applied – and that too many voters would believe the scaremongering.

Brown's concerns were in the opposite direction. The danger he foresaw of giving into the Party's opinion poll pundits – such as Gould – by closing down this tax option was that over time he would be forced to abandon his ability as a future Chancellor to raise any taxes, simply for fear of upsetting potential voters. He would be a neutered Chancellor, unable to pull any tax levers to manage the economy or engineer social change. It was striking, for example, that the Tories had never given a tax pledge of this sort – and the Chancellor of the time, Ken Clarke, would have fought tooth and nail against doing so.

There were other Brown arguments. One was that a 50 per cent band raised a useful sum of money, somewhere over £1bn. It wasn't huge – and actually if the government were to do it now, the annual amount that would be raised would be far higher, at more than £5bn. Every little would have helped. And if voters thought Labour was going to do this kind of thing anyway (which they probably did), why not set the levy at a threshold that could not be described as punishing ordinary people?

Finally, Brown was adamant that if a new top rate of tax was ruled out, it had to be done on pragmatic grounds. One of his friends explains: "His position was to prevent us sacrificing the principle of fairness and taxation. And therefore we weren't going to rule it out as a matter of principle: that was the wrong thing to do. We would never ever say that it would be unfair for ideological reasons to have a top rate of tax that is higher than this or that number. Everything we did we would want to be judged by its effects."

Around this time, newspapers created the images of low-taxing Blair versus high-taxing Brown. But the truth is more subtle. Whenever I've talked to Brown over the years, I've always been struck by how reluctant he is to contemplate pushing up taxes. It has certainly entered his soul that if taxes on individuals and companies are raised to relatively high levels by international standards, many will relocate themselves or their wealth to another country where taxes are lower. So he always has an eye on the international tax norm, with a view to keeping British tax rates a little below that.

He's also persuaded that the "democratisation" of taxation since the second world war has limited Labour's room for manoeuvre. In the

1940s, it was relatively safe for the Party to campaign on an explicit platform of redistribution because only a minority of voters were taxed in any serious way to pay for limited public services that were used by the majority (Inland Revenue figures show that there were just 3.8m taxpaying households in 1938-9, which had risen to 14.5m precisely ten years later). The "giving" was to the many and the "taking from" affected the few, so redistribution could have mass-appeal. But by the 1970s, almost everyone was paying a sizeable amount of income tax – whose significance was quickly learned by the Tories but not by Labour (by 1979-80, when Thatcher won her landslide, there were 21.6m households and 25.9m individuals paying tax, numbers which barely changed for two decades). The majority was at this point being taxed to pay for the majority – although the general perception was worse than that for Labour. The Tories' successful propaganda implied that the majority was being taxed to pay for "handouts" to the minority. So Labour's traditional vision of social justice suddenly didn't seem very just or fair at all. One minister puts it like this: "If everybody's taxed then everybody feels vulnerable. You know a hundred years ago the Labour Party could argue for taxation because it was a minority that was having to pay it, not the majority. It was always going to change as an issue."

There was, however, an important difference in their respective attitudes to tax between Brown and Blair. Brown's caution about tax increases was pragmatic, while Blair's was almost that of a right wing ideologue. Blair seemed to believe that New Labour could achieve its social goals merely by being a better manager of the economy than the Tories. Philip Gould, Blair's influential adviser whose views are probably a reasonable proxy for those of the Labour leader, put it like this: "In the long run, sustainable additional resources for education and health had to come through reducing the cost of welfare, increasing investment to increase the rate of growth, through 'save and invest' not 'tax and spend'" [*The Unfinished Revolution*]. By contrast, Brown was never persuaded that the National Health Service could be rebuilt without an increase in personal taxes.

As the 1997 general election loomed ever nearer, Brown was increasingly persuaded that the battle over tax rates involved higher stakes. He was less worried about Labour ruling out any increase in the basic rate of tax, given the need to position the Party as on the side of the vast majority of taxpayers. What concerned him was that Mandelson and Gould were trying to move from a pledge on tax rates to a pledge not to increase the tax burden.

There is a world of difference between the tax rate and the tax burden. The burden is the amount of tax taken by the Exchequer as a proportion of the economy as a whole, whereas the rate is the percentage of the income of a company or individual that is paid in tax. And the burden can actually rise when the economy grows fast, without any deliberate increase in tax rates by the government, as individuals' growing income takes them into higher tax bands where they become liable to higher rates, or companies move from profit into loss. Also the tax burden can actually fall for a while as an economy slows down, when businesses become loss-making or the stock market slumps and revenues from capital gains tax and stamp duty drop. The point is that the tax burden cannot be manipulated up or down with ease – and even if it could, no prudent Chancellor would wish to be put in a taxation straitjacket that prevented him or her from raising or lowering taxes to promote economic stability.

Also Brown had an understandable aversion to engaging in a debate on what was precisely the right proportion of GDP that could be taken in taxes: there was no magic number, no percentage that would be correct forever. Mandelson, however, appeared unmoved by these points. "Peter through those two years was desperate for us to say there would be no rise in taxation, no rise in the tax burden," says a colleague of Brown. "We kept saying this is absolutely crazy, you can't possibly say that. You can't simultaneously be committed to fiscal prudence and stability, and also make pre-commitments on tax burdens. Nor can you be committed to delivering Labour goals in government (such as improving education and health) while being pre-committed on tax."

There had been a spat about all this in Blair's parliamentary office in the summer of 1996, tied to the publication of a Labour document called the "Road to the Manifesto". This was a preview of Labour's election manifesto and was supposed to lead to a national debate on big policy issues. Anyway, when Mandelson said that there had to be a commitment to not increasing the tax burden, Balls did not mince his words. He said that would be a terrible thing to do, to which Mandelson replied that he could not see why, since surely Labour was not going to raise the burden. That, replied Balls, was what John Major had thought was achievable in the run-up to the 1992 general election and he had turned out to be wrong. Brown sided with Balls and Blair refused to back his friend Mandelson – at which point Mandelson stormed out.

The final deliberations on the income tax question took place in December 1996 and early January of 1997 during a series of meetings between Brown and Blair in the Labour leader's Islington house (some of which were attended by Balls). At the last, Brown surrendered and accepted that the Party would commit itself to not increasing the top rate of income tax for the lifetime of the next parliament, since this was plainly of enormous importance to Blair. Brown was satisfied that his political point – that "fairness" for him was still a guiding principle when adjusting taxes – had been made loud and clear in the press. He also feared that if he insisted on his right to impose a new top rate, Blair and his allies would find other ways of shoring up their position. So his surrender was conditional on there being no promises made on the tax burden or on the hundreds of tax allowances and reliefs that existed; he would retain the right to raise or lower these at his own discretion. On January 19, 1997, he sent a fax to Blair stating that he would be announcing all this in a speech the following day (although it's not clear whether Blair received it).

Brown's historic address, made in an unremarkable modern conference room at the Queen Elizabeth II centre opposite the Houses of Parliament on January 20, began – in characteristic fashion – with an assertion that he would not be put in a taxation straitjacket:

I will not make blanket commitments on each and every one of more than 200 tax exemptions, reliefs and allowances in the system before we know all the economic circumstances we will face, including the true state of the public finances.

It was not for another 20 minutes that he uttered those words which were music to Blair's ears, although there was a typically Brownite preface, that social justice would not be forgotten: "We have already made it clear that our approach to taxation will be based on our values: that the tax system must encourage work and opportunity for all, it must encourage investment and it must promote a fair society." Then came the pledges:

Because we want to encourage work, and after 22 Tory tax rises since 1992 which have hit hard-working families, I want to make clear that a Labour government will not increase the basic rate of tax. It is because we understand the importance of work that there will be no return to penal marginal tax rates at the top. As a signal of the importance we attach to rewarding work, I want to make clear that I will not increase the top rate of tax.

And to reinforce the impression that Labour was now a tax-cutting party, he dangled one further carrot: "My tax-cutting ambition is to introduce a new lower starting rate of tax of ten pence to encourage work and to help all hard-working families." The 10p starting rate – which some economists regard as something of a gimmick that adds unnecessary complication to the tax system – was finally introduced in the budget of 1999. Anyway Blair was deeply relieved. He had feared that no Chancellor would ever agree to be tied down in this way. So in giving him this victory, Brown then won the freedom to do pretty much whatever he liked with other taxes. After the election, he took full advantage of that freedom.

As it happens, this landmark speech was probably more important for what it said about constraints on public spending (see pages 164-5). Apart from anything else, Brown's commitments on tax would have had far less credibility if he hadn't simultaneously promised to keep tight control of public spending and to stick to the spending targets set by the Tories for the first two years after the election. But even though this tax and spending package was a notable break with Labour's past, Philip Gould was not satisfied.

In the run up to the launch of Labour's pledge card in March 1997, which summarised five big themes for the general election, Gould kept trying to harden the promise from "no rise in income tax rates" to "no rise in income tax". Gould argued that the slogan "no rise in income tax rates" on billboards would be seen to be disingenuous (what's amusing about his analysis is that the slogan was indeed disingenuous, in that it did not prevent Brown pushing up taxes in other ways, but oddly it was not perceived as such at the time). Still Brown could not possibly concede: dropping the "rates" word in this way would have committed him to keeping the tax burden in check, which was what he had been fighting to avoid. And Balls continued to make the point that if the economy were to perform better than expected, the tax burden would automatically rise (which Balls believes is a good thing, because it means there is an automatic braking system that prevents a boom from getting out of hand: these are the "automatic stabilisers" discussed on page 175).

In the end, the "rates" word was retained in the policy formulation, because it was precise and unambiguous. The best proof of its efficacy is that Brown now looks relaxed when interviewed about taxes on television. Less than a decade ago, he was a rabbit in the headlights whenever David Frost or one of the Dimblebys asked what he wanted to do with income tax. If he'd said a word out of turn back then, it could have damaged Labour for years.

***

The evolution of the windfall tax on the privatised utility companies –

the electricity companies, water businesses, gas companies, the British Airports Authority, Railtrack and British Telecommunications – again highlights the very different instincts on tax of Brown and Blair. This was the only commitment to actually raise taxes that Labour made in the run-up to the 1997 general election and it was the very first tax policy made by Brown as Shadow Chancellor. It was not an optional extra: Brown desperately needed the money to fund the New Deal, his scheme to subsidise work or training for the young unemployed or the long-term unemployed. But as the 1997 general election loomed nearer, Blair became more and more reluctant to impose any new taxes, especially on the Party's new friends in business. Up to almost the very last moment, Blair tried to persuade Brown to dump it. However, the levy eventually raised just over £5bn in two tranches over 1997 and 1998.

It was dreamed up in 1993 as a populist wheeze. Although Brown, compared with most politicians, is an impressive long-term strategist, he also has a taste for flashy gimmicks, of which the flashiest and least socially progressive was the announcement in his November 1999 pre-budget statement that he would be giving free television licences to those aged over 75. Indeed he believes that this TV licence gift and – especially – the payment to pensioners of a winter fuel allowance resonate more on the doorstep at election time than almost anything else he has done.

Anyway, the windfall tax – which was originally announced when John Smith was still leader, back in January 1993 – was created as a device for kicking the least popular businesses in the UK, the utility companies that had been privatised by the Tories. These companies were typically floated on the stock exchange as *de facto* monopolies facing little competitive pressure. And although the Conservative government had established regulatory bodies to curb their tendency as monopolies to rip off consumers, for years the companies ran rings around the watchdogs: a typical energy company, for example, would cut its overheads and then generate spectacular profits, rather than passing the benefits of increased efficiency to the consumer in the form of lower prices. But what in the early 1990s turned the power and water companies into national objects of opprobrium was that the executives who ran them were awarded spectacular pay rises – which seemed unfair, since their businesses had not become significantly more difficult to manage since privatisation. It was like winning the lottery for the utility executives. One day they were civil servants on a modest salary running a dull public service, the next they were plutocrats loaded up with share options and earnings hundreds of thousands of pounds a year.

Their greed – and some of them were greedy – presented a wonderful opportunity for Labour to exploit the unseemly politics of envy for a laudable social purpose, to fund its employment programme. Gordon Brown cynically recognised that the more these companies and their executives were despised by the electorate, the less public opposition he would face to his windfall tax – and he happily rode on the back of a trade union campaign against the so-called "fat cats" of the privatised utilities. One executive in particular, Cedric "the pig" Brown – the Chief Executive of British Gas – bore the brunt of a media frenzy that the other Brown helped to whip up. However the tactics had long-term repercussions: Gordon Brown helped to reinforce the enduring image of businessmen in general as out to line their own pockets with scant regard for the interests of their shareholders. So this was the last time that Brown played to the mob in quite this way, since he soon recognised that he needed a constructive and amicable relationship with the private sector.

Anyway, winning public support for a punitive tax on the utilities was one thing. Imposing it was more easily said than done. Although there was a precedent set by the Tories in 1981, when Geoffrey Howe as Chancellor imposed a one-off levy on the excess profits of the giant clearing banks, there were technical, legal and moral obstacles to what Brown had in mind. First, just defining what was meant by "excess profits" would not be simple. And once that had been done, the tax had to be constructed in a way that did not allow any company to prove that it was being put at an unfair disadvantage relative to its competitors. There was also a risk that the tax could fall foul of European Community law or even the European Convention on Human Rights, despite centuries of precedent of the British parliament being able to impose whatever tax it liked.

Brown and Balls – who became intimately involved in constructing the tax – needed high-level specialist advice from accountants and lawyers. Happily for the Shadow Chancellor, his friend and fellow MP, Geoffrey Robinson, was willing and able to recruit them (and pay for them, when their services were not offered *pro bono*). Robinson approached Stephen Hailey at the tax consultants, Arthur Andersen (a firm whose famous name has been erased, because it was the auditor to the collapsed US energy firm, Enron, and went down in 2002 shortly after a financial crisis engulfed its client). In his memoirs (*The Unconventional Minister*, 2000), Robinson recalls his initial meeting with Hailey:

> Stephen stressed that he would have to clear the situation with colleagues and was most anxious to know what figure we had in mind for the tax. I came straight out with the £10bn figure. Stephen seemed mildly discomfited.

Andersen agreed to do the work and put together a team of experts, led by Chris Wales who later moved full time to the Treasury after Brown became Chancellor. Their first meeting with Robinson – attended by Balls – took place at his Grosvenor House flat on June 12, 1996. By November, they had a clear idea of the way forward. But a briefing paper they put together highlighted formidable problems with most of the obvious ways of constructing the tax, either as a levy on the companies' turnover, or assets, or profits.

There was one credible solution – the inspiration of Wales – which this briefing paper calls "taxing the privatisation 'windfall'". The way it worked was that the Inland Revenue would calculate the "true value" of a utility at the time of privatisation, by reference to the profits it had generated in the years after privatisation. It would then levy a special capital gains tax on the difference between this true or intrinsic value and the much lower price at which the company had in fact been sold to investors in the privatisation.

Intellectually the approach was robust. And depending on the assumptions used in valuing the utilities, it could yield between £6.4bn and £11.1bn. But Andersen recognised that the tax would be controversial. The briefing paper highlighted a number of arguments against it, most notably that "the burden would fall on current shareholders, not necessarily those who benefited from high returns [at the time of privatisation]" and "it would breach the government's contract with shareholders at privatisation" (the City would take the view that the *ex post* imposition of such a tax amounted to a breach of contract, even though the sale had been made by a Tory government, rather than a Labour one).

However, Robinson and Balls had also taken advice from leading counsel, Michael Beloff QC and Rabinder Singh, on whether such a tax would be lawful (interestingly Brown was not involved in this technical preparation: it was important that he could deny knowledge of what would be a controversial impost, in the event that there was a leak). Their joint opinion was unambiguous. They stated that the windfall tax "could not even attract a challenge under domestic law; should not attract a challenge under EC law, but if it did, such challenge would fail; [and it] would withstand any challenge which may be made under the ECHR (European Convention on Human Rights)". However, they said that Brown should not even think about using the proceeds of the tax for anything apart from the New Deal and schemes to help the young unemployed find work: the New Deal provided the vital "public interest" justification under the ECHR.

While Robinson and Balls were steaming ahead on the development of the tax, Blair was getting the willies. Within just a few weeks of the general election, the Labour leader's Chief of Staff, Jonathan Powell, sent Ed Balls a fax urging him to weaken the commitment to the windfall tax in vital respects. Blair was particularly anxious to exempt British Telecommunications from the scope of the levy, since BT had been useful to him over the preceding couple of years in allowing him to concoct a headline-grabbing but specious plan to connect schools, colleges, libraries and hospitals to the "information superhighway" (the clichéd phrase for the internet and other electronic data services made famous in the mid 1990s by Al Gore, the former Democratic Vice President). The deal with BT – which would have dangerously increased the company's market power and, fortunately, was never implemented – was that Labour would lift the prohibition on the telecoms giant entering the cable TV market if it wired up these public institutions. Anyway, on March 24, 1997, Powell asked Balls to ensure that in any briefings given on the windfall tax, Brown's team would make clear that although "all privatised utilities will be considered for inclusion within the remit of the windfall levy" that "does not mean to say they will all be liable at any particular rate or even that they will necessarily be liable at all".

Powell's intention was to make it possible for BT to be exempted. But what it illustrated was how distant he and Blair were from the detailed process of preparing the tax, because the clear legal advice was that the tax would be open to challenge if any utility was arbitrarily excluded or the rate of tax varied from company to company. In other words, the tax had to be levied on all or none: BT could not escape.

After the general election, Robinson, Brown and Balls showed their preparatory work to the relevant team in the Treasury, led by Steve Robson. The career civil servants were in general impressed by the quality of what had been done. "Obviously we refined it," says one. "But the basic methodology remained intact. Given that Gordon's team in opposition was tiny compared with our resources, we were impressed."

The issue of the quantum of the tax was still to be decided. After talking to the regulators of the relevant sectors – Oftel for telecommunications, Ofwat for water, Ofgas for gas and so on – Robinson and Balls concluded that £6bn could be raised without damaging the businesses. This was far less than the £10bn they had originally sought, but was almost double the estimated £3.5bn cost of the New Deal.

However, Downing Street feared that even £6bn would be viewed by business in general as redolent of a new government that was hostile to its interests – and Blair made one last attempt to kill the whole thing off, although without a great deal of conviction. "Do we really have to do this?" he asked Brown. The Chancellor stood firm. Eventually Blair and Brown agreed on a figure of £5.2bn to be levied in two tranches. And what was astonishing was that, after all the fuss and the controversy, the money was raised with barely a whimper from the companies and with next-to-no criticism in the press or in parliament.

***

Another tax bomb that went off with a phut rather than a bang came in the budget of April 17, 2002. That's when Brown said:

> From April next year, there will be an additional 1 per cent National Insurance contribution from employers, employees and the self-employed on all earnings above £4,615... I believe it is right that when everyone – employees and employers – benefits from the insurance provided by the National Health Service, everyone who can should make a fair contribution.

It was a new, direct, personal tax, which was different from the existing National Insurance arrangement because there was no ceiling on it for employees, no maximum contribution. It was more or less the same as putting 1 per cent on the basic rate of income tax, except that it applied to employers' contributions as well as employees', and was therefore a personal tax and a business tax at the same time. And – because it was a National Insurance contribution – it was not paid by pensioners or on income from saving.

The sum to be raised was significant, as Brown made clear:

> The overall effect of the tax and other decisions I have made today is to raise net revenues by £6.1 billions in 2003-4, £7.6 billion in 2004-5 and £8.3 billion in 2005-6.

The reason for raising all this money, as Brown said, was that the government wanted to spend more on the NHS – and not just a little more. He announced the largest ever sustained increase in health spending since the NHS was created by the post-war Attlee government: a growth in its budget of a staggering 7.4 per cent a year in real terms (or adjusting for the effect of inflation) for five years. This was a big moment, for two reasons: it was less than ten years since Brown had made a very public confession on behalf of Labour in opposition that the Party was not trusted by the electorate to spend wisely even an extra fiver of tax revenues; and it made Brown vulnerable to the charge that he was playing fast and loose with the spirit, if not the letter, of the commitment Labour had once again given to the electorate – this time in the election campaign of 2001 – not to increase the basic or top rates of income tax. But Brown and Balls carried it off after long and painstaking preparation. And once again, Brown – not Blair – was in the driving seat.

However, these events also show a limitation to Brown's writ, in the way he had glossed over a promise he had made in opposition about how a Labour government would be a wise and efficient spender before it became a big spender. "Government has a responsibility to the public to use its money as efficiently as possible," he said in the landmark speech of January 1997 that set out his approach to income tax and public expenditure. "Indeed, those who believe in public services have the greatest interest in ensuring their efficiency and effectiveness. In other words, waste and inefficiency must be stamped out." But, although in July 2000 the Prime Minister announced a national plan for reviving the NHS, what was conspicuous was the absence of any substantial structural reform that might guard against much of the cash being dissipated in hair-brain schemes, admin and wage inflation (see page 290).

Anyway, Brown had been engaged in trying to find extra money for a sustained long-term increase in NHS funding as far back as 1999 (and from 1996 onwards, he was examining ways of obtaining useful increments for health – see page 167 on allocating the reserve). His initial priority was to avoid a scare about taxes going up, once it became blindingly obvious – as it would – that Labour had to spend massively more on health. Inevitably, his concern was as much about a backlash from his own colleagues – notably Gould and Mandelson – as about attacks from the media or the Tories. He worried that in the run-up to the 2001 general election, he would face a rerun of the internal argument about what kind of commitment to make on personal taxes – and his biggest worry was that Blair would this time throw his authority behind Mandelson's desire for a pledge not to increase the tax burden, rather than just tax rates (after the nationwide protests in the autumn of 2000 about the burden of petrol duties, Blair's reluctance to do anything that could be interpreted as increasing personal taxes became acute). "We thought we were going to have the same debate as in the run up to the 1997 election, except that this time everyone [in the media] was going to focus on the tax burden," says a Labour member. "So we feared we would be forced to pre-commit on tax in a way that would have made things very difficult in the second term."

They needed a new way to give a non-answer to questions from journalists about whether taxes would be increased, because they were unsure whether the tried-and-tested phrase – viz "we are not going to make promises on all the umpteen taxes" – would be effective this time. So Brown, Balls and Miliband (who was intimately involved in the NHS work) set about looking for a way to defuse the inevitable pressure to include a stronger and more sweeping promise not to increase taxes in the 2001 general election manifesto. And they somehow had to take attention away from all the changes that Brown had already made to tax allowances and reliefs, which had yielded significant sums, because they wanted to avoid speculation about what other "stealth tax" initiatives could be in the pipeline.

This need for a new general formula on their tax plans became more urgent after Tony Blair appeared on the BBC's *Breakfast with Frost* on January 16, 2000 and said that he wanted spending on the health service to rise over the subsequent five years "to the average of the European Union – it is too low at the moment". This was quite an ambition, since total British expenditure on health (public and private) was then equivalent to 7.2 per cent of GDP, compared with 9.3 per cent in France and 10.6 per cent in Germany (according to OECD figures). As analysts quickly pointed out, Blair seemed to be making a promise to raise NHS spending by more than £9bn a year in real terms over five years – a staggering and unprecedented increment – although it was hard to be sure, since he had not defined his terms very precisely. Brown and the Treasury were surprised by Blair's very public promise, not least because they were still some months from finalising that year's Comprehensive Spending Review which would set three-year spending budgets for all departments. The Chancellor had already agreed with Blair that health would be the big winner from the Spending Review. He just hadn't expected Blair to make any kind of announcement at that moment. "We were shocked," said an official. "It came out of nowhere."

What was motivating Blair? Well, one of the odd myths that was circulating at the time – which allies of Blair seemed to believe – was that Brown did not like spending money on public services. The widespread presumption was that the Chancellor would not give large amounts of additional cash to funding the public services because he could not control them: he would rather direct scarce resources to tax credits for people in low-paid jobs, his anti-poverty programme. Blair was trying – in a crude way – to put Brown on the hook for a truly stupendous increase in health spending (it tells you something about their strange relationship that he had to have this conversation with Brown via a national television programme). Anyway, with just a year and a bit to run before the general election, Blair also wanted a big media splash to show that he, not Brown, was in charge of the big items on the agenda.

The *coup de theatre* backfired when it turned out that officials in 10 Downing Street didn't have a firm grasp of European health-spending statistics and therefore couldn't say what the exact financial implications of the Prime Minister's words were. By default, therefore, control over the health service spending plans returned to the Treasury.

Just over two months later in his budget of March 21, 2000, Brown announced a significant increase in NHS spending, though there would be more to come after the election. He disclosed average annual growth in its budget, adjusted for inflation, of 6.1 per cent – so health spending would grow by more than double the rate of growth of the economy as a whole. In political terms, just as significant was this rather dull sentence in Brown's budget speech to the Commons: "I am also commissioning a long-term assessment of the technological, demographic and medical trends over the next two decades that will affect the health service."

This was Brown's insurance policy, his protection against pressure from Blair to rule out tax rises – and almost nobody noticed it. The Treasury was already aware that taxes might have to rise to pay for the long-term increases in health service spending. But before the election Brown did not want to announce the rises or even admit they might be needed (it was just possible they would not be necessary, if economic growth was faster than the Treasury expected, or revenues from existing taxes were higher than anticipated). So the idea of the NHS review – which was Brown's, but stemmed from a conversation between Miliband and Balls on an airplane flight to the US just before the Christmas of 1999 – was devised to serve two purposes. Its more important, longer term one was to provide the intellectual underpinning, if there was one, for a rise in taxes to fund health spending. And it was a ruse to get Labour through the general election campaign without having to answer the terrible question, viz "will taxes rise to pay for the health service?" If Brown were ever asked this, he could always reply, "It's impossible to know until we have completed our review."

Now with the election still more than a year away, there was no point in rushing this review. So it was another 12 months before Brown announced in the budget of March 7, 2001 that it would be led by Derek Wanless, the former Chief Executive of National Westminster Bank. Wanless is a bright and personable Cambridge mathematics graduate from the north east, with a strong Geordie accent. But a characteristic of his time at NatWest, which only became clear after he was forced out of the bank during a takeover battle in 1999, was that he had failed to make it as efficient and productive as it should have been. Its new owner, Royal Bank of Scotland, pushed up its profits by hundreds and hundreds of millions of pounds through ruthless cost-cutting. So Brown was not appointing someone likely to offer a blueprint for taking costs out of the health service or improving its productivity – although in fairness to Wanless, that was not his mandate. He was asked to assess the scale of increased resources likely to be required by the NHS over the following two decades and – within that context – take a view about whether there was a fairer and more efficient way of funding any increased health spending than through general taxation. Brown's presumption was that Wanless was unlikely to be a zealot in favour of "privatised" models for financing health provision (such as the provision of tax breaks for private insurance or a universal health insurance scheme with limited state-backing) since at NatWest he had taken a gradualist approach to change. The Chancellor hoped that the traditional system of funding the NHS would receive the businessman's imprimatur – and he wasn't disappointed.

From that moment to the general election on June 7, Brown was in a state of full readiness for a public spat with the Tories and the media over Labour's NHS spending plans and how they could be afforded. But it never really happened, largely because the Tories got into a frightful mess over their proposals to limit the growth in public spending and cut taxes. The Conservatives' official position was that they would maintain spending on health, schools, the police and defence, but would find £8bn of savings elsewhere over two years to finance equivalent tax cuts. Even these savings were not particularly credible, because many of them were of the supposedly "painless" variety, such as reducing bureaucracy and benefit fraud (which are often promised by politicians and rarely delivered). However, in mid-May, the Shadow Chief Secretary to the Treasury, Oliver Letwin, blabbed to the *FT* that a Tory government would actually look to find £20bn of tax cuts by the end of the parliament – which allowed Labour to turn the focus away from the implications for higher taxes of its own spending plans by creating a scare about alleged Tory plans to massacre core public services (rebutting this was hard for the Conservatives, since the Tory leader of the time, William Hague, appeared to be more in sympathy with the tax-cutting instincts of Letwin than with the caution of the Shadow Chancellor, Michael Portillo). It was a great escape for Brown, who never once had to use the "Wanless defence" during the election campaign. When he and Balls were interviewed by journalists about the implications of spending increases for taxes, they would chant the mantra that decisions could not be taken because of uncertainties about the outlook for the economy. But they always had a device in their back pockets called Wanless, as an ally of Brown elucidates: "We could always say at any point, 'Look we can't make a commitment because we've got to see the result of this Wanless report'. And we never ever used it, because the Tories were so useless."

However, there was one very nasty moment for the Labour general election campaign that was tangentially related to the NHS plans. Labour had repeated its 1997 manifesto pledge not to raise the basic or top rate of taxes but had said nothing about National Insurance. So it was natural for journalists to probe ministers about whether the cap on National Insurance payments might be raised (the more so since abolishing this ceiling had been at the heart of the Party's disastrous shadow budget in 1992). The Treasury's response to such questioning – the preferred line of Brown and Balls – was a refusal to rule in or out any tax cuts or rises, in advance of a budget. But that's not what the Trade Minister, Patricia Hewitt, said on May 29, 2001, when interviewed on Channel 4. She said something more categoric: "We've no plans to raise the ceiling on National Insurance contributions." This put Brown in a tricky position. Although it was true that there was no intention of abolishing or raising the ceiling on NI contributions in general, as long before as 1999 the Treasury had been considering a special 1 per cent NI levy without a ceiling. What Hewitt said was therefore not exactly the whole truth – and Brown and Blair were forced in their subsequent statements during the campaign to distance themselves from her remarks, while trying desperately not to give a clue as to what the Treasury really had in mind. Blair – who would have loved to issue a statement corroborating what Hewitt had said – resorted to the tried and tested formula of saying, "We are not sitting here writing a budget," before adding that, "We have got no intention of clobbering higher tax earners." And with just three days left before the poll, Blair resorted to amazing linguistic contortions in an interview on the BBC's *Newsnight* programme to imply that such a change to NI payments was not on the agenda, mostly by stressing how dangerous it would be for the economy to impose too high a tax burden on high earners. In the process he came up with one of the more eccentric quotes of the campaign and of his career: "It is not a burning ambition for me to make sure David Beckham earns less money."

What's striking is that – in an almost exact re-run of his neuroses during the 1997 campaign – Blair remained worried that Labour could lose the election and that its vulnerability was the same as it had ever been: personal taxes and NI. Blair's general lack of confidence had become clear to Brown on May 16 when Blair's closest advisers were demanding that he sack John Prescott after the Deputy Prime Minister was caught on film swinging a punch at an egg-throwing protestor in Rhyl, North Wales. The influential pollster, Philip Gould, warned the Prime Minister that Prescott's behaviour could lead to a fatal swing in the polls, which rattled Blair. But Brown urged Blair to keep his nerve – which he did. However, the atmosphere in Blair's immediate circle was febrile. As one Labour frontbencher says: "In the court of King Tony, there is a continual competition to be heard. You have to be heard by playing to a fear. And the fear is that everything is about to go wrong. And therefore there is always a competition to be the person to say it is all about to go wrong. It was always mad."

The election came on June 7 and Labour won by another colossal landslide, with Brown's position on National Insurance intact. So now was the moment for an important shift in emphasis, in respect of what the Treasury would say publicly about how to finance NHS renewal. The initiative was taken on October 1, at Labour's annual conference in Brighton, by Balls. In the briefing he routinely gives after the Chancellor's more important speeches, he helped political journalists translate what Brown was implying in an elliptical part of his speech when he asked conference delegates to start "building public support for the budget and spending decisions we will have to take in the coming months". The following day, pretty much every newspaper ran a story saying that Chancellor had hinted at tax rises – though it's very doubtful that anyone who had missed Balls's briefing would have spotted the hint.

These were nerve-wracking times for Blair, who was still unpersuaded that it was sensible to raise personal taxes and was casting around for "painless" ways to raise money for health. But the Treasury campaign to do just this was now well into gear and unstoppable. On November 27, in his annual Pre-Budget Report, Brown publicly endorsed the findings of Derek Wanless that the NHS was no longer fulfilling patient expectations, that health provision in the UK was inferior to what was available in comparable countries, and that it would take significant investment over two decades to repair the damage wreaked by years of insufficient spending. Wanless also said: "There is no evidence that any alternative financing method to the UK's would deliver a quality of health care at a lower cost to the economy. Indeed other systems seem likely to prove more costly. Nor do alternative balances of funding appear to offer scope to increase equity". Or to put it another way, the NHS should continue to be funded from general taxation.

For Brown, the man from NatWest had provided sterling service – although Wanless himself began to feel a bit manipulated and abused. When he was sitting in his car listening to the Chancellor's speech, he was horrified that his name was cited 16 times by Brown (the official version of the speech on the Treasury's website has only eight references to Wanless, but Brown rarely delivers an address precisely as it is written). Wanless was being used by Brown as his human shield for a planned increase in taxation that would be highly controversial and the poor former banker hadn't really been asked if he was happy to lend his reputation for this purpose (he had also been disappointed that when he saw Brown in the preceding few days, the Chancellor had seemed reluctant to accept his assessment that the NHS was not the absolute *nonpareil* of fair and efficient health services).

However, the way was now clear for the Chancellor – three and a bit months later in his budget of March 2002 – to make tax history, for better or worse. His introduction of the special 1 per cent National Insurance levy to pay for the NHS would challenge one of the great givens of British politics since the advent of Margaret Thatcher in 1979, that direct taxes could not be increased in an explicit way without wreaking huge damage to the Party in government (although they could be raised in inconspicuous "stealthy" ways, by abolishing allowances or failing to raise thresholds, for example). It was the first proper test of whether voters now had confidence in a British government to spend their money wisely and Labour's sustained lead in opinion polls suggests they did (and do) have that confidence. What is less clear, and will not be determined for many years as investment pours into the NHS, is whether such confidence is well placed.

***

Probably the most politically explosive tax that was considered by Brown and Balls was a wealth tax. It was proposed to them as part of a sweeping review of the tax system, given the codename, Cascade, which they commissioned in the year before the 1997 general election. The review – which proposes a number of reforms that were implemented, including changes to capital gains tax and corporation tax – was overseen by Chris Wales, a tax expert at the now defunct accountancy firm, Arthur Andersen who was hired by Geoffrey Robinson. The wealth tax idea was still being discussed in 1997, not long before the general election. The policy document says:

> The Cascade proposal envisages an annual tax on personal wealth primarily as a replacement for inheritance tax, which has a low yield and is widely regarded as ineffective in its expressed object of taxing estates at the point of death.

Instead of the levy on the estate of a deceased, there would be a tax of at least 1 per cent – and "the possibility of higher rates of 1.25, 1.5 and/or 2 per cent" – on wealth held by individuals and trusts worth more than £100,000 per individual or £200,000 per family (which is defined as comprising one or two parents with one or more children under 21). The tax would have applied to the worldwide wealth of UK residents and British property held by others. Collection would have been monthly, or annually with the addition of an interest charge. The paper also provided details of how houses and household effects were to be valued for tax purposes.

The annual yield of a 1 per cent tax was estimated to have been around £3bn. And the document says that, "There is an argument that, for that level of yield, bearing in mind that it should be netted against current receipts of inheritance tax... the benefit might not be worth the political cost" – which is something of an understatement. Had it leaked before the 1997 election, the furore generated by the Tories would have been quite something. It's a tragedy therefore for the Conservatives that the wealth tax is now in the graveyard of tax might-have-beens – although the concern manifested in the Cascade document about the low yield from inheritance tax has been pursued in a series of attempts by the Inland Revenue in recent years to close loopholes to payment of death duties and in tentative plans to reconstruct the tax after the next election so that the take from larger estates increases. Meanwhile, the burial of the wealth tax says much about Brown's basic precept on taxation: if a tax is perceived as stifling enterprise, and could lead to an exodus of wealth-creators from the UK – as this tax would have done – then the revenues it would generate are not worth having.

By contrast there is one tax reform made by Brown that defines his term in office as Chancellor: the introduction of tax credits, which, unlike the abandoned wealth tax, is progressive taxation without the tears. In fact, it's a reform of tax and benefits, because it initially involved the replacement of a welfare payment for those in work – family credit – with the Working Families Tax Credit.

275

Since the introduction of the WFTC in October 1999, tax credits have gone through a series of iterations, so that today they are payable to 90 per cent of families with children and also childless working people in the form of a Working Tax Credit and a Child Tax Credit (any family with children and with an income of less than £58,000 is eligible for some support). Today, an estimated 20m people in 6m families receive these state payments, which can be as much as £5,420 per annum for a low-earning household with three children (or £7,435 if the traditional child benefit payments are factored into the calculations). The annual aggregated cost to the Exchequer of both the Working Tax Credit and the Child Tax Credit is at least £16bn per annum. And by 2004-5, financial support for children through tax credits, child benefit and other benefits will have increased by more than £10bn, adjusting for inflation, or a bit over 70 per cent since Labour came to office in 1997. All this represents, in the words, of a Treasury official, a "quiet revolution".

There has also been a "quiet revolution" in Brown's own thinking about them. When I first started talking to him about them in the mid-1990s, his enthusiasm stemmed from the powerful symbolism of rewarding work, of reinforcing moral pressure on the unemployed to take work with financial incentives. At the time, he appeared to have almost a passionate hatred for the unemployed, and an ethical view of idleness as evil. My sense was that he had some kind of mental block on the idea that there could ever be a good reason not to work. He's mellowed a bit since then. And these days he defines the importance of tax credits in a different way. This is what he said to me more recently:

I think tax credits have been misunderstood. People have focused on the mechanism, a bureaucratic issue, when it is in the end about citizenship, integrating tax and benefits. In the long term, these will come to be accepted as part of the economic and social framework of the country.

The phrase that always comes up when talking to him or his close colleagues about tax credits is "progressive universalism", which may be the closest that Brown will ever get to defining a political philosophy à la Thatcherism. Progressive universalism is brunch for welfare theoreticians: it's not classic means testing; and it's not a universal payment. It is financial help for the vast majority of people that tapers down to nil for those whose earnings are well above the average. And the credits themselves are a practical manifestation of Brown's enduring obsessions:

- The working tax credit is a reward for having a job, any job, so to that extent it reflects his Scottish Presbyterian horror of feckless unemployment
- Because the credits are paid to the majority of people, they are an attempt to destroy the notion that only the poor and wretched should receive support from the state
- They are an attempt to bind people more closely into the state, to re-cast government as a benign provider rather than a meddling interferer, to undermine the widespread belief – that took hold under Thatcher – that there is no credible political alternative to individualism and rolling back the public sector
- In a relatively uncontroversial way, the credits distribute the fruits of economic growth to the low paid (a kind of palatable "socialism-lite")

It was "the other Ed" who worked closest with Brown on tax credits. He's Ed Miliband, who's been an adviser to Brown since 1995 (having originally been recruited as a Labour Party aide by Harriet Harman, when she was part of Brown's shadow Treasury team). Miliband is like Balls's gentler twin: they have the same policy interests, but Miliband – who was educated at a North London comprehensive and is the son of a prominent Marxist theoretician, the late Ralph Miliband – dislikes the brawling of party politics and is rather more cerebral than his namesake.

He and Brown imported the tax-credit concept from the United States, which has been paying a tax credit to families with children – called the Earned Income Tax Credit – since 1975. They initially viewed it as just one part of their ambitious programme to create employment, reduce the incidence of chronically low pay and make work financially worthwhile for those on the lowest incomes. The other elements in this programme were the introduction of a national minimum wage, the halving of the so-called starting rate of income tax from 20 per cent to 10 per cent (which was implemented in 1999) and the New Deal package of training or job opportunities for the young unemployed and the long-term unemployed.

Their initial priority was tackling two causes of unemployment and deprivation: the unemployment trap (or financial disincentives to take work) and the poverty trap (financial disincentives to increase earnings by working longer hours or learning new skills). The poverty trap was particularly acute when Labour won the 1997 election, in the sense that – before the budget in 1998 – some 130,000 people on low incomes lost 90 pence in withdrawn benefits and tax for every additional pound they earned and 300,000 people lost 80 pence in the pound (social security benefits were slashed when a recipient started working more hours). These "marginal deduction rates" are the equivalent of penal tax rates for the very poor. It was a scandal that for so many people it was only possible to take home 10p or 20p of every extra pound they were paid in work.

The impact of Brown's tax credits and of his new lower 10 per cent starting rate of tax (which was announced in 1999) was to slash the numbers suffering from penal marginal deduction rates. Thus by 2003/4, just 30,000 people were victims of a 90 per cent deduction rate and 135,000 were liable to an 80 per cent rate. The most startling and impressive improvement was in respect of those paying a 70 per cent marginal deduction rate, down from 740,000 in 1997/8 to 185,000. So it was a serious initiative to reduce poverty.

However, there is still an unfairness when the tax and benefits system is viewed in the round. Today, a staggering 1.5m people lose 60 per cent or more of every additional pound they earn from the combined impact of taxation and the loss of benefits and tax credits. That's up from 760,000 under the Tories. So the paradox of Brown's generous tax credits is that they have made hundreds of thousands of people better off but have left them subject to deduction rates higher than the tax rates paid by genuinely wealthy people. To give a concrete example, a City whiz-kid takes home 59 per cent of the millions he earns in bonuses (40 per cent is taken by the top rate of tax and 1 per cent by the special National Insurance levy announced in 2002), while a couple with several children on a modest income retain just 40 per cent of the incremental pounds they earn.

This disparity does not seem to accord with Labour's concept of social justice. It's likely therefore that pressure will build up within the Labour Party to increase the top rate of income tax to 50 per cent, with the proceeds used to reduce the marginal deduction rate for those receiving tax credits at the bottom end of the income scale also to 50 per cent – though Brown will not signal any moves in such a controversial direction this side of a general election and would always eschew it if he felt it undermined enterprise (these days, unlike in 1997, a 50 per cent tax rate on those earning more than £100,000 per year would yield a useful some of money, more than £5bn according to the Institute for Fiscal Studies).

But a mission to widely share (if not "redistribute" in the classic socialist sense) the cost of lifting up the lowest paid is one that Brown has pursued. It is part of the rationale for a national minimum wage, which Brown saw as the natural complement to the Working Families Tax Credit. The minimum wage imposes on employers some of the costs of improving the rewards of work for the least well-off: the higher the minimum wage (it was initially set at an adult rate of £3.60 per hour in April 1999 and has been raised incrementally to £4.85 in October 2004), the less that the state needs to pay out in employment subsidies through the tax credit system.

At the birth of tax credits after the 1997 general election, Brown also forced employers to take on the responsibility and costs of administering the Working Families Tax Credit, so that it could be paid in the wage packet through the PAYE system. This was deliberate: Brown wanted the credit to be viewed by recipients as the fruits of work, not as a state handout. However the burden was hated by employers. And it was criticised by equal opportunity campaigners, because the abolished family credit had typically been paid to the woman in a household, whereas the WFTC tended to go to the working man.

Another unexpected critic of tax credits in general was the Prime Minister. According to Treasury officials, Blair and his allies were always grumbling that tax credits were an expensive distraction. "They thought it was a waste of money," says one. "It was money they could have spent on public services rather than poor people."

However, tax credits became impossible to resist after Blair made a famous commitment – in March 1999 – to abolish child poverty over 20 years. A friend of Brown recalls conversations about all this between the Chancellor and the Prime Minister: "Tony would ask, 'Why are you wasting all those billions on that?'" In reply, Brown and Balls would point to Blair's pledge to abolish child poverty in a generation and tell him that they were jolly keen to help him keep that promise.

In fact the dye had largely been cast three months earlier, on the morning of December 16, 1998. That was when Brown and Balls – who had just flown in from the US – held a secret meeting with a quartet of senior officials (including Miliband, Nick Macpherson, then in charge of "working incentive policy analysis" or "weeper", and his counterpart at the Inland Revenue, Tony Orhnial). The big question was how to increase payments to families with children and ensure that the bulk of the increments went to poor families. This was a complex and politically explosive issue, because of the symbolic importance within the British welfare tradition of child benefit – which is paid to all parents and is not means-tested. Simply increasing child benefit was not on, because it meant that wealthy families would receive just as much as poor ones. So the Treasury looked at taxing child benefit for those on higher earnings. But that didn't work either: under a system where wives and husbands are taxed independently of each other, couples with a single earner on a middling income of around £35,000 a year would have their child benefit taxed, whereas households with two earners on £30,000 each would receive the benefit tax-free.

The alternative – which was adopted at the airport rendezvous – was to create the Children's Tax Credit, payable only to households where the combined salary of earners was less than £38,000. Brownism was acquiring a recognisable form: the merger of the tax and benefits system was well under way; and the regressive aspects of independent taxation were under attack, through linking entitlement to the tax credit to total household income.

But, as the scale of Brown's social engineering ambitions grew and grew, so the mechanics of administering tax credits have changed. The administrative burden has been taken off employers: Brown is now convinced that the credits are widely viewed as a reward for work, so the fact that they will be paid directly by the state should not transform their image into handouts for the feckless (recipients will deal directly with the Inland Revenue and payments will go directly into their respective bank accounts). One benefit of this reform is that the bias against the money going to the woman of the household has been removed.

However, there have been cock-ups, precipitated by the introduction of Child and Working Tax Credits in 2003, which increased the numbers eligible for the credits by several million. In particular, the Inland Revenue has been brutal in some cases in the way it has reduced payments to families whose pay has risen or whom it deems to have received excessive tax credits – and some of these households have found it hard adjusting to the sudden drop in income. Even so, the evidence suggests that the system has had a positive impact on reducing poverty and increasing employment – and it seems to have had a particularly strong effect in encouraging lone parents to take work.

***

If Brown's approach to increasing the rewards from employment for those at the lower end of the income scale has been strategic, the same cannot be said of those of his initiatives that have an impact on current and future pensioners. Uncharacteristically, he's muddled through when designing his pensions policies. At best, what he has done can be described as pragmatic. At worst, he's been opportunistic and short-termist. And, what is perhaps even more troubling, he has – until very recently – been in denial about this failure.

To be clear, none of his actions have been intrinsically disastrous, despite the jibes of a financial services industry desperate to distract attention from its own lamentable performance as a provider of retirement savings plans. Even Brown's 1997 raid on the income of pension funds, when he seized £5bn of income per year from them by abolishing the tax credit on company dividends, was not as damaging as is often alleged. Around £3bn of these proceeds were channelled into a cut in corporation tax, which increased the intrinsic value of companies and therefore boosted the value of pension funds' assets. By the same token, the Treasury's notorious decision in the autumn of 1999 to increase the basic state pension by a paltry and insulting 75 pence per week – which was prompted by a mad fear that a dangerous precedent would be set by waiving the mechanistic up-rating formula linked to retail price inflation – was only half the story. Brown also announced a couple of populist wheezes: pensioners aged 75 or over would receive a free television licence; and there was a significant increase to £100 per annum in an allowance for every pensioner household to cover winter fuel costs.

There was some method in this mass of contradictions. Brown wanted to direct scarce resources towards the neediest pensioners. So his so-called minimum pension guarantee – the aggregate of the basic pension and social security payments – was raised in line with average earnings. Here he was again extending the use of means testing (though, as ever, he hated that description). And the trend was reinforced in 2003 with the introduction of the Pension Credit, an income top-up for poor pensioners that was supposed to be analogous to the Working Tax Credit and the Child Tax Credit. Brown's "progressive universalism" now stretched from cradle to grave.

However, this putative familial relationship between the Pension Credit and tax credits was spurious. In practice, they were almost mutually contradictory in their effects on people's behaviour. Tax credits are an encouragement to take work and be self-sufficient. By contrast, the Pension Credit serves as a disincentive to save for those on lowish incomes, because only those with negligible savings can receive it in retirement. So the Pension Credit is a discouragement to thrift and self-sufficiency, virtues that Brown would claim to be the very essence of Brownism. As it happens, there is very little evidence that – just at this moment – the Pension Credit is having a profound influence on the savings habits of employees. But even the possibility that it will deter saving is cause for concern, given that far too few people are putting enough cash into private pension funds.

In fact, probably the most important domestic policy challenge faced by the government is how to close this gap between what the mass of people have tucked away for their retirement and what's needed to deliver a comfortable and respectable post-employment income. The Treasury hasn't ignored the yawning hole, but all its prescriptions for filling it have been ineffectual. Thus the take-up of so-called Stakeholder Pensions – a Brown initiative to promote saving by imposing a ceiling on the fees payable to the pension provider – has been miniscule. And a recent simplification of the tax system as it applies to pensions may inadvertently lead to a reduction in the number of company pension schemes.

It's an uninspiring story. Will it have a happy ending? That's doubtful, given that the development of pensions policy has recently been engulfed in the power struggle between 10 Downing Street and the Treasury. In between the battalions is Adair Turner, the former Director-General of the CBI, who has been mandated to assess whether we should all be compelled to make contributions to pensions schemes and whether the normal age for retiring and drawing a pension should be raised (*inter alia*). His task is unenviable, because it is inconceivable that his recommendations, whatever they turn out to be, will please both Brown and Blair.

A colleague of the Prime Minister says: "Blair doesn't want compulsion. He doesn't want a rise in the pension age. I'm not sure what he wants to be honest." Which is not a great surprise, since any decision to force us all to put money into pension schemes would probably be widely viewed as a *de facto* tax increase: not a prospect that would bring joy to Blair. On the other hand, Blair seems determined to characterise Brown's Pension Credit as malign and is likely to push for its abolition. "Blair is going to be year zero on pensions," says a government member. "He is going to say that the Treasury and Gordon Brown screwed up pensions. And there'll be a big attack on the pension credit and on all Brown's schemes to promote saving."

As for Brown, one of his allies says that – after the election – he will probably embrace a combination of savings compulsion and a rise in the retirement age. But guess what? He'll fight to preserve his cherished pension credit – which isn't completely irrational, since the pension credit would not tend to undermine saving in a lethal way so long as we were all forced to save. All in all it's doubtful that Brown will be motivated purely by reason: dumping a policy stamped with his brand at the behest of Blair has never yet happened, and would probably only happen over his politically dead body.

***

There is only one important sense in which the pension credit and tax credits can be seen to spring from a common political source. They are Brownite in the sense that they aim to close the gap between rich and poor. But although income redistribution is for many people at the very essence of what Labour will always be about, that is not a view held by Blair. When I asked him in a press conference in the run-up to the 1997 general election whether he would deem himself to have failed if, by 2001, he hadn't narrowed the income gap (assuming he became Prime Minister), he neatly sidestepped the question, answering only that he wanted to lift up the poorest. This prevarication was more-or-less repeated during the 2001 election campaign, when Blair was asked a similar question on BBC2's *Newsnight*.

It may be slightly odd that a leader of the Labour Party should be too embarrassed to discuss whether he would like to reduce inequality. But, as it turns out, the very richest have in fact accumulated a larger share of the cake since he took power. A study by the influential Institute for Fiscal Studies shows that the incomes of the richest 1 per cent have grown at 4.2 per cent under New Labour, or 25 per cent faster than for any other percentile group (each 1 per cent of the population, as grouped by income). Meanwhile, for reasons that are difficult to explain, the incomes of the very poorest – those in the bottom two percentiles – have actually fallen.

Now, few of Brown's policies have done much to stem the trend of the very wealthiest becoming even wealthier – which has becoming a defining trend of recent years, especially in the US, where almost a century of steady convergence between rich and poor has been reversed (a study by the left-leaning Institute of Public Policy Research, "Rethinking Social Justice," showed that the share of national wealth, as opposed to income, held by the very richest in Britain has also risen). But Brown's redistribution – or more properly his distribution, since there's not been a great deal of taking from the haves (with the exception of his sharp increases in stamp duty payable on sales of residential property) – has not been trivial. And it has not been confined to helping the working poor, to the exclusion of the unemployed, quite as much as his public pronouncements might suggest. With a deliberate absence of fuss and publicity, almost all the increments in tax credits have been replicated in increases in income support to the non-working impoverished.

On the other hand, the extremely indigent, the absolute poorest, seem to have missed out, according to the IFS's figures – and Treasury officials admit to being nonplussed by this. But what is perhaps even more surprising is that the very rich have actually benefited from Brown's conviction that economic growth requires the encouragement of entrepreneurialism and enterprise. So where he has felt that a tax incentive for the haves would yield dividends for rich and poor alike by increasing the underlying growth rate of the economy through productivity improvements, he's been prepared to provide rewards for the wealthy.

His most conspicuous measure in this respect has been to cut the rate of Capital Gains Tax from 40 per cent to 10 per cent for investments of two years or more in what the Inland Revenue defines as business assets. These include shares held by employees in their companies, any business created by an entrepreneur and stakes in unlisted companies. On the margin, Brown may have sparked the creation of some new companies through the CGT overhaul, but its more visible short-term effect has been to massively enrich wealthy individuals who already owned stakes in companies (among others, the directors of the Queen's stockbroker, Cazenove – which has been around for 182 years – have reason to thank Brown for his largesse). It has also encouraged the takeover of old-established companies by small groups of well-heeled investors, in a process dubbed as "privatisation" (not the Thatcherite version of selling public sector assets, but the transformation of sleepy publicly quoted companies, those listed on the Stock Exchange, into secretive 'private' companies). Thus any billionaire would pay CGT of just 10p in the pound on the disposal of a UK business (on the unlikely assumption that any of his or her wealth were parked here for tax purposes rather than in low-tax regimes off-shore).

So there is a risk that this CGT reform is simply enriching small numbers of privileged people in a regressive way, while doing little of benefit for the economic performance of the UK – which would be an indictment of Brown and New Labour. Many of its supporters would wonder why on earth they should elect a Labour government, if it makes little inroads into inequality. However, what's been happening to incomes at the extremes of wealth and poverty turn out to be untypical. Or to put it another way, tax credits have had a significant effect.

What the IFS shows is that if the population is split into quintiles (or groups of 20 per cent, determined by income), the incomes of the poorest two quintiles have risen faster than the rest, since Labour took office. And households with children have done particularly well. Interestingly, it's the middle-middle classes who have done worst, those in the third and second richest groups – which suggests there is an electoral opportunity for the Tories, if they can whip up resentment among these middling income groups.

There has been genuine redistribution compared with the Thatcher years from 1979 to 1990, when economic power brought disproportionate returns: back then, the poorest 20 per cent saw the tiniest real income increases, and each ascending quintile progressively did better (with the richest doing very nicely indeed). And what has been noted with considerable satisfaction by Brown and his friends is that the Gini coefficient, a statistical measure of income inequality, fell by a tiny amount between 2000 and 2003 – suggesting there has been a modest reduction in inequality. However that fall is described by the IFS as not statistically significant, whereas the overall increase in inequality since 1997 is statistically significant.

Brown's attempt to distribute the fruits of economic growth through tax credits, in order to lean against inequality (in the centre-left tradition probably best described by Tony Crosland), has so far been a moderate success on any kind of egalitarian measure. For Brown, whatever his future political role, this is unfinished business.

CHAPTER NINE
Brown's Britain

T hrough most of the 1990s, the tensions between Gordon Brown and Tony Blair stemmed mostly from Blair's frustration with Brown's determination to retain the policymaking autonomy he had won as part of the Granita deal. With no serious parliamentary opposition to speak of and his massive majority in the Commons, it was irksome for the Prime Minister that the Treasury was so little under his sway. However, when it came to the policies themselves – as opposed to the process of making them – there was not a great gulf between the two of them. Like most Prime Ministers, Blair was more reluctant to raise taxes than his Chancellor. He couldn't understand why Brown was keeping quite such a tight control on public spending in the early years. And he has never liked Brown's redistribution to those on low incomes through his system of tax credits.

But these disagreements were not of a life-or-death significance, even if they could occasionally become heated. Blair and Brown were conspicuously playing for the same team and their joint project was to prove to the electorate that it was possible to combine sensible management of the economy with progressive social policies. Although it's true that their relationship was (and is) irrevocably damaged by Brown's resentment of Blair for stealing his crown and Blair's resentment of him for stealing the Prime Minister's proper powers, it's only in the last three years that they have also been fighting over the more fundamental question of New Labour's political destination.

After the 2001 election landslide, the nature of their disputes became altogether more serious. The Prime Minister and the Chancellor began to fight over the very measures that the government should adopt. One example, described in Chapter Six, was Blair's fury with Brown for refusing to rig the Treasury's assessment of the euro in favour of British membership. That was not an ideological rift, but was centred around Brown's conviction that it would be disastrous for the British economy if we joined at the wrong time, while Blair felt that the economy would muddle through and that the price of not joining in terms of lost political influence in the EU was excessive.

However, their clashes over health service reforms and a new funding system for universities were much more about their respective political values – though in both cases there were also arguments about practicalities. Labour's second term in office was to a large extent characterised by Brown exercising his right under the Granita deal – as he saw it – to act as the Party's conscience and criticise the Prime Minister when he perceived him to be veering too far to the right and away from Labour's essential tenets. As the Granita briefing note shows (see pages 66-7), his role was to a large extent as New Labour's Jiminy Cricket and the guarantor that Tony Blair would not be swayed from a path of promoting social justice. It didn't say "GB shall have the power to overhaul the NHS". But it did imply that if Blair wanted to change health service provision in a way that jarred with Brown's notions of Labour's fundamental mission, Brown was entitled to frustrate and block.

That said, Blair viewed Brown's behaviour as neither legitimate nor principled. He interpreted it as Brown pandering to the left in a divisive way to shore up his power base. "Blair always characterises the rows as being about personalities, about Gordon's ambitions, in order to trivialise them," says an ally of Brown. "But they were much more than that." Anyway it was their mutual inability to engage in an open policy debate, untainted by mistrust of their respective ambitions, which finally led to the collapse of the Granita deal in 2004 and a new and dangerous standoff between them.

So how was the great impasse reached? Well, one cause was Brown's unwonted and short-sighted decision not to seize the initiative in a debate on the future of the National Health Service by coming up with detailed reform plans at an early stage. Many billions of pounds of new money were going into health from 2001 onwards and much of it was bound to be wasted – or at least so Brown's own officials warned him quite explicitly – because controlling an organisation as vast as the NHS from Whitehall was grotesquely inefficient. Why on earth didn't Brown come up with a plan in the late 1990s to improve the efficiency of the NHS, in the way that he had shaken up the tax and benefits system, or taken bold initiatives to create employment, or inaugurated a new competition policy, or even overhauled the functions of the Treasury itself? He had never before been put off by the notion that he was over-reaching the bounds of the Treasury's formal responsibilities. Why didn't he act? The reason, in part, is that – at the relevant moment – it would have been a battle too far. Given the resentment felt by the Prime Minister and his close allies at Brown's unprecedented autonomous control over vast swathes of government business, he couldn't set the pace for all necessary reforms – although there is now a recognition by his team that he made a mistake in holding back.

Brown contented himself with interventions in the government's debate on NHS reform of a "thus far and no further" sort. He has strong reservations about so-called market solutions for the NHS's problems (see pages 295-309) – which led him to frustrate some elements of the "modernisation" programme of 10 Downing Street and Alan Milburn (until Milburn resigned as Health Secretary on June 12 2003, ostensibly to spend more time with his family, after a series of clashes with Brown). Here we can see why Blair finally came to hate the Granita agreement, in that it held back the implementation of important new policies by legitimising Brown's interventions when he believed that Labour's commitment to "equity" (a favourite Brown word) was being sacrificed in the pursuit of free market solutions. If Brown has not transformed the

NHS, he has certainly made it far more difficult for Blair and Milburn to undertake a wholesale transformation.

But if Brown had all the levers of power at his disposal, what would he actually do? This chapter will look at what kind of Prime Minister Brown would be. As it happens, Brown has recently started to set out his personal manifesto in a more explicit way, having belatedly reached the inescapable conclusion that Blair will not smooth the way to his taking over as Prime Minister and that he will only become Premier if he fights for it. Much of his newish agenda focuses around the notion that the mission of the left is to prove that the ethos of public service can be harnessed to provide top quality health and education services in an efficient way. It goes against the tide of free-market ideology of the past 25 years, which claims as fact the idea that efficient outcomes can only be provided by the imposition of market structures, and it will be a hard sell outside the ranks of traditional Labour supporters. Also – and this is no coincidence – it's a deliberate challenge to Blair, his Health Secretary, John Reid, and his new policymaker-in-chief, Alan Milburn (who has returned to the Cabinet as Chancellor of the Duchy of Lancaster), who are proponents of providing "choice" in the NHS via a wholesale privatisation of medical services.

Some of what differentiates him from Blair are personal political obsessions of older vintage: an obsession with stimulating charitable giving and encouraging the voluntary sector, for example, and with endeavouring to eliminate the crippling burden of debt on impoverished African nations. His charity initiatives range from the relatively small and personal (such as allowing any credible charity to use Number 11 Downing Street for a function, free of charge) to a massive extension of the tax relief available to donations under the gift aid scheme by abolishing the ceiling on such charitable gifts (although the income of charities, like pension funds, was initially hurt by his abolition in 1997 of the so-called tax credit on dividends).

Also, since 1997 he has worked with great zeal and imagination to persuade the developed world to forgive most of their loans to poor countries. On September 26, 2004, it was striking to witness the excited and warm reception given to Brown by seasoned anti-poverty campaigners – who are cynical about most elected politicians – when he sermonised to them. The meeting was held in a vast, lavishly decorated church in Brighton, St Bartholomew's, on the opening day of Labour's annual conference. Thousands of protestors associated with the Trade Justice Movement had been on the sea front since 11.30, making a great din about the need for the leaders of the wealthier countries to stop forcing the developing ones to open their markets, to curb the alleged depredation of big companies on the environment and weak economies, and also to bring greater democracy and transparency to the making of international trade policy. Only the most hard-nosed and committed remained to hear the Chancellor, but they were surprisingly willing to give him the benefit of the doubt, almost to regard him as one of their own – which is slightly odd given that he would find it difficult to sign up to every element in their manifesto, as a proponent of free trade. What was impossible to miss, however, was the sincerity of his speech (a quality that is not always present in his general political addresses), which included a tirade against the west in general for failing to provide the necessary resources to honour promises, known as the Millennium Development Goals, to end avoidable infant and maternal deaths, ensure primary schooling is available to every child in the world and halve global poverty, all by 2015. He was at ease in the pulpit – which says something about the empathy he felt for his late father, the Rev John Brown – and was apparently more comfortable with this audience than when addressing a crowd of Labour activists.

Brown has put Britain's money where his mouth is over the past seven years. As well as pushing the Group of Seven leading industrial nations to adopt strategies to help impoverished nations build their economies, rather than simply forcing these destitute states to tighten their belts in the traditional way, he has written off 100 per cent of Britain's bilateral debt to the heavily indebted countries. He has come up with a range of suggestions for slashing multilateral debt (loans from international financial institutions such as the World Bank) and on September 26, 2004 he said that the UK would pay 10 per cent of the interest and debt repayments that the poorest countries were obliged to make to the World Bank and African Development Bank. Another of his initiatives, which has not yet been adopted, is a clever piece of financial engineering, called the International Finance Facility, whose aim is to boost aid to Africa and the poorest nations by $50bn per annum for 15 years and put the west back on track to achieve the Millennium Development Goals. The plan is that the developed countries will channel $16bn per annum of increased aid – which they promised to make at the Monterrey Conference on Financing for Development in March 2002 – into servicing the principal and interest on new international bonds. Launched at Chatham House in January 2003, the proposed IFF stems from a year of detailed technical preparation by the Treasury in consultation with the US investment bank, Goldman Sachs, and credit rating agencies, to verify that the financial markets will provide the $50bn per annum on reasonable terms. It's probably his single most important political priority (apart from becoming Prime Minister) as he made clear in an important speech he gave on October 22 2004, when he attempted to set out a distinctive Brownite vision for Britain (see page 318). He described the IFF as "a new Marshall Plan (the US post-war reconstruction plan for Europe), as bold a step in this generation as the very creation of the UN and World Bank was for the last, a new deal that emphasises the responsibilities of the developing countries to root out corruption as much as our responsibilities to provide aid for development."

Earlier on July 12, 2004 in his announcement of government's spending plans for the subsequent three years, he committed to continue to raise the share of British national income devoted to overseas aid from the 0.26 per cent he inherited to 0.42 per cent in 2006-7 and 0.7 per cent in 2013. That had a powerful symbolism, because in 1970 the United Nations General Assembly adopted a target of 0.7 per cent for aid as a percentage of gross national income, but major industrial countries have consistently provided only a fraction of that. Brown estimates that if his

Finance Facility were adopted, the UK would reach the 0.7 per cent objective much earlier, in 2008-9.

There is a double significance to Brown's work in the aid arena, which is that he sees the creation of mass-movement, anti-poverty pressure groups as a model for how to restore faith in traditional politics. He is deeply worried by voter apathy, as he said to me in an interview for the *Sunday Telegraph* on September 24, 2004:

> It was the last general election where the number of young people voting was less than 40 per cent. This is a long running problem and challenge which has got to be met. I think we have got to look at the energy and the dynamism of local community, NGO and voluntary organisations and the activity that they generate. Some of our great pressure groups have managed to attract members just as political parties have been losing them. So we've got a lot to learn from organisations outside politics and that make us think about how we can deal with the future of traditional politics.

Brown's new agenda includes plans for rebuilding trust in politics and politicians through radical constitutional reform – including, possibly, the codification of the UK's sprawling constitution, or what's usually called (slightly misleadingly) the preparation of a "written constitution" (which is discussed in more detail on pages 319-20). But to learn about Brown and his convictions, it's also instructive to look at his more traditional political activities. His punch-ups with Blair since 2001 over the future of hospitals and universities (the sort of infighting which is supposedly a great turn-off to the electorate, though my view is that voters are not repelled by honest arguments like these over matters of principle) also give insights into what the map of Brown's Britain would look like.

Brown has never shown a world-class talent in the display of unity with 10 Downing Street, for all his sincere rhetoric about the importance of Party unity. But even the pretence of solidarity with Blair and his people more or less disappeared during his second term of office. For the good of the Party, Brown would imply, he had to resist what he perceived as the reactionary, right-wing instincts of the premier. Briefings by Brown's allies have been increasingly sharp-edged and explicit about the policy gulf with Blair. And Brown hasn't been coy about the hiatus. Probably the most important speech he has given since 1997 – which was on the role of market mechanisms in the delivery of public services and was delivered in February 2003 at a meeting organised by the Social Market Foundation – was a very public declaration of independence from the Blairite policy agenda, though it received surprisingly little attention in the media.

The SMF speech was prompted by almost a year of wrangling over the future of the NHS. But to digress for a moment, there could well have been a ruction over the basic direction of the Party much earlier. If Brown had known about Blair's ambitions in the mid-1990s to bring Liberal Democrats into a Labour Cabinet as a possible precursor to a full merger of the two parties, he would have objected: Brown preferred to conquer and marginalise the Lib Dems rather than court and marry them. As it happens, he knew nothing about Blair's secret talks with Paddy Ashdown until they were disclosed by the former Liberal Democrat leader after his diaries were published in 2000. "Tony kept asking Gordon to meet this guy Ashdown, but he never really knew why," says one of his friends. "What Gordon now thinks about all this is that if Tony really wanted to realign the parties of the left in the way that he claims, his big opportunity was in 1997 and he fluffed it."

The divergence over the health service started to become conspicuous after the 2002 budget, the one that included the National Insurance levy that paid for a long term surge in NHS spending. Brown's statement to the Commons raised the prospect of giving greater management autonomy to hospitals that had proved their clinical and management competence (the phrased used by Brown in his budget speech was "greater freedoms for high-performing hospitals and trusts"). But he did not explicitly refer to "Foundation Hospitals", Milburn's big idea which he had been floating as Health Secretary since the beginning of the year.

Foundation Hospitals, under Milburn's vision, were to be not-for-profit companies, that would be given almost complete management autonomy so long as they met national clinical standards and were financially competent. Milburn also wanted these hospital-companies to have the freedom to borrow privately from banks, to buy and sell assets and to keep the proceeds of land sales, on the basis that the discipline of behaving like a company – especially the discipline of having to make debt payments – might improve their efficiency.

In the spring of 2002, Brown and his officials thought this was a classic attempt by a minister at a spending department to break free from the limits on expenditure set by the Treasury. They thought that what Milburn wanted was simply to allow the Foundation Hospitals to spend and borrow without being subject to Treasury controls. There was nothing terribly novel about such a demand: there is a great tradition of ministers urging a Chancellor to set free this or that arm of their respective departments, on the basis that the public good would be served if, as one example, a new-fangled public housing institution or some transport service were to be able to invest more by borrowing from the City.

The Treasury's response is usually a simple "no". And so it was for Milburn, as one of Brown's colleagues recalls: "We said, 'There is no way they should be able to borrow off budget, because that would break down public spending discipline'." The Treasury made this point to Milburn on the afternoon of April 18 2002, which was the day after the budget. "We were all in favour of top-rated Foundation Hospitals having more freedom and flexibility," says a Treasury official. "But Milburn was told that any debt taken on by these hospitals would come out of his budget."

It was the kind of argument that Treasury officials would push irrespective of which party was in power, because what was at stake was its ability to keep public sector borrowing within prudent limits. But the argument soon shifted from narrow technocratic issues into more ideological ones. "In July 2002, after the budget, Milburn moved from a position of 'high-performing hospitals should be allowed to borrow more', which is a traditional attack on the Treasury," an official recalls. "He started to argue that the borrowing should be classified to the private sector and therefore not on the government balance sheet, on the grounds that Foundation Hospitals are really private companies." What was worrying for Brown is that there were precedents for treating Foundation Hospitals in this way: for example, universities are not classified to the public sector, because they have independent sources of income, such as fees from foreign students, and they have their own estates (a fact which the Treasury is desperately keen to keep quiet, for fear that other state bodies will notice and start lobbying for their financial fetters to be cut). "Milburn shifted towards the argument that Foundation Hospitals should be like universities, not public sector," an official says. "In a draft guidance note about Foundation Hospitals which he circulated, one of the explanations which he put for this was that they would be able to justify this borrowing on the basis of the income they would generate from private practice."

It was at this point that a conventional spat between the Department of Health and the Treasury escalated into a much more serious dispute. Brown had two profound objections to the notion that Foundation Hospitals should be encouraged to carry out more private work: at a time of scarce health resources, it would lead to rampant inflation of healthcare costs and would diminish resources available through the NHS; and he was worried that Foundation Hospitals would become like NHS dental practices, offering a topnotch service to those who pay extra for private treatment and a very basic one for those insisting on a pure NHS service. "We said that was completely unacceptable," an official says.

Milburn, who was increasingly viewed by Brown as a licenced vanguardist for Blair under the tutelage of Peter Mandelson, drew the battle lines as he saw them in an article in the *Times* on August 7, 2002. His piece was all about the need to extend the involvement of the private sector and the voluntary sector in the delivery of public services, especially health, and also about how we should all be able to exercise more choice over the schools and hospitals we use. What particularly infuriated Brown was that Milburn set up an argument between the so-called "transformers" – those, like Milburn, who allegedly had the courage and vision to see that New Labour must be bolder in its reforming ambitions – and the "consolidators". This last group – implicitly Brown and the Brownites – was defined by a strategy of "accepting the reforms made so far and relying on increased public spending to deliver an expanded service, but one whose culture remains essentially unchanged". Brown vehemently denies that his position was quite so conservative. But he was in no doubt that Milburn was painting him as the leader of the antediluvian consolidators. "A deliberate attempt was made to characterise Gordon and the rest of us as centralisers and anti-reform," says a colleague of the Chancellor.

Milburn's argument was conducted mainly in generalities. His notable claims were these:

> Patients need greater freedom to choose where and when they are treated and resources must follow... While those who favour consolidation imply that choice is neither possible nor desirable in a public service like the NHS, the experience from other tax-funded healthcare systems such as those in Denmark proves them wrong. We should never have let the Right occupy this territory. Choice and diversity of provision should be the preserve of the Centre Left in this country, just as it has been in Scandinavia...
>
> In Britain we have allowed choice over schools or health provision to be the exclusive preserve of those who can pay directly. Embracing diversity can extend choice beyond the ability to pay... Ensuring high quality but locally delivered public services run in the public, private or voluntary sectors is true to our socialist values, but breaks from our overly centralised, paternalistic, Labourist history.

What did Milburn mean by all this? This is what Brown thought it meant, according to an official:

> Blair and Milburn developed a view that the NHS should not be a

provider of services, it should be an 'organising idea'. So having a competition between public and private within the NHS was the way to go because private was necessarily better. Also the rhetoric suggested that 'choice' was going to be about vouchers and using the price mechanism for people to choose which hospital they wanted to go to. That quite quickly gets you to an American-type insurance model, which is hugely expensive and unfair.

So for Brown, Milburn was arguing for a demolition of the very essence of the NHS. The stakes could not have been higher. "Part of the problem we had with Blair and Milburn is their wanting to say 'private good, public bad'," says an ally of the Chancellor. "It was also them wanting to say that choice and the price mechanism and the market system is the best way to deliver public services. We said that would cause us real problems on equity grounds and was also going to turn out to be very expensive by raising costs and expectations".

To be clear, Brown's position is not "public good, private bad". In fact the notion that he is uncomfortable with the private sector and wealth creation is wrong (though this is not the same thing as saying that he has an empathetic bond with the private sector, which he plainly does not). It's striking that, even when he's goaded from the left wing, he resists the temptation to say that there should be any limit to how rich any individual should become. He has frequently been a bold proponent of privatisation, as manifested in his unwavering and unpopular insistence on a private sector solution to the renewal of the London Underground in the late 1990s (against some strong practical arguments that it would not work) and his contentious decision that 46 per cent of National Air Traffic Services (or the air traffic control system) should be sold to a consortium of airlines (which took place in July, 2001). But – in contrast to the position he believes is Blair's – he does not see public sector ownership as always the second best option. This is how he put it on September 27, 2004, at Labour's annual conference in Brighton: "I have seen… that there are values far beyond those of contracts, markets and exchange and that public service can be a calling not just a career". His view is that there are certain public services which are not amenable to privatisation without excessive damage to "equity" – which broadly means that he fears the poor would suffer – and without excessive cost.

If that's a credible position, in the autumn of 2002 there was still a risk that Milburn and Blair would succeed in characterising him as a dinosaur who would never break up the unwieldy and inefficient NHS monolith, while they were the imaginative, decentralising progressives. And, as the newspapers were recording every skirmish throughout September, Brown became increasingly concerned that the Prime Minister himself was encouraging this factionalism. Brown and Balls held meetings with Blair and Jeremy Heywood, during which Brown would insist that the core issue was a technical one about public spending control and that the Treasury could not possibly lose this control without wreaking havoc on the government's economic credibility. Brown and Balls were sure that Heywood agreed with his analysis. So why was the Prime Minister not closing down Milburn? Why was he allowing the argument to rage? The only reason that they could identify was that he wanted to embarrass Brown.

As summer turned to autumn, the Prime Minister still refused to intervene. Brown's patience was exhausted and at the end of September, just before Labour's annual conference – and hours before he and Balls were due to fly out to Washington for the annual meeting of the International Monetary Fund – his private office sent Heywood a letter and a separate Treasury paper on Foundation Hospitals. It was copied to every member of the Cabinet and set out the Treasury's objections to Milburn's version of Foundation Hospitals, highlighting in particular the risks for the control of public spending and pointing out that costs for the rest of the NHS, the "core" NHS, might soar. This was a highly inflammatory act, especially since Brown's *modus operandi* was almost never to put anything down on paper. Blair was furious, interpreting Brown's intervention as profoundly hostile. The Prime Minister's advisers counselled him that the only reason Brown would have done this was as a prelude to leaking the paper, to destabilise and embarrass Milburn (the paper was in fact never leaked or even mentioned in the press). So Number 10 simply decided – in a surreal tactic that it has used on a number of occasions – that the Treasury paper had not been formally received by it. Blair's officials rang round the Cabinet to tell other ministers that they should treat the paper as not having arrived. In fact, lots of ministers never got sight of it, because 10 Downing Street succeeded in nobbling their respective private offices. As far as the Chancellor was concerned, however, the paper had been distributed and his battle position had been staked out.

The climax of the conflict came when Brown, back from Washington, made his speech to Labour's annual conference in Blackpool on September 30. Balls gave a briefing to journalists about his speech, as he always does, and was asked by a reporter whether Foundation Hospitals would have the freedom to borrow. He said "no", that NHS hospitals were in the public sector and that borrowing by NHS Foundation Hospitals would be included in the public sector accounts. At that point, the dispute was out in the open and Milburn's officials started briefing against Balls and Brown in a conspicuous way. All of a sudden, what started as an apparently dull argument about the management of hospitals was being portrayed in the media as full-scale internecine war in the Cabinet. The *FT* wrote:

The simmering row between Gordon Brown and Alan Milburn over financial freedoms for new Foundation Hospitals boiled over yesterday, with allies of the Cabinet heavyweights openly briefing against each other on the fringes of the conference.

The dispute went on throughout the week and was only settled the following Monday, October 7, at a meeting between Blair, Brown, Milburn and John Prescott, the Deputy Prime Minister. Milburn secured his aim that top-performing hospitals should become independent, locally based "public interest" companies, no longer owned or run by the NHS but still largely serving NHS patients. And these new Foundation

Hospitals would have the right to borrow from the financial markets. But Brown retained for the Treasury the ability to control how much they would borrow. Their debt would remain on the public sector balance sheet. And whatever was borrowed by them would reduce the amount available to Milburn for spending on other parts of the NHS. Brown was probably the victor, as a government member explains:

> If Foundation Hospitals wanted more funds, it came out of the NHS's allocation. Which is why it became a debate in the Labour Party about why hospitals which aren't Foundation Hospitals should lose out to hospitals that are. And that suited Gordon fine.

However the victory was short-lived.

Brown recognised his vulnerability to the charge that he was opposing reform out of a fear of change, so he needed to present his own, alternative view of the future of public services. In a speech in early 2003 for the Social Market Foundation – the think tank whose politics have veered around the centre ground for some years – he went back to first principles to come up with a clearer theory of what the relationship between public services and the private sector should be. Called "A Modern Agenda for Prosperity and Social Reform," it was long and cumbersome. It was also rather dull for anyone unaware that his insistence that he is a true radical and not an unimaginative "consolidator" was a direct and personal riposte to Milburn's swipe at him.

The main point of the speech was to demolish what Brown perceived as the Blair/Milburn/Mandelson vision of the future of public services. He made this clear at the outset by saying: "We risk giving the impression that the only kind of reform that is valuable is a form of privatisation." However, his argument is not primarily about the pros and cons of transferring the delivery of public services to the private sector, it is mostly about whether it makes sense to create a *de facto* pricing mechanism for these services and sell them to consumers through "markets."

Brown starts with an apology on behalf of the Labour Party as a whole:

For nearly a century the left in Britain wrongly equated the public interest with public ownership and at times came near to redefining one means – public ownership – as a sole end in itself [or to put it another way, any system of ownership should be judged by its impact on society]...The left has too often failed to admit not just that, in order to promote productivity, we need markets, but also that we should normally tackle market failure not by abolishing markets but by strengthening markets to enable them to work better...But there are some areas where markets are not appropriate and where market failure can only be dealt with through public action.

Markets are part of advancing the public interest and the left are wrong to say they are not; but also markets are not always in the public interest and the right is wrong to automatically equate the imposition of markets with the public interest.

When Brown says "the right is wrong", it's transparently obvious that he means "Blair and Milburn are wrong". And he then moves through several layers of argument to come down against the creation in the NHS of a health market in which patients would "buy" treatments from the hospitals of their choice and private and public hospitals would compete freely in the sale of these services. This is how he sets up the debate:

The free market position, which would lead us to privatised hospitals and some system of vouchers and extra payments for treatments, starts by viewing health care as akin to a commodity to be bought and sold like any other through the price mechanism. But in healthcare we know that the consumer is not sovereign: use of healthcare is unpredictable and can never be planned by the consumer in the way that, for example, weekly food consumption can.

On the other hand, it is rational for all of us to insure against our future need for medical attention. So why shouldn't the bulk of this insurance be provided by the private sector? Well, the huge and rising cost of treatments – as medical science makes great strides through genomic research – means that privately provided insurance would be prohibitively expensive for many of us. So the case for a public insurance policy like the NHS is, Brown argues, unanswerable.

Even so, it would still be theoretically possible, even with a public insurance policy, for patients to shop around, for the NHS to be the organiser of health services supplied by independent entities, in the private sector, the voluntary sector and the public sector. As it happens, this is the model which the government seems to be on the verge of adopting. But this model would not be efficient or fair, according to Brown, if the suppliers of health services could vary their charges, because the ordinary patient simply does not have the detailed expert knowledge to know when the supplier, the hospital, is ripping him or her off or providing a sub-standard service ("there is an asymmetry of information" is the way Brown usually puts it). For this and other reasons, he is convinced that the "price mechanism" does not work properly in the provision of health services, that it cannot do what it is supposed to do, which is to deliver the spoils to the most efficient providers of high quality services and drive the substandard ones out of existence.

To be clear, his quarrel is with those arguing for a market in health, which is not quite the same as opposition to all use of the private sector in the NHS. He says:

Where the private sector can add to, not undermine, NHS capacity and challenge current practises by introducing innovative working methods, it has a proper role to play – as it always has – in the National Health Service. But it must not be able, when there are, for example, overall capacity constraints, to exploit private power to the detriment of efficiency and equity."

The speech is not completely negative – not simply an argument against "the assumption that the only alternative to command and control is a market means of public service delivery". There is the outline of a Brownite programme for reform, in his case for a "non-market means of delivery that does not have to rely on the price mechanism to balance supply and demand." He wants public services like the NHS to import the management techniques and structure of a "modern company", with a lean headquarters setting "clear targets" for local managers charged with hitting those targets. And, contrary to Milburn's charge that he is a centraliser, he suggests a devolution of decision-making away from Whitehall, with local communities setting performance standards for local services, greater flexibility in the setting of pay, and a reduction in ring-fenced budgeting:

> The accountability of local service providers to patients, parents and local communities would be improved through greater transparency and a deeper democracy, tailoring services to needs and choices expressed both individually and collectively.

There would be national standards, to which all hospitals would have to adhere ("otherwise it would no longer be a *National* Health Service," he says). But this is not the vision of a ruthless control freak. In fact it comes perilously close to a "Third Way" between traditional public sector centralised structures and a market solution – which is a wonderful irony, since Brown was always scathing about Blair's search in the late 1990s for the elusive Third Way between Old Left and New Right. But it may not be much more practical than Blair's Third Way, in that it relies on the notion that local activists will be able to gather appropriate information about the health needs of their communities and transmit the information efficiently to the suppliers. Recent experience of local government is not wholly encouraging about the efficacy of such a system. That said, the break-up of the NHS into smaller self-governing units would probably lead to more efficient outcomes than the status quo, with or without the simultaneous introduction of competition on a large scale from private sector hospitals.

And to be clear, Brown has not been opposed to the re-introduction to the health service of what used to be known as the internal market – a system in which hospitals compete to "sell" their services on the basis of quality and efficiency to Primary Care Trusts, or local NHS institutions that "purchase" these services on behalf of groups of general practitioners, who in turn offer them to their patients. Competition between public sector hospitals, with more resources going to the better ones, is something they would encourage. And they belatedly recognise that Labour made a terrible mistake in 1997 by abolishing the original version of the internal market created by the previous Tory government. Where they part company from Blair, Milburn and the current Health Secretary, John Reid, is over the extent to which private hospitals should be allowed to compete within this internal market. It's the wholesale importation of the private sector that they believe will lead to higher healthcare costs and detriment to the poorest patients.

There is, however, a significant hole in the SMF speech, in that Brown doesn't provide an answer to the central practical dilemma for this government, which is how far and how long it should tolerate differences in the quality of services offered by institutions providing health or education services:

We have to get the balance right between responsiveness to choice and efficiency [on the one hand] and equity. Local autonomy without national standards may lead to increased inequality between people and regions and the return of the post code lotteries. And the view we take on the appropriate balance between efficiency, diversity and equity will be shaped by the values we hold. The modern challenge is to move beyond old assumptions under which equity was seen to go hand in hand with uniformity... We should seek the maximum amount of diversity consistent with equity.

Shortly after this speech, when Milburn resigned as Health Secretary in July 2003, it was widely thought Brown had triumphed in the battle over the future of the NHS, that the onward march of profit-making companies into the provision of NHS services would be halted. This was wrong. Reid, the new Health Secretary, has been rather more deft than his predecessor in the tactics he has used to enhance the role of the private sector. He has adopted the seductive rhetoric of extending greater choice to health service patients as a cover for a plan that 15 per cent of all waiting-list operations – around 1m per year – should be provided by the private sector. The ostensibly attractive idea is that private companies will act as a service benchmark to the public sector, so that standards across all hospitals will eventually be raised. But what worries Brown is that this will eventually lead to a two-tier hospital service – very similar to the structure of British dentistry – in which those on lower incomes will have access only to a very basic service.

The logic of the argument put by Brown goes like this. The private sector is being encouraged to make a substantial investment in new capacity to serve the NHS. And for a while, several years probably, private sector companies will be prepared to provide their services to the NHS at a price identical to the cost of a pure public sector service. But there will come a time when they start to argue – in a way that would be completely fair and rational from their point of view – that they should be allowed to earn an acceptable rate of return on their massive investment. And if the NHS itself does not want to pay them more, they will urge that they should be allowed to charge top-up fees to patients who want a superior service. If a Labour government – or, one day, a Tory one – were to allow this, the spirit of the health service would be lost forever, in Brown's view. In theory, hospital treatment would still be universally available for free at the point of use. But the best treatment would not be available to those unable to pay.

In unpublished extracts from an interview he did with me for the *Sunday Telegraph*, Balls explains the relevance of the dentistry precedent, where there is a mixed economy within each surgery, and each dentist can provide NHS and private work to the same patient:

> When you go the dentist, the dentist says 'you can have that crap crown if you want, but I recommend you have this better one that the NHS won't pay for.' And it's quite hard for you to say 'well I've looked at the detail and I'm going to go for the NHS one rather than the other'. The market doesn't work and prices don't work, because the consumer is not sovereign, and the dentist or doctor has all the information and power. So in that world, the service becomes very expensive, the coverage becomes partial and the poor lose out.

In the end the disagreement between Brown and Blair over the future of the NHS has come down to one very simple point. They both believe in giving greater choice to patients about where they can have their respective elective treatments. Thus they want to extend the right of everyone to choose to go to a hospital some way from his or her home if that more remote one has a better reputation than the local one or it is able to offer a shorter waiting time. But Brown sees a much smaller role for the private sector in satisfying patient choice than Blair or Reid do. Brown wants to limit the private sector to simply filling gaps in the capacity of the NHS. When there is a severe constraint on the ability of an NHS hospital to provide a certain kind of operation, then Brown is happy for the private sector to step into the breach. But what he opposes, on principle, is Blair's plan that the private sector should be a provider of core services to the NHS, in constant competition with public sector providers.

At the time of writing Brown is re-inventing himself as a genuine alternative to Blair – no longer a *de facto* Blairite – partly on the basis of his different vision for the future of public services and the NHS. His platform for a future leadership election – whenever it comes – is that the ethos of public service, as distinct from the profit motive, is redeemable. He made this explicit in a speech on October 22, 2004, at a conference organised by Compass, the pressure group for the "progressive left":

We must win our argument that the ethic of public service, distinct from the operation of the market, is sufficiently powerful and can be modernised and come alive in this new generation to ensure that public services, with public money well spent, will deliver not only more equitably but more cost effectively than privatisation, and that we can find for our generation a means by which non-market but non-centralist provision can provide choice through capacity, local accountability and excellent personalised services for all.

Long-winded as he was, this was a direct challenge to the agenda being set by the Prime Minister.

A related ideological difference between Blair and Brown was highlighted by a battle over the funding of another public service, the universities. In ultimately acceding to the reform, the introduction of so-called top-up fees of up to £3,000 per annum financed by loans to students, Brown is vulnerable to the charge of inconsistency. The reform is regressive, in the sense that the proportionate burden of debt repayment falls heaviest on graduates earning lower incomes – and that runs counter to Brown's most basic convictions. Also, implicit in the argument for permitting universities to charge variable fees is the idea that they operate in a price-driven market, that there is proper competition between them and that all applicants for places will behave like genuine "buyers" (or that teenagers and their parents possess sufficient knowledge of the cost and quality of the services being "sold" and are endowed with the financial and intellectual resources to purchase these services) – and again Brown would have difficulty in accepting all of this. But in late 2003 and early 2004, Brown was prepared to put the unity of the Party ahead of principle. And the reason was partly selfish. At the time he thought he would replace Blair as leader within the year (see Chapter Ten), and he did not want to inherit a party weakened by civil war over an issue as basic as access to education.

Brown and the Treasury were never opposed in principle to allowing universities to charge differential fees for courses. He recognised that they needed a new source of funds for the long term, if they were to have a fighting chance of retaining a world class reputation. But in 2000, he was increasingly concerned at the growing evidence that the existing system of university financing – which involved students taking out substantial loans to cover the costs of maintenance and living – was discriminating against teenagers from poorer homes. Some were put off from applying for higher education by the prospect of running up substantial debts and others dropped out before completing the course when confronted with the reality of those debts. But if Brown was concerned about this unfairness, Blair was more worried about a separate element in the system, which was that students had to pay an annual tuition fee of up to £1,000 per annum (which is now £1,100), on a sliding scale from zero to the full amount depending on the income of their parents. Blair was worried that this up-front fee was eroding Labour's support among middle class voters, who had flocked to it in droves in 1997. And he could not blame the Tories for the increasingly heavy financial burden shouldered by families for encouraging their children to better themselves. Although the review by Sir Ron Dearing that paved the way for these new funding arrangements was commissioned by a Conservative government in 1996, it was a Labour Education Secretary, David Blunkett, who implemented them the following year. "In the run up to the 2001 general election, Blair wanted to abolish fees, because he thought middle class parents hated them," recalls a government member.

So the Department for Education, the Treasury and 10 Downing Street inaugurated a joint project to review the financing of higher education. The plan was to see if it was possible to increase the fairness of the system while allowing universities – especially the acknowledged centres of excellence – to vary their charges. "Gordon had come round to believing that – given that we had these loans that were paid back through the tax system – there was potentially a fairer way of repayment that would be less loan-like and therefore less like the working class was taking on a big burden of debt," says an official.

Against this background, Jeremy Heywood, Blair's Principal Private Secretary, David Miliband, the head of the Prime Minister's policy unit and Ed Balls were amazed when – during a meeting in February 2001 – they learned that David Blunkett had categorically ruled out that top-up fees would be introduced for the lifetime of the next parliament. On February 8, Blunkett told the Commons: "I can now this morning make the government's position clear that in the next parliament there will be no levying of top-up fees if we win the next general election." The pledge would be in Labour's manifesto for the election, which would be held in just four months. Blunkett, who precisely a year earlier had said, "We will not have top up fees while I am Secretary of State", appeared to have won a notable victory. He seemed to have drawn a line under a heated debate that was only just getting going – except that what had really happened was that the issue was killed off for a few months, or for the duration of the election campaign, but pressure from the universities for the ability to raise more from fees would not dissipate and would ultimately prove to be irresistible (and in fact Blunkett hinted as much, because when he said in 2000 that he would never introduce such fees, he pointed out that "I won't be Secretary of State forever"). The government, if it so chose, could later exploit the political scoundrel's option of sticking to the letter of the manifesto pledge while breaching its spirit – by drawing up a plan to introduce the charges but saying that they would not be levied till after the following election (which is precisely what happened).

Anyway, for a year or so after the election of June 7, 2001, the Treasury worked on a proposal for what was effectively a graduate tax. It was designed to appeal to Blair, by involving the abolition of the upfront tuition fee. Loans for maintenance would also go. And the hope was that the new tax would not only rise in a progressive way linked to graduates' income, but there would also be a mechanism to allow recognised centres of excellence to charge more for superior services. "We always wondered whether there was a way of having a differential fee or differential income for universities depending on their world-classness," says an official. If the Treasury could pull that off, it could perhaps quieten the noisy clamour for more financial freedom from the Russell Group of leading universities. And, in the initial phase at least, the Department for Education and Skills – under Estelle Morris, who had replaced Blunkett as Secretary of State – was enthusiastic about the plan.

However, the Prime Minister started to become wary of the tax idea. "Number 10 kept producing these focus groups which said that middle class families were very against a graduate tax in place of loans," says a colleague of Brown. "We never really believed it because our focus groups always told us the opposite."

In the summer of 2002, Blair announced that it was important to be "bold" in the reform of university finance. "He had been got at by the universities. The Russell Group had been very active, because its members had been very angry about the manifesto," recalls an associate of the Prime Minister. "Suddenly there was this new enthusiasm for fees, which was driven by Andrew Adonis (the newly promoted head of Blair's policy unit) who had been to Australia to look at differential fees there." In response, Brown and the Treasury urged that Blair take a deep breath and not rush into anything. The Chancellor pointed out that even if the new system was introduced in 2006, there would be no repayments by students – and thus no new money for the government – until 2009. So they could afford to take their time and make sure that the proposals would not discriminate further against poorer students and that universities would use any new resources efficiently. Brown's recommendation was that the government launch a formal review of the funding needs of universities, the way that these institutions are governed, and the state of competition between them. On the basis of that, a decision could be taken shortly after the following election – which was likely to be in 2005 – on whether or not to go with fees or some other system. In other words, he was suggesting that Blair adopt the model that he had used successfully in the run-up to raising National Insurance for funding the NHS in the budget of 2002 (as described on pages 269-73, in March 2001 Brown had commissioned the former banker, Derek Wanless, to write a report on the financial needs of the health service, which allowed him to demonstrate that he was taking the issue of inadequate health resources seriously, without committing himself to a particular solution).

Blair was adamant that boldness was the order of the day and he turned Brown down flat. He had become persuaded by the noisy lobbying of Richard Sykes – the argumentative rector of Imperial College who created Europe's largest pharmaceutical company, GlaxoSmithKline (and agonised about it later) – that British universities were falling behind the international competition largely because of their inadequate resources. Blair put remorseless pressure on Estelle Morris at the DFES to adopt top-up fees. But out of the blue, on the evening of October 23, 2002, she quit. Her stated reasons for going did not include her reservations about variable tuition fees, though she had serious qualms about them. However, she had lost confidence in her own ability to manage her department, hated the intrusion of the media into her private life and needed time out to take stock.

Morris was replaced by a more formidable character, Charles Clarke, who initially declared a preference for Brown's graduate tax idea and on October 25 he said he was "generally anti" top-up fees. This was in no sense an attempt to curry favour with the Chancellor, since Clarke has a conspicuous dislike for Brown. But he was not definitive on what system of university funding should be adopted and Blair did not give him long to make up his mind. On October 30, Blair announced that a blueprint for the new system would be announced in January 2003 (in fact, this represented a postponement; the plan, while Morris was in the job, was to publish the relevant proposals in November).

Brown was worried about the pace. "We kept saying 'it doesn't add up, it's mad'," recalls one of his allies who has a powerful position in the Labour Party. "There were no pages written by the DFES, nothing had been circulated." So the Chancellor once again broke the habits of a lifetime by committing his views to paper and writing a letter to the rest of the Cabinet which expressed his concern that top-up fees would reduce access for poorer students to universities. Relations between Downing

Street and the Treasury deteriorated again. "Gordon was presented in the newspapers as a centraliser, a control-freak, who hates universities and wants to stop all reform," says an official. "But we kept saying to Blair, 'You need to have a political strategy for this which is not going to split the parliamentary Labour Party and turn Labour-voting students and their families against us at the next election. You need a policy strategy on this which deals with the issue of access for teenagers from families on lower incomes. And you need to think about implementing this in a staged way'."

Again Blair – now supported by Clarke, as well as Alan Milburn and also Peter Hain, who had joined the Cabinet as Welsh Secretary – snubbed Brown and reiterated that he would be taking "the bold route". So in mid January 2003, John Prescott – as chairman of the Cabinet committee on domestic policy – endeavoured to bring the warring sides together. Clarke was by now clear in his own mind that the government must press ahead with the single option of top-up fees, while Brown argued that it was too early to rule out a graduate tax. Blair, furious with Brown for the way that the dispute had become public knowledge, was not going to side with the Chancellor. It all became fraught, according to a ministerial eye-witness: "I mean you had amazing things going on, like the radical lefty, Peter Hain, agreeing with Charles Clarke that he would support this thing in the Cabinet so long as Charles Clarke agreed that Wales would be exempted. Absolutely astonishing stuff. Quite astonishing."

On January 22, 2003, Clarke announced that universities would be free to charge tuition fees of up to £3,000 a year from 2006, provided that they signed agreements with a new government regulator to ensure that there was no discrimination against poorer candidates. The upfront annual fee of £1,100 would be abolished. But debt on graduation stemming from fees and maintenance would rise to £21,000 for many students – and graduates would repay loans at a rate of 9 per cent of any income they earned above £15,000 per year. As Brown had predicted, the fury provoked among Labour's own MPs was greater than anything Blair had experienced since 1997.

What the new system means is that – as a proportion of lifetime earnings – women pay back more than men, because their earnings are significantly lower than men's. And nurses, by the same logic, pay back more than doctors. It seemed to run counter to everything Labour held dear, which is why so many of its MPs were livid.

So what was Blair's problem with a graduate tax, which would have linked the amount that anyone paid much more directly to their earnings? Here is the explanation of one of Blair's colleagues:

Blair, when he finally thought about it in that period 2001 to 2002, decided he was against a graduate tax because he did not think it would be possible to persuade middle class families that they should pay more than poor families. His argument was that those on higher earnings wouldn't think it was fair that they were being asked to pay back more than they owe.

The Prime Minister acknowledged, however, that his argument would not be accepted by all the parliamentary Party. So there was then a year of preparation for the fateful moment that Labour MPs would be asked to go against their most basic beliefs and vote for the policy.

Meanwhile, it did not escape Blair's notice that one of the leading organisers of a threatened backbench rebellion was Nick Brown, the former Agriculture Minister who is one of Gordon Brown's closest allies. Blair, egged on by his advisers, concluded that the Chancellor was surreptitiously running the revolt. Nick Brown insists that wasn't true. He says: "I am friends with Gordon. I support his agenda. But I do not take instructions from him… On student fees, the idea that I was working for Gordon is absurd. All through it he said, 'Would you mind packing it in.' But I couldn't support such a regressive tax."

Clarke and Blair heaped concessions on top of concessions, in order to win over the malcontents. They promised that the very poorest students would have their £3,000 fees entirely covered by a combination of a

£1,500 grant for living costs, a £1,200 discount on the fees themselves and a university bursary of at least £300. They said it would be written on the face of the bill that the mechanism that could trigger an increase in the £3,000 ceiling on the fees would not be used until 2010. They pledged that the impact of the system would be assessed in a thorough independent review in 2009, three years after launch. And there would also be an interim enquiry to assess whether students from middle income backgrounds were likely to be deterred from going into the public sector and the professions and whether there was likely to be a future shortage of doctors and teachers.

Their desperation to buy off their opponents undermined much of the *raison d'être* for the unpopular reforms: the costly additional help for the poor meant there was little saving to the government from imposing the fees on better-off students, while the universities themselves were gaining far less financial independence than they wanted. "We ended up with it costing us more money, with it not raising much for the universities: it was all mad," says a government member. Another says: "If you want to criticise tuition fees you would say that simultaneously we caused a massively unpopular thing for the next election while not giving that much freedom to the universities: we had the worst of all worlds."

But what was more embarrassing for Blair, the bribes did not look as though they were going to be enough – defeat when it came to a vote still looked a very distinct possibility. And given that he disapproved of the entire adventure as a matter of principle, Brown could have kept a clear conscience and watched from the sidelines as Blair suffered a humiliating defeat.

Anyway, Blair met the two leading rebels, Nick Brown and George Mudie, twice from January 24 to January 26, in a last-ditch attempt to woo them. All to no avail. They would not be swayed from going into the no-Lobby. So after Blair had collided with these seemingly immovable objects, Gordon Brown met with as many of the unhappy backbenchers as he could. He talked with Mudie but could not move him off his chosen course of action. However, Nick Brown, after seeing the Chancellor, decided to change sides.

Was it all a piece of theatre cooked up by Gordon Brown to demonstrate to Blair that he dare not attempt to muddle through without him? Absolutely not, says Nick Brown: he dropped his opposition for two proper reasons. First, he became persuaded that the basic method of financing the top-up fees could be changed after the promised review into a more progressive impost (his own preference is for graduates to pay marginally more national insurance than non-graduates). Perhaps more relevantly, Nick Brown says he feared that if the bill were defeated, "Blair would be so angry, beside himself with rage, that he would put the bill back as a confidence issue and withdraw the concessions." He calculated that "quite a few MPs", fearful of being expelled from the Party for voting against a confidence measure, would change sides.

But if that was really the logic behind Nick Brown's change-of-heart, the other rebels did not see it. They were furious with him for what they perceived as his turncoat behaviour. So even if Gordon Brown was not the decisive influence on Nick Brown, it's weird that he should even have thought about asking his old friend to risk such unpopularity by going against his principles. Why on earth should the Chancellor have exorted such a sacrifice from him? On one interpretation, Gordon Brown gained nothing from it – and many of the Chancellor's friends wish that he had sat on his hands to the last. "Some of us felt it would be much better if we lost," says one. But what Gordon Brown would reply, according to a government member, was that "in the end, the moment a Labour government is defeated by its own side, it never recovers." His conviction is that the second that a vote of that significance is lost, "the divide in the Labour Party becomes the new media thesis." And once the idea of the split Labour Party takes hold, it is very hard to knock it down. However much Brown wanted to lead Labour, he did not want to lead a bifurcated, enfeebled Labour Party.

***

After these struggles over precise proposals to reform public sector institutions, how different really are Blair and Brown in respect of their more basic views on the direction in which Labour should be heading? Having been united in the early 1990s by their near-contempt for those in their party who did not recognise the imperative of ditching traditional "baggage" – especially the Party's knee-jerk instincts to raise taxes and to spend – they have steadily grown apart, not just as friends but also as politicians. This has become increasingly evident as Brown, since 2002, has embarked on a personal mission to rediscover the basis of his beliefs, to make respectable his periodic opposition to the policy initiatives taken by Downing Street or other ministerial departments and to rebut the predictable charge from the Prime Minister and his allies that he is simply playing to Labour's left to further his personal agenda.

Brown has come to the conclusion that Blairism is fatally flawed. For example, Blair – and Brown – failed to embrace the true significance of Labour's landslide victory in 1997. Brown made this critique surprisingly explicit in that important speech to party sympathisers and activists on October 22, 2004 organised by Compass, the left-wing pressure group:

> We have not done enough to respond to the yearning in 1997 not just for different government but for a different way of governing, not just for different policies but for a different politics.

He argued that the exponential rise in voter apathy – the stark facts that in the 2001 general election, the turnout was just 59 per cent and only 40 per cent of those under 25 bothered to vote – was not an accident. It represented "disaffection from our current political system."

He has not elaborated in public about how Labour's behaviour in office has reinforced widespread disillusionment with the political process. But I understand that his concern has two principle elements. One of his criticisms of New Labour's style of government, which is particularly difficult for Blair, is implicit in the Compass speech:

Our shared task, united as a party, is to build the public's confidence that politics in our country is a force for good and for achieving a British progressive change based on progressive values. We must build trust in a British way forward. We must reach out far beyond our traditional constituencies. We must show we are rooted in our communities, not remote from them. If we are serious about a new kind of politics we must be serious about addressing the undemocratic nature of some of our institutions...We must re-invigorate the constitutional reform agenda we began in 1997.

This linking of the collapse of trust in politicians to the future of the British constitution is, at the time of writing, one of his most pressing preoccupations, though he is still wrestling with precisely what he should say about it in public. His agonizing stems in part from the implicit criticism of Blair in his private analysis – which is that the recent collapse in the public's trust in the Prime Minister is directly linked to a widespread view that this government, and perhaps any government, will ride roughshod over the UK's sprawling constitution as and when it suits. This widespread cynicism, in Brown's view, was reinforced by the perception that inadequate information was provided by the government to public and parliament, in the build up to war with Iraq, and that neither parliament nor the Cabinet were consulted properly on the decision to go to war. A minister explains:

People might say that there should be a statutory duty on the part of a government prior to any declaration of war normally to have a procedure by which parliament is properly consulted and provided with the information on which a decision could be based. You could argue that as far as the executive (especially the Cabinet) is concerned, a more structured approach to decision-making is not only essential in order to get the right decisions but is also necessary because it's the only way people will think that your decisions are properly made.

So far, what he's said in public about the renewal of the constitution has concentrated largely on the importance of finishing the process of turning the House of Lords into a more democratic and accountable chamber, as well as the need to reinvigorate local government and decentralise decision-making to much smaller, localised bodies. His espousal of the cause of "localism" is an explicit attempt to rebut the consistent charge against him that he is an incorrigible centraliser and "control freak".

And, as we've seen, his promotion of the notion that an element of local democracy could be injected into the management of hospitals is part of his alternative to privatisation as the key to reforming the NHS. But where he may go from here is to argue that the time has come for the UK to codify the many and disparate elements of its constitution. Such ambitions are normally referred to, in short-hand, as pressing the case for a written constitution, but that is slightly misleading, in that most elements or our constitution are written down in assorted acts of parliament, treaties, conventions, codes of practice, and so on. What Brown is likely to call for is an explicit, comprehensible statement pulling together the basic principles of our constitution.

He's halfway there in terms of some of what he has been saying in public. Thus he has been arguing that he rebuilt public confidence in the ability of any government to manage the economy, after decades of mismanagement by governments of both main parties, by putting in place clear new rules about what Chancellors can and cannot do. One example was his decision to transfer control of interest rates to the Monetary Policy Committee of the Bank of England and publish a clear framework for the way that the MPC would then set rates. "We put transparency and accountability right at the heart of decision-making and in this way sought to build support for difficult long-term decisions," he said in the Compass speech.

But, for Brown, rebuilding trust will flow not simply from putting in place more explicit rules that limit elected politicians' scope to act and exercise power. He is also a staunch critic of "triangulation", the approach to political positioning imported by Blair and Mandelson from the US President, Bill Clinton, and his advisers. This is how one minister summarises Brown's critique:

> Triangulation is basically where you say, 'Look, I've got a problem here, the country does not like what we are doing,' and what you then do is move one step to the right and announce a particular policy. And you justify your positioning by saying 'I know the Labour Party is going to hate it, because it's a step that's quite difficult because we are modernising and they are reactionary in the old sense and they are trying to stop this change.' But the right-wing newspapers support your position because they think it's good that you are taking on the old Labour establishment so it must be worth supporting.
>
> You end up with moving to the right and not necessarily doing the right thing. But the real problem is that you have no chance of building a progressive consensus, because you have founded the whole policy on a split between your own view of what the future should be and your party's view. You may have moved the press headlines so that they support you, but you have not shifted fundamental opinion in a way that would allow you to sustain the policy over a period of time. It's an initiative simply taken for presentational reasons.

Brown's view is that such an approach – of formulating policies with the express aim of always being in conflict with Labour's left-wing – may have been successful in opposition as a way of proving to the media that the levers of government were safe in the hands of New Labour, which was conspicuously demonstrating its newfound belief in the superiority of capitalism. But voters were less impressed and saw through it as a cynical attempt by Blair to have his cake and eat it, to woo the right while exploiting the hard fact that his left-wing supporters had nowhere else to go. Triangulation doesn't build a long-lasting consensus for reform of public services, for example, but simply engenders widespread anger and disenchantment with politicians. And for Brown, Blair's push for

Foundation Hospitals and tuition fees were examples of where triangulation goes wrong.

So since 2002, Brown has been endeavouring to demonstrate that there is an alternative to triangulation, that Labour can be true to its core principles without making itself unelectable. And, in order to do that, he has had to re-examine what he holds to be those principles, in the absence of the old simplicities of a long-finished class war. His Social Market Foundation speech of February 2003, examining where the public good is served by allowing markets to flourish and where the writ of markets should be curtailed, was part of this voyage of self-discovery. The Compass speech, as we have seen, was an attempt to see how elected politicians can re-stake their claims to legitimacy at a time when individual campaigning groups, such as Oxfam and Christian Aid, have vastly larger and more committed memberships than either Labour or the Conservative Party. And then there is his other great theme of the moment, the need to rehabilitate "Britishness".

The ostensible point of his exploration of what it is to be British is again to give confidence to voters that they can know what he stands for and – by implication – to communicate the precepts that would be held dear by a government in which he was premier. For Brown, as set out in the annual lecture to the British Council which he gave on July 7, 2004, being British is certainly not a racial thing. It's about values, which he lists as the cherishing of liberty, the promotion of a sense of duty, a commitment to decency and fair play. He also believes that Britons are internationalist, outward-looking, creative, adaptable and tolerant. And he argues that there is something fundamental in the way that Great Britain has consistently rejected crude individualism, the primacy of the state or the tyranny of the collective. His views are hard to summarise without them seeming trite and rose-tinted. But they are a million miles from the simple waving of the union flag which normally passes for patriotic discourse. And they escape from the sterile and false dichotomy often claimed by those on the left between internationalism and nationalism.

As it happens, it's a life-and-death issue for Brown that Britishness is alive and well. If the over-riding trend of our time is the rise of the constituent nations in Great Britain – if Britishness is gradually vanishing as Scottishness, Welshness, Irishness and Englishness all achieve sharper definition – then he has made a huge strategic error in devoting his life to the parliament in Westminster. It's vital for him that English voters continue to feel a powerful bond with the Scots, for example – irrespective of the powers transferred to the Scottish Parliament – because otherwise those English voters might not be enthusiastic about voting for a Labour Party led by a Scot (and, in his case, one who has never even thought about anglicising his accent or outlook). Brown's concept of Britain is one in which anyone of any sex, colour or background can be Prime Minister. It's a Britain that will not recoil when the ambitious son of a Presbyterian minister from Fife presents himself, some time very soon, as the natural candidate to head its government.

CHAPTER TEN
End of the deal

The Prime Minister's official website (www.number-10.gov.uk) records the following exchange from Tony Blair's monthly press conference on July 22, 2004:

QUESTION: Ten years is a very long time in any job, has there been any point when you have thought about moving on?
PRIME MINISTER: No.
QUESTION: Not at all?
PRIME MINISTER: Look, I think that what we have achieved as a government and as a political party over the ten years has been to show people, I think for the first time in the 100 years of our history, that you can combine a strong commitment to economic prosperity with a commitment to social justice. And we have still got things to do. As you see from the presentation on delivery, it is true that we have fulfilled what we said we would do in terms of the improvement in investment in public services and so on, but there are still big challenges that remain. And we want, I want, to see them through.

The background to the question was that over the previous fortnight, newspapers had been filled with reports that a troika of Blair's most loyal Cabinet supporters (Tessa Jowell, John Reid and Charles Clarke) had talked a demoralised Prime Minister back from the brink of quitting.

These articles had been precipitated by a confident broadcast to that effect by the BBC's political editor, Andrew Marr. But, according to the Prime Minister himself, it was all a load of nonsense.

Blair, however, had said something starkly different to Gordon Brown ten days earlier on July 12, the day that the Chancellor delivered his three year public spending plans in the Comprehensive Spending Review. Blair told the Chancellor then that he was still minded to stand down in the autumn, just a few weeks later. As it happens, Brown – who had heard this from Blair several times over the previous nine months – was growing increasingly doubtful that the resignation would actually take place. But there was no ambiguity in what Blair said. The intriguing question is whether Blair misled the media on July 22 or misled Brown on July 12. It's quite difficult to reconcile the spirit of the separate messages he was communicating on the two occasions. Of course, there is nothing in the constitution which says that Prime Ministers must tell the full, unvarnished truth to the press, or even to their respective Chancellors. And in one sense it's an academic issue now.

In a statement made on September 30, 2004 which has no precedent in British constitutional history, the Prime Minister tried to put paid to all speculation about when he'll depart by saying that he plans to serve a "full" third term in office, but will not fight a fourth election as Labour leader. His pledge is to stand down at some unspecified time before 2009 or so.

Blair's declaration that he won't be moved was the long-anticipated serving of the divorce papers on Brown. Their dysfunctional marriage is now at an end. Brown and Blair are no longer partners in a mutually agreed political project, the most effective double act in parliamentary history. Brown remains as Chancellor for no other reason than that it is too dangerous for Blair to sack him. The formal dismissal of Brown would foment a revolt among Labour MPs that would probably do for Blair. So Brown and Blair continue to cohabit, although there is no affection between them any longer and they rarely communicate, except through intermediaries. The occasional meetings they have are stilted, characterised by the withholding of information rather than the sharing of confidences.

For now at least, Brown is probably even more powerful than ever, in the sense that he no longer even has to pay lip service to the notion that he should show deference to a Prime Minister. From his point of view, Blair has ripped up the contract that they should be mutually supportive of each other. "The thing which is guaranteed now – which didn't have to be the case – is that, whatever happens, Gordon Brown will not be a Blairite successor to Blair," says a senior member of the Labour Party. "Which is madness." And Blair has also demonstrated that he cannot commit the final *coup de grâce*. As Brown told one of his closest friends on September 9, when he began to understand that Blair was in the process of reneging on the Granita pact: "It's a liberating moment."

The Granita dinner was not the last occasion that Blair exploited Brown's hopes and expectations by making what the Chancellor understood as a promise that he would stand down in good time for an elegant handover of power. It happened again in mid November 1999, when Brown – who had by then been Chancellor for two and a half gruelling years – toyed with the idea of quitting the government to become managing director of the International Monetary Fund in Washington DC.

Running the IMF is a huge and influential job. Finance ministers of the leading economies would have backed him to do it: he had a formidable international reputation, even if his blunt negotiating style could put the backs up of his peers in foreign governments just as much as he excited jealousy and resentment in the British Cabinet. In many ways, it was the perfect job for Brown. He has devoted much energy to helping design new "international financial architecture", or rules to avert international financial crises when whole economies run into difficulties, and he has a genuine passion for helping to lift up the impoverished economies of Africa and the less developed world. As Balls confirmed to me in an interview for the *Sunday Telegraph* (July 4, 2004), Brown gave serious thought to taking it, even to the point of having detailed discussions about its structure. Balls said it was a "worrying time" for him, since he had no desire to quit the Treasury at that juncture.

Was Brown really ready to leave, having completed only half of the giant task he had set himself, having established the economic credibility of the government without yet having done much to exploit that credibility to execute a significant transfer of resources from rich to poor? Well, he was fed up. His father – the dominant influence on his moral outlook on the world – had died just under a year before, on December 8, 1998. And after the Prime Minister had deliberately presented the reshuffle of July 1998 as a snub to his influence, Brown had been suffering growing doubts about whether Blair would continue to honour the Granita agreement in all its rich detail, especially the clauses that mattered to him most, that he would have autonomy on economic and most social matters and that the two of them would work in harmony in deciding the composition of the Cabinet. The interminable skirmishes with 10 Downing Street, especially over the role and influence of Peter Mandelson – with whom Brown would never be reconciled – were also taking their toll. If Brown ever thought he would be rid of Mandelson, that notion was knocked on the head in early November 1999, when Blair appointed him as head of Labour's general election planning group, alongside Brown, who was to be chair of the Party's election strategy committee (this incident now looks like a dry run for Blair's neutering of Brown's influence in the build-up to an election expected in 2005).

On the other hand, my own view is that Brown was quite a long way from actually packing his bags for Washington. He was trying the idea of doing something else out on himself, to see what it felt like. And he also tried it out on Blair in a private meeting. He sold it well to Blair. "Tony thought the job sounded great," says an MP. "He said, 'Do you think I could do it?' To an extent they were both having a laugh". However, Blair recognised that his old friend was capable of calling it quits. What he spotted was that even if Brown would not go to the IMF, there was a risk that he might quit at an inopportune moment. "Tony was very worried about the prospect of Gordon leaving" says a senior Labour member.

To a certain extent this can be seen in the heavy-handed way that the government endeavoured to kill off speculation that Brown might go to the IMF, following a story written by me in the *Financial Times* of November 19, 1999 that he was contemplating such a move. Officials encouraged the *Sun* to write a leader, under the headline "*FT* bilge", denouncing my article and making the hilarious claim that "he [Brown] revels in being a heartbeat away from the Prime Minister" (which was true, but not in the simple and touching sense that the *Sun* implied).

Anyway, Blair has periodically remembered that as a team, he and Brown are unbeatable. It therefore made sense to bind Brown in for the long term, to provide him with a powerful incentive not to do anything silly like resign. So Blair significantly toughened up and refined his 1994 offer to hand over to Brown during the course of the subsequent parliament. "At that point in the autumn of 1999, Blair hardened the position considerably beyond what he had said before," says a friend of the Chancellor. "He said he was going to leave in the spring of 2003."

This was quite a big moment for Brown. "Gordon has a strong moral sense of word and truth," says one of his friends. "He has a tendency to think too much, 'That's what he's said, so that's what he'll do.'" In other words Brown believed Blair – though his allies, such as Nick Brown, Ed Balls and Wilf Stevenson, were always much more cynical about the Prime Minister's tantalising offers. On the other hand, they all calculated that it was in Blair's interest to effect a smooth handover to Brown, as the best way of defining Blair's period in office as a notable political success, as the famous era when the building blocks were put in place for a long and stable period of Labour success. They assumed that Blair would want to pass the baton to someone who defined himself as a Blairite. And they tried to make it crystal clear to Blair that Brown would contemplate subjugating his pride and proclaiming himself the Blairite heir if Blair gave him the baton in an elegant and selfless way, rather than taunting Brown to snatch it.

But even by now Brown had long since lost his blind faith in Blair. He transmitted the details of his conversations with Blair to several friends, to make them proxy witnesses. And within a couple of years, it became relatively common currency in the Treasury that there was a "deal" on the succession – though the details were never divulged. As and when Blair reneged on it, Brown would not have to suffer in total silence and isolation.

In fact, on the day after Labour's general election landslide of June 7, 2001, Blair came close to cancelling the Granita pact in every one of its elements. On June 8, Blair reshuffled his Cabinet – and for 90 minutes the biggest beasts in his Cabinet, Brown, Robin Cook and Jack Straw, all sat in separate rooms in Downing Street unsure what jobs they would be given. Blair was contemplating two ruthless initiatives which would have reclaimed power for himself and for Downing Street. Brown was to be moved from the Treasury to be the Foreign Secretary. And the post of Chief Secretary to the Treasury, in charge of negotiations on public expenditure, was to be stripped from the Treasury and moved within the axis of 10 Downing Street and the Cabinet Office, in order to give Blair the financial levers that would facilitate his burning ambition to be the great moderniser and reformer of public services.

Although Blair was being egged on by his closest colleagues to neuter Brown in this way, in the end he couldn't bring himself to do it. Brown stayed put as Chancellor and the post of Chief Secretary remained in the Treasury (as it happens most of the public expenditure functions normally associated with that position were carried out by Balls before he quit the department). However, Blair was still able to give the impression of ruthlessness, by shunting Cook from the Foreign Office to be Leader of the House of Commons, and giving the post of Foreign Secretary to Jack Straw – whose role of Home Secretary was taken by David Blunkett.

This was probably the last occasion when Blair could have ousted Brown and not destroyed himself in the process. "In retrospect, Blair ought to have done it," says a senior member of the government. "But he can't do the thing he ought to do." Brown learned about the secret plan to defenestrate him many months after the event, via a discreet message sent on the Whitehall mandarin's net. Meanwhile towards the end of that year, he was to discover that Blair regarded the Granita and IMF offers to stand down as conditional deals. On December 2001, Anji Hunter — Blair's special assistant, a kind of Ms Fixit and the most important gate-keeper to him — contacted Brown's office. She informed a stunned official that Blair would quit so long as Brown ensured that the Treasury came down in favour of the UK joining the euro (see page 228). "Why are you telling me this" asked the Treasury aide, to which Hunter replied: "Tony wants there to be witnesses."

Hunter and the Chancellor's aide then arranged for Blair and Brown to have a dinner, held at the Prime Minister's request, on December 18, 2001 in Downing Street. They were alone. And Brown categorically refused to make the trade. "History would never forgive us for having that conversation," he said, a theme he repeated whenever Blair put pressure on him in the succeeding months to fix the outcome of the Treasury's evaluation of whether the time was right to join the euro.

Was Brown being astonishingly virtuous in apparently putting the interests of the country ahead of his personal ambition? Not really. He calculated that if it was bad economics to join the euro, it would be worse politics. If he endeavoured to prejudice the Treasury's verdict on the single currency, there would be no point in becoming Prime Minister in the aftermath. In the worst case, he could be taking over as Prime Minister just as the potentially disastrous economic consequences of joining the euro at the wrong moment were turning the electorate against the Labour government. So if joining the euro were not in the economic interests of the UK, it was not in his interest either.

However this was an argument that carried no weight with Blair, who spent much of 2002 trying to barter the keys to Number 10 for membership of the euro. For example, Clare Short recalls in her memoirs (*An Honourable Deception*, 2004) how in February of that year the Prime Minister asked her to be an envoy to Brown, to communicate the message that "he really did not want a third term but he wished Gordon would work more closely with him so that he could make progress on the euro and, if he did, he would then be happy to hand over to Gordon." When

Short saw Brown at a specially arranged lunch in 11 Downing Street the following week, his answer was, "First, such deals were not worth talking about because previous agreements had not been kept; and second, he would not contemplate recommending that we join the euro in order to advance his own position rather than advance the economic interest of the country."

At Blair's behest, Short repeated the offer again, in a further meeting with Brown during September of the same year, during which she also voiced strong criticism of the government's approach to Iraq, saying it would divide the Labour Party, damage the world economy and inflame the Arab world (she was right). A note in her diary made at the time records: "GB said he would think and get back, but on the euro it would take time for the economy to converge."

So Short's attempt to effect a rapprochement between Blair and Brown ended in failure. One of Brown's friends is caustic about the episode: "She was persuaded by Tony that only she could bring Tony and Gordon together. It was a joke. Tony says to her – and others – 'Everything will work out for Gordon if only he would help me, if only he wouldn't frustrate what I want to do'. Which is why he tells her to tell him that if he fixes the euro, he'll keep his word and stand down. It was always a joke, never believable."

Short also records Brown as saying that Blair had sent two other cabinet emissaries to offer him the same trade, of the governance of Britain for a fistful of euros. They were Alistair Darling, the long-serving cabinet minister who is a supporter of Brown but who has been adept at remaining on amicable terms with Blair, and John Prescott, the Deputy Prime Minister. Neither of them was any more successful than Short in persuading Brown to trade a positive economic assessment of the euro for personal advancement.

***

As autumn turned to winter in 2002, Brown was wondering how long he could or would remain in the government. An entry in Clare Short's diary for November 22, 2002 says:

> Had startling discussion with GB this week. Said not too worried about economy but sick of fighting against bad proposals: removing child benefit from parents who truant; Foundation Hospitals; top-up fees... Number 10 briefing against him would get worse and nasty. He wouldn't take any other job. Was in a hurry to move forward on extra $50bn ODA (an international scheme promoted by Brown to increase aid to poor countries) because he did not know how long he would have... TB doesn't listen to him any more and was listening only to non-Labour voices and thinking about his reputation in history.

One of Brown's colleagues recalls the sense of being in the bunker: "All the time a campaign was being fought against us, claiming that we were anti-reform – equating reform with 'marketisation' and privatisation and then saying we are anti-reform and centralisers on that basis. There was a limit to how much we could do while staying in the government."

There was no healing of the relationship in the early part of 2003. As described in Chapter Seven, Brown's total refusal to influence the assessment of whether the time was right to join the European single currency, which was being carried out for him by Treasury civil servants, led to the sharpest ever disagreement between Blair and Brown. On Wednesday April 2, after Brown had delivered the Treasury's verdict – which was unambiguously that it would be wrong to go for the euro – Blair said to him, "If you are not going to give me what I want, then you should consider your position". Brown replied: "I'll do just that". A dispassionate observer would have concluded that Brown had just been sacked – although Blair's survival instincts persuaded him to come back from the brink within a couple of hours. If he had dismissed a Chancellor for refusing to steamroller the UK into the European currency – when monetary union was hated by most of the media and not much loved by most voters – his own longevity in office would have been sharply curtailed.

The summer came and went, without Blair honouring what Brown regarded as his promise of standing down by the middle of 2003. So Brown was no longer in much of an emollient mood. Barely one of Blair's important domestic initiatives found favour with Brown – and what was more damaging for the Prime Minister, Brown no longer made much effort to hide his unhappiness with many of the policies cooked up in 10 Downing Street.

The Prime Minister was intent on defining his second term of office as being "radical" in the reform of public services, to make the most of all the increased resources that were being pumped into hospitals and education. But, for the reasons set out in Chapter Nine, Brown kept raising objections to a plan that would allow better-performing hospitals to have greater financial and management freedom as Foundation Hospitals. Brown was also concerned that a proposal to allow universities to charge top-up fees of £3,000 per annum would place a disproportionately heavy burden on students from poorer backgrounds.

What was Blair to do? Most Prime Ministers would probably have sacked a Chancellor so out of sympathy with what they wanted to achieve. But that was impossible for Blair. Brown and the Treasury have given shape and direction to the government in respect of its economic and social agenda – the kernel of all its domestic policies – in the absence of coherent leadership from 10 Downing Street. It's not clear that Blair had the ideas or infrastructure to fill the yawning gap that would be created once Brown had gone. Still, there comes a moment in many marriages when the fetters imposed by one of the spouses become intolerable, whatever the risks of removing them. The problem for Blair in the autumn of 2003 was that it was only the stability of the economy and the lack of a powerful and credible opponent on his own backbenches that was keeping him in office. The fallout from his relatively unpopular war against Saddam Hussein had precipitated a sharp slide in his personal popularity ratings. The polls showed that voters had increasingly lost trust in him. And it was unclear whether he or the BBC would come out worst from an enquiry by Lord Hutton, a law lord, into the broadcaster's claims that a government dossier on Iraq's capability to launch weapons of mass destruction had been deliberately "sexed up" in Downing Street. It would be an act of self-immolation for Blair to reinvent Brown – who could claim to be responsible for the longest period of economic growth in living memory and the extermination of inflation – as his formal opponent outside the tent. Far better to have him inside, even if he was maddeningly unbiddable.

There was a further reason why it was useful for Blair to patch up relations with Brown. The Tories, on October 29, 2003, voted to dump their ineffective leader, Iain Duncan Smith, to make way for Michael Howard, the former Tory Home Secretary. When Blair had been Howard's shadow in the early 1990s, he had not always got the better of him in parliamentary exchanges. However, Brown had been relatively untroubled by Howard more latterly, when Howard had been the Shadow Chancellor. Advice from Brown on how to best Howard at the weekly gladiatorial battle of Prime Minister's Questions would be invaluable.

But how was Blair to get back on terms with Brown? The mutual animosity between the two of them was too pronounced to simply do what they had done for years, which was to patch things up in a private meeting on their own. He needed a third party to help them establish a new way of cohabiting. On this occasion, and throughout the following 12 months, staunch and loyal service was provided by his deputy, John Prescott. As it happens, Brown and Prescott are close. They like each other and there is probably more overlap between their respective political credos than there is between those of Prescott and Blair. But Prescott's primary loyalty is to the Prime Minister who has built him up into a big political figure and has stuck buy him through all the brickbats hurled at him for his eccentric use of English. "He has a profound sense of gratitude to Blair, which means that he will never in the end do anything to destabilise him," says a senior member of the government.

However, Prescott also has a mystical sense that the soul of the Labour Party is in his charge. It's his responsibility, he feels, to ensure that the two biggest figures in the Party – excluding himself – get along. In early November 2003, the private disagreements between Blair and Brown were spilling out in public. Brown's behind-the-scenes opposition to a plan by David Blunkett to introduce identity cards as part of the UK's defence against terrorism – an initiative which was backed by Blair – was being widely reported. More significantly, Brown flaunted his invulnerability by publicly criticising – in a television interview on November 6 – Tony Blair's decision to exclude him from Labour's National Executive Committee, the Party's ruling body. In the same interview, on GMTV, he also made clear that he expected to be put in charge once again of Labour's general election campaign, which was an inflammatory public declaration of his perception of the rights and powers conferred on him by the Granita deal – which was then almost 10 years old. At the time, he and his closest colleagues were acting virtually as a government within a government, showing that they could attack the Prime Minister with impunity, almost daring Blair to sack him.

Prescott became anxious that the dispute might spiral out of control. Just hours after Brown's television interview, in the evening of November 6, 2003, he hosted a dinner for Blair and Brown in Admiralty House, the elegant London residence provided to him by the taxpayer. Blair was forthright about the difficulties he faced. "I know things are very difficult on trust [ie, that the electorate no longer trusted him]," Blair said. "I think in the end I will be vindicated [over Iraq]. But I'm not going to turn this around for a very long time. Therefore I am going to stand down before the election." And turning to Brown, he said: "I know I must leave, but I need your help to get through the next year."

At this point, no precise date was put on Blair's departure. And in early December, Peter Mandelson – who is as close as any politician to Blair and spent much of 2003 working in an informal capacity inside 10 Downing Street – told a private gathering of businessmen that if Blair survived in office till June, or the date of the local and European elections, he would be there for the foreseeable future. Now, this was an odd thing to say if Mandelson knew about Blair's secret talks with Brown on the succession. Brown's allies see it as evidence that the Prime Minister never had any real intention of standing down and that he was simply manipulating the Chancellor in an attempt to bring stability to his government, buy some time, and reinforce his power base. Mandelson, however, insists that Blair's offer to quit was real and sincere, but was conditional on Brown giving him 120 per cent support for the following 12 months – and that Brown did not deliver his side of the bargain.

In the subsequent weeks, Blair and Brown had a series of discussions on the tactics and timing of the proposed handover. Brown even talked about it with Mandelson in January, in a meeting also attended by Prescott. And, for a while, the relationship between the Prime Minister and the Chancellor improved markedly. In particular, Blair had long conversations with Brown about how best to fend off Howard from the Commons Despatch Box. Then, early in the new year of 2004, the Prime Minister's mood took a sharp turn for the worse, after Hutton on January 28 published his verdict on whether the government had intentionally exaggerated the ability of Saddam Hussein to launch devastating weapons. Blair's immediate reaction was relief that the government was cleared of acting disreputably, either in the preparation of a controversial intelligence dossier on the threat posed by Saddam or in the way that it had outed an official based at the Ministry of Defence, David Kelly, as a source for a contentious report by the BBC journalist Andrew Gilligan (in other words, blood was not on Blair's hands for Kelly's subsequent suicide, according to Hutton). But his elation soon turned to despair. Hutton's report had been so forgiving of the government that it was widely derided as incredible. Far from restoring the Prime Minister's reputation, voters' confidence in his stewardship of the country fell even further.

Evidence mounted that the infamous dossier on weapons of mass destruction was a false prospectus for war, even if it was not cooked up as a work of fiction. Also, the fury with which Blair's former head of communications, Alastair Campbell, turned on the BBC after Hutton criticised the corporation had the reverse effect of what he intended.

Sympathy for the broadcaster was created and, much to Blair's dismay, Labour's polling showed that the public's trust in him had fallen again.

The mood in 10 Downing Street was dire. Labour Party officials based there were increasingly demoralised by the Prime Minister's unwillingness or inability to grapple with new policy ideas and start preparing seriously for the general election – which was likely to be held not much more than a year later. Even relatively recent recruits, such as Matthew Taylor, head of the Prime Minister's policy unit, toyed with the idea of quitting.

However, relations between Blair and Brown were still – on the surface at least – less fraught than they had been for years. They were in regular contact, to a far greater extent than had been the recent norm. It was clear to the Chancellor that Blair was more fed up than he could remember. But even he was taken aback by a proposal that the Prime Minister put to him as part of their discussions on the mechanics of the succession. It was shortly after the budget of March 17 and the two were – as usual – talking alone. Blair said that in May, after the Easter parliamentary recess which ran from April 2 to April 19, he was determined to make an announcement of his determination to retire in the autumn, to "pre-announce" a decision to quit. And this wasn't something that Blair said casually. "During that phase in March, Blair raised pre-announcing more than once," says a government member.

Brown did not know quite what to make of it. It would suit him to have it out in the open that Blair was going. In fact, surely this would make all his dreams come true. What he feared however was that he was being set up. He calculated that the so-called "pre-announcement" would fire the starting gun on a bitter and divisive campaign by all the pretenders to the throne. Brown would not have a clear run. A number of senior ministers – including John Reid and Charles Clarke – would bitterly resist a seamless transfer of power to Brown. In fact Blair reinforced those concerns, by saying, "I'm going to support you but some of these members of the Cabinet are going to be very difficult."

There was a serious risk that the Party would be gravely weakened if a vicious leadership contest raged from the spring to the eve of winter. So Brown did something that he now regrets. He said: "Don't do that, it would be crazy. You'll make yourself a lame duck. You'll send the Labour Party into turmoil." Instead he wanted Blair to take a much more conventional approach, which was simply to stand down towards the end of the year and allow a leadership contest on the normal short timetable to begin. Blair, however, claimed to be unpersuaded by the arguments. "I can't get through on Iraq, I'll never turn it around," he said. So Brown advised him to spend the Easter holidays thinking it over, which Blair did. Brown, meanwhile, was wracked with doubts about the advice he had given to the Prime Minister. He repeatedly asked one of his closest confidants "I am right, aren't I? It's the wrong thing (for him to pre-announce his departure)?" To which the confidant replied: "So long as we know what he is going to do, it's better that he sits tight."

Now the presumption among many MPs and in the media has been that Blair's big wobble, the moment he came within a whisker of quitting, coincided with two upsetting events for him. One was a family drama which took place on Monday April 19. What actually happened that day has been widely discussed by journalists, but has never been printed, because Sir Christopher Meyer, the chairman of the Press Complaints Commission, urged restraint on newspapers. However, all the gossip about it in and around Westminster generated speculation that the Prime Minister could quit at any moment.

The other demoralising event for Blair was the disclosure that Britain's ally in the Iraq conflict, the US, had treated some of its Iraqi prisoners in a brutal and inhumane manner – and there were allegations, which turned out to be untrue, that British troops had also behaved abominably.

In fact, the evidence suggests that Blair's lowest point, when he was closest to simply packing it all in, was earlier. The view of Brown and his allies – and I have heard from several of them on this – is that by the time that Blair's public demeanour was showing the strain of his hellish months, he was in fact already well on the way to reneging once again on his promise to stand down before the election. "The apparent wobbling in April was not Blair deciding to go, it was the process of him being persuaded not to go," says a friend of Brown. The reason for their contrarian view is that – out of the blue – Blair stopped talking to Brown. "Suddenly the conversations stopped, suddenly the discussions stopped," says a government member. Brown began to fear, not only that Blair wasn't going to "pre-announce," but that he wasn't going to stand down at all.

What happened at Easter was that Blair's closest allies in the Cabinet and Brown's most fervent opponents suddenly began to realise the gravity of what was going on and worked hard and successfully – in conjunction with Blair's wife, Cherie – to persuade him to stay on. Among these is a caucus which actually defines itself as Blair's cheerleaders. They consist of John Reid, the Health Secretary, Tessa Jowell, the Culture Secretary, and Lord Falconer, the Lord Chancellor who is also one of Blair's oldest friends. "We meet regularly to discuss how the Blairite agenda is advancing and to think of ways to shore up Tony," says one of these ministers. Alan Milburn has become a fully paid up member of the group since returning to the Cabinet in September 2004. And David Blunkett – until he resigned as Home Secretary on December 15, 2004 – was an *ex officio* member, who did not attend its meetings but was briefed on its deliberations. Anyway, the cheerleaders trooped in to see Blair one after another to urge him to buck up and not to hand over to the beastly Brown.

Meanwhile, Charles Clarke – who replaced Blunkett as Home Secretary, and operates independently of the Blairite cheerleaders – also urged Blair not to quit. Clarke has a conviction of almost visceral intensity that Brown will never be leader and should never be leader, which is slightly odd in that their politics are similar in many respects. Brown's allies believe that Clarke's animosity towards the Chancellor is rooted in Labour's defeat in the 1992 general election. At the time, Clarke was the Chief of Staff to the Party's leader, Neil Kinnock. They believe that Clarke concluded from that painful electoral humiliation that Labour could never win if it was led by a politician with a regional accent – and it didn't matter if the accent was Welsh (as it was for Kinnock) or Scottish (for Brown). "His view is that we can only win if the leader is someone who looks and sounds like an English public schoolboy," says a senior MP.

At the time, the "Save Blair" campaign was largely undetected by the media, although every now and then a small clue to what was happening crept into the press. Thus on May 15, 2004, John Prescott implied – in an interview with Tom Baldwin of the *Times* – that a change at the top of government would not be far off. What Prescott said – in a relatively translucent phrase – was, "It's true that when plates appear to be moving everyone positions themselves for it." And the following day the *Sunday Herald* reported that Prescott and Brown held a discussion on May 9 about the Labour succession in the back of Prescott's official car, a black Jaguar, in the car park of the Loch Fyne Oyster Bar in Argyll (the Health Secretary, John Reid, and the junior minister, Douglas Alexander, were sitting in a parked car behind them).

They had both been in Scotland for a memorial service on Iona to mark the 10th anniversary of the death of John Smith. According to a government member, the actual conversation with Prescott at Loch Fyne was not significant, although the leaking of the story about it was. He says:

The Loch Fyne thing suddenly appeared. It was out of the blue and looked like someone wanting to raise fears of a Brown/Prescott plot. We assumed the leaker was someone who had got wind of what was going on and decided to try and blow it up.

I mean Gordon and Prescott have had so many conversations about this over the past year, as have Gordon and Prescott and Blair. The idea that there was one significant conversation with Prescott in a car is absurd. And the idea that they would pick a day when there were two other ministers in the car behind is equally ridiculous. What that story did was expose that these discussions had been going on, but to present them in a bad light as a Brown/Prescott plot.

What finally convinced Blair that he could and should stay were the results of the local and European elections, which took place on June 12. Although at first blanche Labour did appallingly in both, winning only 26 per cent of the vote in the locals and 23 per cent in the Europeans – which was its worst result in any national election since shortly after the second world war – the revival of the Tories under Howard was not as strong as Blair had feared. The Tories received 38 per cent of votes cast in the locals, well short of the 42 or 43 per cent it needed to win a general election. Given the unpopularity of the government's approach to Iraq, this was disappointing for the Conservatives. To be confident of ousting Labour in elections for parliament, the mid-term protest vote would have had to be greater.

In the European poll, the outcome for the Tories was even worse: their share of the vote actually fell compared with the previous European elections, from 36 per cent to 27 per cent, largely because the UK Independence Party – the youngish anti-European Party – garnered a remarkable 16 per cent of all votes. A government member elucidates: "Over the weekend, the local and European elections weekend, there was all this bleating about it being a bad campaign. But Blair concluded that the result was nowhere near as bad as we thought." It was at this point that Brown began to listen more seriously to those in his circle who consistently argued that Blair was duping him, that he had never had any intention of resigning if there were a reasonable probability that he could survive.

Brown and Blair had stopped talking face to face. But in the great tradition of celebrity couples going through a fraught time, they started to communicate through the media. Their "friends" – especially at this stage chums of the Prime Minister, though Brown's people would not be napping for long – started placing stories to set the tone for the divorce battle that seemed increasingly inescapable. The first significant one was a broadcast report on July 10 by Andrew Marr, the BBC's political editor, that four cabinet ministers – Reid, Jowell, Clarke and Patricia Hewitt, the Trade and Industry Secretary – had all lobbied Blair not to fall on his sword (unlike the others, who met with Blair, Hewitt's intervention took the form of a letter). Marr's source may have thought that he or she was sending out a message that was positive for Blair, to the effect that the Prime Minister was going on and on. In fact, Marr's report had precisely the opposite effect, creating fevered speculation that Blair's grip on office was increasingly tenuous. And that impression was reinforced on July 11, when Patrick Hennessy – political editor of the *Sunday Telegraph* – reported that Cherie Blair had also been putting pressure on her husband not to make way for Brown. Hennessy quoted an ally of Blair as saying: "It's been speculated that Cherie was putting pressure on Tony to go. Well, the opposite is true. Cherie was not going to allow Gordon to take over this early. She can't stand him."

None of this was conducive to creating the impression that Blair was in charge of his own destiny. But there was rather less ambiguity to a report the following day by Trevor Kavanagh, the political editor of the *Sun* who has a daunting reputation for garnering Grade A scoops. Under the headline "Blair's shock blow for Brown", Kavanagh wrote:

Tony Blair has vowed to be Prime Minister for five more years, in a crushing blow to Gordon Brown. The PM has told allies that if he wins the next election he will serve a full third term.

The article appeared shortly after Blair had had a drink and discussed his future plans with Rebekah Wade, the *Sun's* editor. "It was supposed to be an off-the-record chat," says a friend of the Prime Minister. "But Trevor said he got the story from another source, not from Rebekah." Either way, the *Sun's* report was strikingly similar to what Blair eventually declared he would be doing, immediately after the close of Labour's annual conference late in September – although he had not given a hint of these plans to Brown, who was exercised by the *Sun's* story and keen to get to the bottom of it.

Brown and Blair spoke almost immediately, in advance of the Chancellor's announcement that same day, July 12, of how much each government department could spend over the following three years. Blair said to him about Kavanagh's story: "It's wrong, I'll correct it". But it wasn't wrong – as Brown was to find out the following Sunday. Before then, however, on July 14, came the judgement of yet another enquiry into the preparation for war with Iraq, this time on the quality of the intelligence used by the government to justify its decision to strike against Saddam. Lord Butler, the former Cabinet Secretary who headed the enquiry, cleared Blair of "deliberate distortion or culpable negligence" – which was all that Blair needed to live another day – although Butler's report raised serious concerns about the processes that had allowed flimsy intelligence claims about the threat posed by Saddam to be presented by the Prime Minister and his government as hard fact.

Four days later, on July 18, Prescott hosted another of his family-therapy dinners at Admiralty House. At this one, Blair implied to Brown, without making it completely definitive, that he had changed his mind about quitting. What he said to the Chancellor was that he needed to take a different approach, in the wake of the Butler report. He appealed to any residual affection Brown might feel for him by saying: "To go now would look like I've been defeated over Iraq." He would evaluate the situation over the summer. "I need more time, I can't be bounced," he added.

Brown could not help but feel that the Prime Minister had once again cheated him. He was low, although his colleagues dispute how gloomy he became. One of his closest and oldest friends says: "When I spoke to him in July he was really fed up, thinking of quitting. He had surrendered all hope that Blair would ever quit. We talked him out of that."

The Chancellor's sense of bitter frustration increased the following day, July 19, when a senior cabinet member divulged to him that Blair was planning to bring Alan Milburn back into the Cabinet as soon as he could. At that time, this would have been an unusually inflammatory act, given that Brown and Milburn had fought a very public battle over the future of the health service, until almost the moment of Milburn's resignation from the government on July 12, 2003. The return of Milburn would have happened towards the end of that very same week, since Blair was working on carrying out a reshuffle before the summer recess. However at the last moment he chose not to change the composition of his ministerial team until the autumn.

On the other hand, he did make one significant political appointment on July 23. He named Peter Mandelson as Britain's new European Commissioner. Blair was honouring a debt to an old friend and supporter. But, in his heart, he did not want Mandelson to go, telling him that he preferred to have him in closer proximity. According to a cabinet minister close to Blair, the Prime Minister even gave serious thought to appointing Mandelson as Secretary of State for Work and Pensions, in succession to Andrew Smith, but was counselled by several senior ministers that there would be uproar among Labour MPs if Mandelson was brought back into government at that moment. Instead, Blair urged Mandelson to hang around as a backbench MP and informal adviser, with the promise that he would bring him back into the Cabinet for a third time after the next general election. What's striking was that Mandelson, after much deliberation and after taking advice from friends, decided to take the bird in the hand. He apparently recognised – in a way that Brown should have done years earlier – that Blair's promises of future advancement cannot always be banked, even if the Prime Minister means them at the moment he makes them.

Brown stayed in Scotland for the summer, in order to spend as much time as possible with his ailing mother (who died on September 19) in Aberdeenshire. Blair returned from his vacations in Barbados and Italy with his confidence restored. Almost his first action after the break was to flout Brown's wishes and bring Alan Milburn back into the Cabinet on September 8. Milburn was given a general role developing government policy as Chancellor of the Duchy of Lancaster and also running Labour's general election campaign. It was probably the biggest slap in the face Blair has ever delivered to Brown, partly because Milburn's view of the extensive role that the private sector should play in the delivery of core public services is one with which Brown profoundly disagrees. Also Brown ran Labour's general election campaign in 1997 and 2001 and regarded the job as his by right. The decision was a flagrant breach of what Brown felt was Blair's duty to reflect his views when making senior government or party appointments, under the Granita agreement. "Blair has crossed the Rubicon," was one remark made by an ally of Brown's at the time. "It's never been as bad as this between the two of them," was another.

However, Milburn's arrival was a notable victory for the Blairite cheerleading duo of Reid and Jowell, who had coached Milburn on what to demand from Blair and had stiffened his resolve to hold out until he had a genuinely powerful role (Stephen Byers, the former Transport Secretary, was also an influential counsellor to Milburn and will be brought back into the Cabinet by Blair immediately after the next election, according to a senior minister). This was the moment that Brown knew that there was no alternative to divorce. Or to put it another way, if he was going to be leader and Prime Minister, that would not happen with the co-operation and help of the Prime Minister. His new strategy would be to offer the alternative way for Labour to go, from within the government. A senior Labour Party member explains:

Six months before we were trying to persuade Blair that his legacy was best secured through unity and transition. He's taken the view that he's not going to get his legacy through unity and transition. And our fear is that the consequence of that is he's not going to get any legacy at all.

So on September 9, the day when most newspapers were reporting on how Brown had been snubbed by Blair with the appointment of Milburn, a slightly threatening message was sent to Blair via the *Times*. The newspaper's political editor, Philip Webster, broke the story that Brown had talked Blair out of pre-announcing in May that he would quit before the election. Blair would have interpreted this leak as a warning from Brown that he would not take his kicking meekly. However, to state the obvious,

Brown's strength is in strategy rather than tactics. And his strategic response to Blair's snub has been increasingly to characterise Blair and Milburn as the ministers espousing divisive and damaging policies, especially on the importation of market mechanisms into public services such as health and education (see Chapter Nine) and the *de facto* privatisation of these services. He is setting himself up as the candidate who gives primacy to the unity of the Party and an ethos of social justice married – as far as possible – to policies that encourage enterprise. Would anyone see a contradiction between that ambition and Brown's willingness to challenge the authority of the Prime Minister? Well, Brown took the view that only those in Blair's immediate circle would shout and scream "hypocrite" and he doesn't much mind about them.

That has become the medium term game. And Labour's annual conference, at the end of September 2004, was the perfect time to try it out. A great deal was riding on how Brown's message to the gathering of Labour's activists would be received, since he was convinced that Blair would attempt to portray him at the great gathering as an increasingly marginal and irksome colleague. In the event, his speech at midday on Monday September 27 went down better than he expected. And the audience revelled in his statement that "there are values far beyond those of contracts, markets and exchange and... public service can be a calling and not just a career" – although only a minority would have understood that this was Brown's explicit critique of the market-based reshaping of Labour's approach to the public sector that he believed was being adopted by Blair and Milburn. The standing ovation he received seemed more than the habitual deference that party members pay to him.

Although Blair's own speech the following day also went down well, Brown and his team were elated. One of Brown's friends says: "They (Blair and his allies) tried to kill us at conference by painting us as the dinosaurs. It didn't work. We out-manoeuvred them." But Blair was deeply annoyed with Brown. He made this clear when Brown went to see him in his suite at the Brighton Metropole at around 3pm on September 29. Blair accused Brown of conducting a deliberate campaign to undermine him throughout conference week and before. This allegation, that Brown had been plotting against him for at least three months, was one that the Prime Minister had also made earlier in September. It's true or false depending on your definition of conspiracy. There were no dirty tricks by Brown, just an increasing reluctance to hide his frustration at the policies adopted by the government and disappointment that his former friend had reneged on their pact. Brown was in a way simply being truer to himself, although it is striking that whenever his unhappiness has threatened to do serious damage to the Party – such as in the vote at the start of 2004 on university top-up fees – Brown has always put Party before self.

Anyway, at the September 29 meeting, Brown asked Blair how he proposed to rebuild their entente. "You've got to work with me," Blair said, which is a phrase he often uses in his meetings with Brown. It's the major condition he almost always sets for delivering what Brown wants most, his resignation as Prime Minister. And what it means – as in 2002 when Blair tried to persuade Brown to fix the outcome of the Treasury's assessment of whether it was right to join the European single currency – is that he will stay on in the top job until Brown has helped him to earn his place in history. But Brown refused to be cowed. He replied that the reshuffle – the bringing in of Milburn – was not consistent with the understanding that his views would count for a great deal when it came to senior appointments. The implication was that Blair had to work with him, as much as vice versa. To which Blair rejoined: "You know I've got to be able to bring my people in. Milburn's very talented, we need campaigning people". It was stalemate.

This was the moment that the Chancellor lost any residual belief that Blair placed any value in a demonstration of unity by the two of them. As of that meeting, Brown concluded that Blair was taking the "divisive, factional route," according to a minister, even though "that is not in Blair's interest... or the Party's." Brown sees Blair as a proponent of "exceptionalism." What he fears is that Blair – and Mandelson – are on a mission to undermine anyone, especially himself, who might be a success as Prime Minister after he has moved on. Blair, not Brown, has decided that the best way to secure his place in history is to ensure that the transition from him to another premier should be as messy as possible and as damaging as possible for Labour – or so Brown believes. "Blair's approach is '*aprés moi le déluge*,'" says a minister.

There was one big thing that Blair had not said in that September 29 meeting. He did not divulge to Brown the historic announcement he was planning to make the following night, that he would fight a third election and only stand down right at the end of the next parliament, in around four years. Brown had some inkling that something along these lines was in the offing. But he did not know the detail and had heard nothing directly about it from Blair. And, as the clearest possible sign of the erosion of all mutual affection from the relationship, Blair had told him zilch about the minor operation he was planning to undergo on October 1 to correct an irregular heartbeat. In the end, Brown was one of the last members of the government to learn about all of this, because he was on a flight to the annual meeting of the International Monetary Fund in Washington when the news started to leak out. When he landed, he was finally briefed by a fellow minister, but not by the Prime Minister.

Brown was irked but unsurprised to learn that Milburn had known all about Blair's determination to fight on for several years a fortnight earlier. As for Blair, his morale was tip top. Andrew Grice, the political editor of the *Independent*, reported that on the morning of October 1, just before going into hospital, Blair left an upbeat message on the mobile telephone of a close friend. According to this close friend, whom I would wager a magnificent sum to be Peter Mandelson, Blair was "chirpy, giggly and elfin-like".

On October 5, on his return from Washington and just before Blair flew out to Africa for a three day-visit, Brown went to see Blair in Downing Street. One item on their agenda was an offer from Blair that Brown could chair Labour's press conferences during the general election campaign – which had been leaked to that morning's *Guardian* ("I don't know how the *Guardian* got hold of that," said Blair). Brown turned it down. Chairing these events had been a natural thing to do when he was running the general election campaign as a whole. But since Milburn was now doing that, Blair's suggestion was contemptible. Instead, Brown would rally Labour's support by spending the campaign travelling around the country. And when Brown asked him why he had not given him advance warning of his announcement that he would be going on and on as Prime Minister, Blair said – to a disbelieving Chancellor – "I told you that before."

According to their friends, the rift between them is now a chasm. One says that Brown used to react to the apparent duplicity of his old friend with considerable pain, but "he's beyond that now". And Brown routinely says to Blair, "There is nothing that you could ever say to me now that I could ever believe." As for Blair, when he is reproached in this way, about his failure to honour promises to stand down, he replies, "You wouldn't work with me." That is his habitual line. And his allies cite a number of examples of Brown's alleged disloyalty as the reasons why Blair failed to stand by the offer he made at Admiralty House in November 2003: first, that Brown whipped up opposition to university top-up fees on Labour's backbenches; second that he forced Blair – against his basic instincts – to promise a referendum on the adoption of the EU's new constitution; and third that the Treasury was obstructive when ministerial departments were formulating five-year plans that would underpin the Party's election manifesto.

One of the Prime Minister's friends elucidates: "Frankly, Gordon should be Prime Minister by now and he only has himself to blame that he's not. All that Tony simply asked was that he should give him total support over the year. And instead of being loyal and helpful, he was obstructive and difficult."

So was it Blair who let down Brown or vice versa? Well, as ever when these two argue, the judgement of where right lies is nuanced. It's true that Brown was deeply unhappy for many months about the proposals for top-up fees. But in the event, Labour might well have lost the vote if he hadn't put huge pressure on his friends in the Commons – especially Nick

Brown – to back the relevant bill (Nick Brown says that it was the concessions he won that persuaded him to vote with the government, though he acknowledges that Gordon Brown was relentless towards the end in asking him to cease his opposition).

As for the pledge to hold a plebiscite on the EU constitution, Brown had indeed argued for many months that the electorate should be consulted in this way, because of the widespread perception – which was impossible to ignore, even if it was exaggerated – that its introduction would lead to a further erosion of the UK's autonomous ability to make laws. It was far better, according to Brown, to challenge the Tories' opposition to the constitution in an open and fair fight at the ballot box, than to ride roughshod over genuine concerns in the wider electorate about the growing influence of the EU. And it's also true that Blair was deeply reluctant to concede this, fearing that it would show the government moving in a eurosceptic direction by manifesting a lack of confidence in the evolution of the EU. However, Brown always feels that announcements of the magnitude of a proposal to hold a referendum should not be pulled like a rabbit out of the hat. His *modus operandi*, as we have seen, is to steadily make the case for a significant shift in policy. So right at the last, in the middle of April – when Blair had been persuaded by Jack Straw that the government needed to hold a referendum on the constitution – Brown actually argued for a delay, on the grounds that the announcement would look like a U-turn made under pressure, given Blair's well-known opposition to holding such a vote. When Blair finally made the announcement on April 20, the fury unleashed on him from parliament, the media and the world beyond for his unexplained volte face was an unprecedented experience for him. Thus it's quite difficult to see Brown's behaviour in this case as disloyal to Blair.

On the other hand, Brown and the Treasury did lay obstacles in the way of departments' five-year plans. In particular, the Chancellor insisted that no spending commitments could extend beyond 2008, or the final year of the latest round of his biennial Comprehensive Spending Review. For Blair this was confirmation of his general critique, that the Treasury under Brown has neutered every one of his pet policies, that it has stopped him being radical and that it plays to the Party's left wing. Brown's typical response is, "Hang on a sec, we announced 84$^1/_2$ thousand civil service jobs were to go: how can you call that playing to the left?"

But Blair increasingly does not hear what Brown says. Instead he is swayed by those in his immediate circle who argue that Brown is plotting to unseat him – which is an over-simplification. Blair sees Brown's principled opposition to policies as evidence of a personal vendetta by his Chancellor. To be gripped by such paranoia is par for the course for occupants of the Downing Street bunker, from Harold Wilson to John Major. But in this case, it's not right. Brown may not be a pliable colleague, but he could have done vastly more damage to Blair over the past couple of years if he had devoted his formidable energy and creativity to that project.

The battle between them is only in part about personal ambition. It's now about ideas and the future of the Labour Party. The Granita power-sharing deal held for as long as it did because – for all the disagreements on policy detail in New Labour's first term – Blair and Brown were largely in agreement about the foundations that needed to be laid to keep Labour in office for the long term, viz proving to the world that Labour was now a prudent and astute manager of the economy, to pave the way for a massive increase in public spending. The rift has come, as it inevitably would, because there is now an important difference in their visions for the second phase of their time in office (see Chapter Nine). Blair behaves like the chief executive of a modern multinational company. I don't say this to belittle him. But he is more pragmatic and less ideological than Brown. His ambition is for the UK to sit at the top table, for his government to have maximum international influence in a globalised world where national barriers are less important than they were. So he wants to be in the euro to strengthen his hand in negotiations with EU partners. And he has formed a close military alliance with a US Republican president because of his conviction that his voice will be heard better from inside the US tent.

As for the reform of public services in the UK, Blair's observation is that the public sector has historically provided an inferior service across the board when compared with private sector businesses operating in a marketplace – so it must make sense to remodel public services such as health and education along private sector lines. It's redolent for me of the kind of unemotional strategic thinking manifested by someone like Lord Browne, the Chief Executive of BP (and it's intriguing that at the end of 2001, Blair's longest-serving aide, Anji Hunter, found a new berth as director of communications at BP's head office).

Brown is more recognisably a scion of the line of Keir Hardie, James Maxton and Anthony Crosland. He is an intensely practical politician. Just like Blair, he has no interest in being in opposition – and would ruthlessly abandon any policy that would catapult his party to the opposition benches. But having obtained power, he is remorseless and obsessive in his pursuit of social justice. It is a mission for him, which can be seen in his dedication to the cause of alleviating poverty in Africa and testing every one of his domestic policies by whether it advances or disadvantages the cause of the dispossessed. That doesn't make him an anti-capitalist or a socialist who wants to squeeze the wealthy till they squeak. Quite the reverse. He is sincerely committed to creating the economic conditions in which entrepreneurs can flourish, even if many of the breed do not always see it that way. And for all that he has raised the burden of taxation for those on above-average incomes through a multiplicity of reforms, he is mindful that the burden should never be raised to a level that discourages wealth-creation or encourages wealth-creators to relocate to low-tax regimes abroad. Subject to that constraint, he has a vision of a more equal Britain, based on maintaining the economic conditions necessary for full employment, investment in public education, the imperative of reconstructing the research and science base of the UK, restoring the ethos of public service and rebuilding faith in government itself by remaking the constitution. He put it like this in a speech on October 22, 2004:

The equality we support is not equality for equality's sake – as if we want to level people down – but equality for liberty's sake, because we wish to lift people up.

As Chancellor, he has made a reality of much of that vision. Even if it turns out not be his destiny to pursue the mission as Prime Minister, Brown's idea of fairness is the closest thing that Labour has at present to an idea that could restore the electorate's trust in politics and politicians.

So it's a slightly odd time to be finishing a book on Brown, because his story is not over. Quite a lot has gone wrong for him over the past year. It is possible that his reputation for financial prudence will be tarnished, because public borrowing has not been falling as fast as he hoped, and he may breach his cherished Golden Rule which stipulates that over the cycle the government's borrowing should not exceed the amount that it invests (although Brown is remarkably sanguine that he won't and the foundations of sound macro-economic management that he laid in 1997 still look robust). Meanwhile, Blair has ruthlessly squished his hopes that he would have fought and won a leadership election by now. But through these setbacks Brown has emerged a stronger politician. So long as he does nothing openly and grotesquely disloyal to the Prime Minister, and so long as he is not engulfed by some unexpected economic disaster, he cannot be sacked. If Blair could have dismissed him without simultaneously sealing his own doom, he would have done so by now.

Brown is now the official opposition to Blairite Labour. From the house next door to the Prime Minister's, the Chancellor is beginning to stake his claim to lead the country in a very different way from Blair. He is offering Labour a new start, an *alternative* kind of government to Blair's – both in style and substance – rather than more of the same (which is how he had always thought, for better or worse, a Brown administration would be seen). And he probably won't have to wait all that long before at last contesting a leadership election, even though Blair has said that he will serve another three or four years after the election. "You could argue that the statement [by Blair] that is interesting is that he is leaving, not that he is staying," says a minister.

The comprehensive ripping up of the Granita pact, performed by Blair in September 2004, will change the direction of British politics just as dramatically as the premature death of John Smith in 1994. It has inaugurated the final struggle between the lawyer and the historian – the two bright young men on-the-make who entered parliament in 1983 – for possession of the Labour Party.

ACKNOWLEDGMENTS

Lots of people have been wonderfully supportive and patient during the two-year preparation of this book. I am indebted to the many politicians and civil servants who made themselves available to be interviewed. Particular thanks are due to the Treasury, for facilitating access to officials and answering my tedious factual queries.

I am grateful to Sir Steve Robson, a former Second Permanent Secretary at the Treasury, for giving me the kind of first-rate advice for which he is renowned after reading an early draft of a couple of chapters.

Thanks also go to my brilliant publishers, Rebecca Nicolson and Aurea Carpenter at Short Books, the outstanding literary agent, Kate Jones, of ICM Talent, and Annie Williamson-Noble (who stepped into the breach to write the index at the last possible moment). Big hugs also go to Dominic Lawson, the superb editor of the *Sunday Telegraph* who encouraged me when I told him I wished to undertake the project.

I need to apologise (again) to my darling boys, Simon and Max, for being too much in my head while writing this thing. And the biggest thank-you of all goes to my beautiful and brainy wife, Sian Busby, without whom nothing would be possible.

SELECTED BIBLIOGRAPHY

Balls and O'Donnell *Reforming Britain's Economic and Financial Policy*, Palgrave, 2002

Balls, Grice, O'Donnell *Microeconomic Reform in Britain*, Palgrave, 2004

Bower, Tom *Gordon Brown*, Harper Collins, 2004

Brown, Gordon *Maxton*, Mainstream Publishing, 1986

Dell, Edmund *The Chancellors*, Harper Collins, 1996

Draper, Derek *Blair's 100 Days*, Faber and Faber, 1997

Gould, Philip *The Unfinished Revolution*, Little Brown, 1998

Keegan, William *The Prudence of Mr Gordon Brown*, Wiley, 2003

Lamont, Norman *In Office*, Little Brown, 1999

Lipsey, David *The Secret Treasury*, Viking, 2000

Macintyre, Donald *Mandelson*, Harper Collins, 1999

Mandelson and Liddle, *The Blair Revolution*, Faber and Faber, 1996

Radice, Giles *Friends & Rivals*, Little Brown, 2002

Rawnsley, Andrew *Servants of the People*, Hamish Hamilton, 2000

Rentoul, John *Tony Blair*, Little Brown, 1995

Robinson, Geoffrey *The Unconventional Minister*, Michael Joseph, 2000

Routledge, Paul *Gordon Brown*, Simon & Schuster, 1998

Scott, Derek *Off Whitehall*, IB Tauris, 2004

Seldon, Anthony *Blair*, Free Press, 2004

Short, Clare *An Honourable Deception*, Simon & Schuster, 2004

Stephens, Philip *Politics and the Pound*, Macmillan, 1996

INDEX